Promised Land

Books by Michael Frome

Promised Land—Adventures and Encounters in Wild America
Issues in Wilderness Management (Editor)
The Forest Service
Battle for the Wilderness
Whose Woods These Are—The Story of the National Forests
Strangers in High Places—The Story of the Great Smoky Mountains
Rand McNally National Park Guide
The National Parks (with David Muench)
The National Forests of America (with Orville L. Freeman)
The Varmints—Our Unwanted Wildlife

PROMISED LAND

*Adventures
and Encounters
in Wild America*

MICHAEL FROME

William Morrow and Company, Inc.
NEW YORK

Library of Congress Cataloging in Publication Data

Frome, Michael.
Promised land.

Includes index.
1. Wilderness areas—United States.   I. Title.
QH76.F765   1985   508.73   84-19074
ISBN 0-688-04173-6

Printed in the United States of America

First Edition

1 2 3 4 5 6 7 8 9 10

BOOK DESIGN BY ELLEN LO GIUDICE

For Eunice, my editor,
friend and advocate of wild nature.
For your encouragement and inspiration,
I extend the warmest appreciation and affection.

Contents

CONTENTS

Promised Land

CHAPTER I

Of Music in the Wind, Of the Message in a Rock

I profess a certain expertise on the subject of wilderness and like to believe the evidence and credentials will support it. My various books and articles, explorations, and the battles and debates to save wild places have all added up. Delivering the Wilderness Resource Distinguished Lecture at the University of Idaho, with wilderness close at hand in all directions, almost made me feel distinguished, at least for a little while. But wild nature is humbling. The more I learn about the principles of wilderness and the more time I spend in the slender sanctuaries that survive across the face of America, the less I actually understand about them.

That little confession may undermine confidence in the expert, but I can't imagine an expert who has all the answers about *anything* these days, let alone anything as intensely subjective as wilderness. The truth is that no matter how many pages I turn in the book of wild places, I can never reach the last page and then feel that *Well, now I've done it; now I can teach it.* Over the years I've acquired knowledge and experience, but this only proves that I may be into the phase of absorbing wisdom. That reminds me of a line spoken by Robert Frost, whom I interviewed in the last year of his life. "You're too young," he said pointedly, "to understand the young."

We're all too young, if you ask me, civilization is too young, to comprehend, scientifically or ethically, values implicit in the earth, let alone the universe beyond, to which the earth is hitched. But who needs all the answers? Wonderment is better equipment with which to perceive adventure and mystery, without requiring firm, factual conclusions.

One of the classic arguments for "opening up" wilderness is to enable grandmother to drive through it in a car. It wouldn't be wilderness any longer, but that's not the point. "The music I prefer," writes John Cage, "even to my own or anybody else's, is what we are hearing if we are just quiet." The statement may be surprising, coming from the master of electronic sound, yet it suggests in the most graceful way benefits derived from listening and observing in a setting free of crowds and mechanical sounds, without pressure to get up and go anywhere.

I value wild country for its own sake, not for any specific or demonstrable utility. It shouldn't be necessary to render all wilderness accessible for human consumption of one kind or another. A fragment of original earth, just by its being there, uncluttered, unimproved, and unmolested, represents living poetry, music, and art.

When I do enter a wilderness I find it a source of sustenance for well-being, of evenness to balance the oddness of life's routine. But that doesn't mean wilderness must be there for my benefit, not when it has inalienable right and reason of its own. Wilderness by federal law is "an area where the earth and its community of life are untrammeled by man, where man himself is a visitor who does not remain," but that's only a legal definition.

Wilderness is what I want it to be, where and how I want to find and feel it. Wilderness is in the cycle of seasons and weather: in clouds descending and gliding, brooding over forests and lakes; in summer rain, soft and warm, splashing the air with smells of new life; in mist rising from a mountain meadow at twilight; and in lightning and thundershowers, blizzards and icy winds, discomforting to convenience and defiant of control.

Wilderness is in the chorus of thrushes, the crashing thunder of waterfalls, the encrusted mystery in a rock that asks me to contemplate its shape, form, composition, history, color, and the influence it exercises on life around it. For that matter, wilderness is in the lichens that decorate the rock surface while drawing from its nutrients to mix with energy from the sun, and in the mosses, humble forms that remind me to be humble. Wilderness is in the rhythms of ponds and swamps, where crawfish, snails, and lizards grow. It's in the semiarid brushy chaparral of the Southwest and West, profuse in colors, sounds, and fragrant scents, with treeless hills peopled by coyotes and jackrabbits. And it's on the prairie, flat, rolling, and broken, where I envision in mind's eye bison feeding on grass, wolf and Indian feeding on bison.

Wilderness spreads across the continent, no longer in large masses, but in bits and pieces, vestigial traces of what America once was all about. Most wilderness with a capital "W" is in national parks and national forests, in those portions not yet overrun and degraded, though I wish there were more of it without signs, labels, or boundary lines.

Wilderness is more than sheer spectaculars, such as Yellowstone or Yosemite. In the Badlands of western Dakota, for example, the raw arid land seems to support little life. It appears like some strange planet, moonscape of alien formations, a variety of spires, towers, and pinnacles. Winter lasts half the year and blizzards go on for days. Temperature on summer days is in the nineties, sometimes over one hundred. During June, thundershowers tear away the soft surface of the earth. Not too appealing on the face of it. Looking closely, though, I observe pastel blues, pinks, greens, and bands of tan engraved in the ridges, low hills, and cliffs. I smell the sweet-scented silver sagebrush and snowberry and begin to recognize the variety of life-forms. Fields of prickly pear and Spanish dagger, and patches of cottonwood along the watercourse are alive with birds, pronghorn antelope, coyotes, and badgers. The seemingly bare cliff faces are not so bare after all, considering that swifts and swallows find them useful places to build their nests, and often rock wrens do the same in crevices, while an occasional eagle perches on a high cliff-top butte.

Far from being sterile, or static, everything in the Badlands creates a mobile image in my mind. As evening advances, pastels yield to bolder-toned grays and blacks. In the process of day to night, forms change, too. What seemed minutes ago like the pyramids of Egypt or the Great Wall of China have become Inca temples. In the moonlight shadows dance across those unworldly ridges and spires. It's a marvelous night for sleeping out, but not for much sleeping, not with the coyotes howling and breeze whistling across the buttes, and the procession of stars, planets, nebulas, and constellations marching across clear Dakota skies.

I've been to diverse wild places in the United States and elsewhere in the world, encountering all kinds of people along the way. They too are part of the wilderness scene. Now that so little remains of a once abundant endowment, more people want a piece, or at least a little taste, of it. Strange in a way, or poetic justice.

People are drawn to wilderness with different motives, goals, and responses. Ralph Waldo Emerson, John Muir, and others conceive it as the call of the wild summoning humankind home. As Emerson wrote in his essay on "Nature":

"At the gates of the forest, the surprised man of the world is forced to leave his city estimates of great and small, wise and foolish. The knapsack of custom falls off his back with the first step he makes into these precincts. Here we find nature to be the circumstance which dwarfs every other circumstance, and judges like a god all men that come to her."

And from Muir:

"There is a love of wild nature in everybody, an ancient mother-love showing itself whether recognized or no, and however covered by cares and duties."

I believe in this idea, but it's been stated so often that it tends to sound simple. Walt Whitman reportedly loved to read poems in the open air with the sound of the sea. I like that image. The wild setting stimulated his psyche and intellect in direct channels of thought and action. At Coney Island following a swim, he would race up and down the sand of a long, bare, unfrequented beach declaiming Shakespeare to surf and gulls. He first digested the *Iliad* in a sheltered hollow of the rocks, in the full presence of nature, under the sun, absorbing a far-spreading landscape, and hearing the sea rolling in. I can picture old Walt, poetic champion of the American epic, exultant and exuberant, likely without a stitch of clothing, king of the universe at last, in contact and harmony with every bit of finite and infinite.

What about us in our time? In the summer of 1982, in the course of my thoroughly subjective studies of people and wild places, I joined a horse trip into the high backcountry of Yellowstone National Park. I had been over much of the same terrain with the outfitter, Ralph K. Miller, two years earlier, and he had invited me to return. I was interested in renewing my contact with him and with Candace, or Candy, his attractive, red-haired cook, wrangler, and roommate, as well as with the Yellowstone country.

It was a small party, six riders and eleven horses in all. Keeping things cozy is part of the attraction. Twenty years earlier I had been on a trail ride elsewhere in Wyoming on which I counted sixty-four horses and eighteen mules. They were carrying twenty-two riders plus wranglers, cooks, equipment, and food. It was more of an urban convention than a wilderness adventure. But a horse trip catered for class carries a price tag with it; it attracts those who have saved their money or who have $1,000 or $1,250 to spend without saving.

We rode high above the concrete and plastic of the Yellowstone tourist loop, the "front country," as national park officials call it to justify writing off wilderness lost. Actually, there were only two cash customers in the party, Jeff and Cindy, a married couple in their early thirties, both lawyers from New England. They had been with Miller once before on a one-week trip and now were back for the ten-day ride. For most people a week is plenty, easier to take, with enough to remember, and significantly less expensive. Jeff and Cindy were not nature-oriented outdoors people, but rather were accustomed to roles among what are called the "upwardly mobile." From conversation I gathered they lived comfortably in a house on the water. They read the latest best sellers and saw the right foreign films. They had chartered a yacht on Nantucket for one vacation and had gone to Italy on another.

Still, I couldn't help contrasting Jeff with another lawyer, Harvey Broome, a particular friend and mentor of mine. In the early 1920s Harvey was a sickly, slightly built boy in Knoxville, Tennessee, who took to the wilderness of the Great Smoky Mountains to build his health in the same way that Theodore Roosevelt had taken to the Badlands of North Dakota. Later, Harvey studied at Harvard and pursued a successful law practice, but his heart and mind were in the wilderness and in protecting it through his activities in the Wilderness Society. He quit his practice to work as law clerk for a federal judge in Knoxville, with the understanding that he could take reasonable time off as needed to labor in behalf of the Society, which he helped found in 1934 and later served as president. On several occasions before his death in 1968, I hiked with Harvey in the Smokies and overnighted at his home. He was anything but robust, but knew the mountains in every season of the year and was indomitable on the trail.

At the end of a day's ride, Jeff expected service (and received it). The fish he caught he expected to be prepared for him, rather than as a sharing for the group. "This is costing me two hundred dollars a day," Jeff announced to me apropos of nothing. It couldn't have been important to me, but it *was* to him, important to hear himself express it. I've heard the same idea elsewhere, as in Africa, from those who want the world to understand: "*My* safari cost me such and such. . . . This is *my* safari jacket . . . *my* elephant gun . . . *my* elephant." It's the possessory way of viewing things that makes buying a piece of naturalness and, of course, the appropriate services, seem utterly logical.

When it came time to head for the hot springs basin to bathe together in the nude, the accustomed style, Jeff and Cindy opted out. They chose to go by themselves, one confided, and then the other, in deference to Cindy's oncoming menstrual period. This could very well have been, but it didn't surprise me. Oh well, there would be more room for the rest of us.

There were four of us, two men and two women, at close range, in a shallow pool only a little larger than a backyard hot tub. There was Ralph, in his late thirties, lean, hobbled, and raw as a cowboy should be, but actually an Eastern cowboy; the son of a Boston physician, he had been through a wild youth, with drugs and reform school, and discovered his purpose by hanging around race tracks and raising horses. Between summers, he now was busy studying veterinary medicine, hoping to be an equine surgeon. Candy, in her early thirties, was slender, bony, and burned, like Ralph, from the rigors of a summer on the trail. Her routine was not easy, but obviously what she wanted, or was willing to accept, out of life. Then there was Mary Ellen, a very healthy physical

16

specimen in her late twenties, crowned with thick black hair; she had worked for Candy at a Berkshires restaurant. She had arrived only a few days earlier, driving her VW camper-van cross-country.

I see such young people everywhere, seeking and searching for space and place. No, not everywhere, I suppose, but at certain spots that are almost designated as sanctuaries by their genre: Big Sur, on the California coast; the San Juan Islands, off the Washington coast; Jackson, Sun Valley, Aspen, Crested Butte, and other outdoor rendezvous in the Rockies; Santa Fe, southwest center of arts and Indians; Vermont, the escape from Eastern cities; and in Jamaica and the Virgin Islands, where it's summer all year. These young people (and some older) consider themselves nonconformists, but they follow patterns of their own. They are groupies, regrouping from a system of formal education that has little to do with learning or fulfillment. They love beauty, which is manifest in the settings where they ski, sail, hike, meditate, and very often share and care in ways that earlier were denied to them.

The pool in which we bathed was fed by two streams. One that flowed from some distant, mysterious underground source furnished hot water, too hot for comfort. Fortunately, it mixed with a clear, cold stream, and the temperature could be adjusted with a barrier log regulating the flow of cold, all in all a deliciously natural experience, a soothing interlude, thoroughly welcome after several days of riding and camping.

I observed these two attractive young women, one fair complected and the other dark. Their skins were smooth, breasts small and firm, stomachs flat and free of strains of childbirth. They were unaffected, as children of nature should be, at home in the wild. I felt conscious of the sensuous quality of this experience, without feeling anything evil about it.

Wilderness is enriched by sensuality, a part of the rhythms and mosaic of life. On almost any night in the wild one can hear an explosion of sounds—of animals crooning in love, calling for mates, or in some violent conflict—that must somehow comprise a rational form and continuum. If valid for other species, so too should love in the wilderness be for ours, whether in a tent at eight thousand feet, or in a waterfall, or in a hot springs basin in Yellowstone (perhaps for me at some future time!).

The point is that wilderness can be scientific, ecological, recreational, philosophical, ethical, political, and polemical. It can be all those and more based on the completeness of life and what one's own mind wants to make of it. Wilderness gives me a sense of freedom, health, hope, and companionship. "Man has lost the capacity to foresee and forestall," wrote Albert Schweitzer. "He will end by destroying the earth." Maybe so, but wilderness is the antidote to pessimism and, as long as it exists, the source of hope.

Hope begins inside oneself. Happily, my hope is founded on the companionship and warmth shared with friends whom I've encountered in the wild, and who presently will people the pages to follow.

These people are integral to my wilderness, but above all, perhaps, I should stress the sense of mystery involved. Willi Unsoeld, a revered professor of philosophy and history at Evergreen State College, was an intrepid mountaineer, a participant in the first United States climb of Everest in 1963. In 1977, while on a return to Nepal, he lost his daughter (a skilled climber like himself) on the slopes of Nanda Devi, for which she was named, then two years later he perished in an avalanche on Mount Rainier. Willi once told me that mountains may be climbed but they're never really conquered, and that he felt humbled by the mystery and power of massive raw stone and ice.

It doesn't take a trip to Nepal or the summit of Rainier to get the same feeling or perception. I mentioned lichens earlier. These little pioneers of the green world need to be examined closely or they're missed altogether. They grow in the shape of rosettes, variously colored in delicate shades of jade-green, silver, red-yellow, and orange. They may be found in the most incredible places, ranging from the cold North to water-logged soils, dry, burned-over land, the bark of trees, and bare sandstone or granite. They grow very patiently, absorbing elements from the air, minerals from rock, and radiant energy from the sun. Lichens cannot be manufactured in a laboratory, yet they open the way for mosses, which accumulate humus, providing seedbeds for grasses, sedges, shrubs, and, ultimately, trees.

Lichens are teachers, in their own way. In the fall of 1970 I learned a lesson from them in a remote corner of the world. I was in Lapland, the Finnish Arctic, traveling with Walter J. Hickel, then Secretary of the Interior under President Nixon. Hickel had been governor of Alaska, and had a passion for the Arctic. As governor he had rightly or wrongly been labeled as a developer and despoiler, but as Interior Secretary he surprised everyone, possibly including himself, with his sensitivity and concern for wildlife, wilderness, and other aspects of natural resources. I got to know him fairly well in Washington and it was a pleasure to travel with him in Finland.

Our destination, the Kevo Subarctic Research Station, lies in the northernmost part of Lapland, wedged between Norway and the Soviet Union, at the edge of the Scandinavian, or Scandes, Mountains, less than fifty kilometers from the Arctic Ocean. En route north from Ivalo, well above the Arctic Circle, we flew over a landscape that reminded me of the Allagash country of northern Maine, or the Algonquin Shield in Canada, with beautiful streams flowing through ever-changing canyons, now steep, then gentle, and over waterfalls, surrounded by marshes, heaths, glacial ridges, and arboreal forests.

At the shore of Lake Kevojarvi, in the remotest part of Lapland, we met Dr. Paavo Kallio, a professor of botany at the University of Turku, who was directing a project at the Research Station. He spoke to us about life, of how the work at Kevo and other Arctic stations around the world relates to the study and perpetuation of life-forms. Here in the Arctic, he said, in broken but always effective English, man is but one part of the natural system. Thus, research efforts were intended to provide correlation between solar energy and the possibility of man's life.

"We are measuring the transformation of solar energy into chemical energy," he said, "through plants and herbs—the growth and production of life, with the effects of temperature and light conditions, of plankton as the basis of life for fish. We are studying mushrooms, including the protein calorie count and the number per square miles. Mushrooms are good food for reindeer, and especially necessary now in autumn so the animals can stand the winter.

"Thousands of measurements are being made of soil, temperature, air, light in all seasons; of lichens, mosses, and herbs as they provide food for reindeer; of soil microorganisms and how they deposit litter, and of carbon dioxide and its effect on the environment."

We walked on trails through bushes of birch. Dr. Kallio pointed to an area of lichens that had been judged to be two thousand years old. He commented on the marvel of the species, capable of growing independently of other plants and of drawing nitrogen directly from the air. This stimulated Hickel.

"Can we plant it in Alaska?" he asked. "Will it grow better than grass?"

"Wait, I will show you where we are culturing lichen," Dr. Kallio replied.

"The oil companies on the North Slope are trying to plant grass where they disturb the land, but they have to reseed every year. Could they use lichen instead?"

"Wait, I will show you."

"But will it grow?"

"There are no fast-growing lichens, you know. They grow very slowly."

The Secretary's aide, Josef Holbert, was walking at his side. He had faith in the ability of his boss to solve any problem. "Wait till Hickel gets hold of it," he chimed in boldly.

But his boss knew better, conceding with a sigh, "And there are no fast-growing Hickels either."

What was it that I learned from this lichen encounter? What is it they have to teach? I could spell it out, as I see it, but why create a blueprint when the lichens themselves have so much to explain that goes beyond science and words?

CHAPTER II

Down the Colorado River with the Crusading King of the River Rats

"I don't look for them. They come to me."

Martin Litton, king of the river rats, was describing the breed that works for him as boatmen on the Colorado River. It was during the course of an interview, but only of sorts, as you can tell from the following bit of dialogue.

"What are the qualifications?"

"They have to be healthy, reverent, well dressed, clean, smart, helpful, loyal, strong."

"Do you ever find that combination?"

"Never . . . but they stay forever. I can't get rid of them. They make more money than any banker takes home because they get it all in cash. They don't have to have anything deducted. They average fifteen hundred dollars a month, free and clear. The trip leaders get a lot more. All their food is furnished. That's not a bad deal."

"And whatever romance they get is on their own?"

"They're not allowed to have romances on the trips."

"Is that rule strictly enforced?"

"Well, that's up to the clients."

Martin lives strictly by the rules, mostly his own. Before chucking normalcy to become king of the river rats, he was travel editor of *Sunset*, an attractive, slick western magazine that became popular in the 1950s, rather like a regional *Better Homes and Gardens*, though more sophisticated.

"As travel editor, my first rule was that we would never publish anything about any place that I particularly loved that was at all vulnerable to overuse. *Sunset* never pretended to be serious. We weren't supposed to write good, but to 'write *Sunset*.' Nevertheless, I would stick in as much conservation and wilderness propaganda as I could.

"I left in high dudgeon over something the publisher, Bill Lane, wanted to do to an article I wrote about the California redwoods and the effort to save them. He wanted to postpone it to avoid offending his influential friends who opposed the idea of a Redwood National Park. I said, 'That does it. I quit.' But they still published the article verbatim, exactly as I had written it, after I quit, and he didn't know it was mine.

"What happened was that Bill had a guilty conscience about my leaving. He called in my successor (who had been my assistant) and told him that I was extreme, that he wanted a more objective article to run the following month. After it appeared, Bill said, 'Now you see, Larry, you see what I mean. This article is exactly the way it ought to be. Martin is just too wrapped up in these things. Now you've been able to take this and distill it into something very innocent.' But Larry said, 'I'm sorry, Bill, what you read is exactly the same article as the page proofs you pulled out of the magazine last month, word for word.'"

Such things happen to Martin all the time because they take shape in his head and then emerge, more or less, according to his design. Martin is one of the superlative wilderness adventurers and advocates of our time, with an independent, unchained spirit. His dory trips down the Colorado River through the Grand Canyon are the longest and most expensive of many offered, but those who take them always say the experience proved better than expected. Boatmen complain, but come back, and those working for competitors yearn for a chance with him on the dories.

His departure from *Sunset* marked the beginning of Martin Litton's Grand Canyon Dories, which he operates from an office at his home in Palo Alto, California, with various field headquarters near the rivers. Starting with the Colorado, Martin expanded to operate trips on the Green River, in Utah, and marvelous wild streams of the Northwest: the Snake through Hells Canyon, the deepest gorge on the North American continent, and the Salmon, Owyhee, and Grande Ronde. Though clearly not accomplished in business ways, his "product line" stands unmatched in his field.

Martin is the kind of character Shakespeare would have loved. When I went down the Colorado with him in August 1981, the *Today* show sent a crew. A few weeks later I watched the results on NBC. Someone timed it and said it was the longest segment *Today* had ever run, and it was virtually all Martin, pictured at the oars, like the Old Man of the Sea, declaiming on the eternal values of the Grand Canyon and of wilderness and denouncing schemes to undermine them, not with diatribe, but with expression and gesture worthy of Shakespeare.

"There will never be wilderness again until humans are gone," he said to me at a later date, "all of them gone, even thee and me, and allow the earth to heal itself."

And again: "Nobody should go there. It's dangerous, full of wild beasts. Yet pure wilderness is the only beautiful thing on earth. Everything man makes is only a copy, an attempt to copy, to bring out the same feelings."

He is variously fatalistic, pessimistic, defiant, determined, self-sacrificing, caring, cantankerous, and unpredictable. These contradictions are in his appearance, dress, and talk. Martin stands about six feet tall, solidly built, with wavy whitish hair, well-tended full moustache, and a leathery reddish face that is a little puffy from too much booze. He walks with a combination of surefooted swagger, roll, and waddle. Away from rivers he dresses well and holds his own in any circumstance, yet as a boatman running the toughest rapids, he seems born to the part. One day on the trip I made with him down the Colorado, he ran his dory into a rock and cracked a gash in the side (proving that it happens to the best of them). That evening in camp he worked for two hours or so patching the boat with epoxy glue and tape, while nourishing himself with vodka or gin, or maybe both, and exhorting members of the party on the evil design of the Bureau of Reclamation, a federal agency, to alter the water flow through the Grand Canyon. An indomitable specimen, at the age of sixty-five.

I've known Martin on and off for years, but our closest encounter off-river was in the fall of 1982. I invited Martin to come to the University of Idaho to speak to various classes and show his spectacular film on the Grand Canyon, which he narrates. He agreed to come at his expense (which is the way our wildland recreation management program would get speakers), flying his own plane. Then he called back with a condition: that I, in turn, would return to California with him to speak before the annual meeting of the Kern Plateau Association, a citizen group committed to protecting wilderness on the east slope of the Sierra Nevada. Martin has given a large measure of himself to such underfinanced organizations and to such causes as the Grand Canyon and the redwoods and the California desert, yet he laments his fate. "I have to get back and rescue my business," he would groan during the course of our plane trip. "We've got checks out all over and we haven't got a dime."

Martin Litton made his first trip down the Colorado through the Grand Canyon in 1955. It was still a rare adventure. Between the pioneering expedition of Major John Wesley Powell in 1869 and 1940, less than seventy-five persons had successfully run the river. The year 1949 marked a record high of twelve. That was the year two daredevils, Ed Hudson and Dock Marston, rode through in a motorboat. It took them only four and a half days. Then an enterprising woman named Georgie White lashed together three inflatable war surplus bridge pontoons and steered them with an outboard motor. She was able to carry up to fifty passengers and gear. It signaled the end of the era of wilderness adventure in solitude and the beginning of the era of thrill riding with lots of company. By 1966 the number of people riding the river through the canyon topped one thousand, and in 1980, fifteen thousand—per year, that is. Aluminum, fiber glass materials, and rubber rafts gave a tremendous boost to river running, if not quite to the welfare of rivers. The American wild river, due to one cause or another, has largely gone the way of the Indian, buffalo, and grizzly.

Nobody knows who named this canyon the Grand Canyon. It

was the only region missed by the trappers and traders in the era of Jim Bridger, Jedediah Smith, and the Sublette brothers. "It seems intended by nature," wrote Lieutenant Joseph Christmas Ives in 1858, "that the Colorado River along the greater portion of its lonely and majestic way, shall be forever unvisited and undisturbed."

Then along came Major Powell, driven by scientific curiosity and courage. He was a Union veteran who had lost his right arm at the Battle of Shiloh. With nine companions Powell started from Green River, Wyoming, rowing and dragging narrow round-bottom boats. They followed the Green to its confluence with the Colorado in southern Utah, exploring wild country that few, if any, white men had seen before—a lonely land characterized by treacherous canyons, isolated settlements, Indian shepherds, and hardy wild animals.

They were river-wise by the time they reached the Grand Canyon, that is, at the point now called Lee's Ferry, where Navajo sandstone of Glen Canyon yields to Kaibab limestone. Mishaps and near starvation still lay ahead. Three of Powell's men quit the party and tried to climb to the rim in hope of reaching a Mormon outpost. They were never seen again and Powell concluded they were slain by Indians. Despite the hardships, Powell studied the canyon walls stratum by stratum and accumulated a wealth of data. Three months after they began, on August 29, 1869, Powell's crew rowed out of the Grand Cayyon at a point sixty-five miles from Las Vegas, Nevada. The two books Powell subsequently authored, following this trip and his second, in 1872, *First Through the Grand Canyon* and *Exploration of the Colorado River and Its Canyons*, are American classics of science, history, literature, and hair-raising adventure.

One hundred summers later, in 1969, Powell's expedition was reenacted covering three months in time from Green River, Wyoming, to Echo Bay, Nevada. Everywhere the new Powell went, crowds came to greet him. People thought it was a great stunt, a tourist promotion or chamber-of-commerce celebration, but the idea behind it was to dramatize irreplaceable natural wonders and the need to respect and protect them. The new Powell (who had dreamed up the whole thing and had built somewhat of a replica of the original boat) was larger in bulk than the original, and two-armed, but he played the role to the hilt. It couldn't have been anyone but Martin Litton.

Martin had already been scrapping for years to keep dams from changing the wild face of the Colorado River country. For almost three hundred miles the Colorado still flows free, from Lee's Ferry, just below Glen Canyon Dam, to the Grand Wash Cliffs. For millions of years the water of the river and its tributaries has been carving canyon, but now that's all that's left of it. Change has imprinted civilization on the wild country.

First, Hoover Dam at the western end created a reservoir 115 miles long called Lake Mead. Then, at the eastern end, Glen Canyon Dam and the reservoir behind it, Lake Powell, in 1964 opened access by powerboat to remote crannies such as Rainbow Bridge, the largest known natural stone arch, and Hole-in-the-Rocks, where a Mormon party once made a daring, seemingly impossible crossing of the Colorado with eighty wagons, plus hundreds of cows and sheep.

This was followed by the huge power plant at Page, adjacent to Glen Canyon Dam, part of the electricity generation and transmission system that has transformed and tamed the Four Corners of the Southwest. All these benefactions are presumed to enrich and enhance the quality of life in America, except for the local Americans, the Hopi and Navajo, traditional peoples standing in the way of power demands of distant supercities.

Almost all the rest of the Colorado River has been tamed, and so too the Columbia, Snake, Stanislaus, Klamath, Trinity, and other western rivers. A natural river has a life of its own, with rhythm and vibrance, but these no longer flow free. Their flows are closely controlled, with priority uses assigned to power production and irrigation, while recreation "lakes" behind dams are primarily holding pools.

Dam building for years was equated with progress. It was part of the New Deal design of helping people during the 1930s and '40s. But there was no end to it, and by the mid-sixties the Bureau of Reclamation, an agency with political punch and large appropriations, was prepared to build two dams within the Grand Canyon. Arizonans might have asked, "Why do we really need these dams? What effect will they have on the values we treasure?" Instead, most wanted these dams to proceed, or thought they did, like a panacea, or religion, that is sure to guarantee a better life, inducing prosperity, boom, bank deposits, freeways, congestion, and sprawl. It took the weight of public pressure from *outside* the Southwest to save the Grand Canyon. I can't imagine anyone today who isn't grateful. Harnessing natural features and improving upon rivers may represent man's ingenuity, but the greater ingenuity is to show that man can survive while leaving some few features of the earth to their own devices. This is the true test of our mechanical, intellectual, and moral skills.

Martin Litton was one of the chief troublemakers who blocked progress in order to save the Grand Canyon. David Brower, executive director of the Sierra Club, was another. Brower, the Club's first full-time executive, was largely responsible for converting an essentially social organization devoted to outdoors play and pleasure into a force of conservation activism variously respected and feared. Tall, erect, and prematurely gray, Brower cast a striking figure, even while lacking an outgoing personality. He always impressed me as reserved or aloof, possibly shy, a poor communicator in conversation and speeches, although extremely literate. His genius lay in his clarity of purpose. The Sierra Club had actually endorsed the dams in the Grand Canyon ("The knowledge of the board members was so fuzzy and so thin," according to Litton, who was one of them, "they didn't even know where the Grand Canyon was"), but this didn't stop Brower. Without consulting the board, he took an advertisement in the Club's name in *The New York Times*, comparing damming the Colorado River with flooding the Sistine Chapel. It might not have been sound organization procedure, but it helped stir the nation.

Brower and Litton had been through an earlier battle in the 1950s over proposed dams in Dinosaur National Monument in western Colorado and eastern Utah, embracing deep canyons of the Green and Yampa Rivers and the world's most concentrated deposits of petrified dinosaur bones. The idea of a dam was a threat to the integrity of the National Park System, but only a handful had the courage, at least at first, to stand up and defend it. In those days Martin was working for the *Los Angeles Times*, not as a staff reporter assigned to cover such events as news, but as a field man boosting sales in the circulation department. On the side he would contribute freelance articles and photographs to his own paper.

"I was writing responsible, inflammatory articles, thoroughly objective," he told me. "I gave both sides and said one was right and one was wrong. They were always big Sunday features with lots of pictures, taking the front page of the second section and continuing inside. Even the headlines were full of fire, about overcrowding in Yosemite, the impending doom of Dinosaur, threats to the Grand Canyon. I wrote evenings and weekends, not with the idea I was going to get a job anywhere else, but because there was something I wanted to say in print, and I wanted it to reach people.

"Brower saw the series on Dinosaur in 1952, got in touch, and asked me to join the Sierra Club. I said I could do more on my own, but he insisted that now that he was executive director things would be different. He made up the slate for the board and I was on it before I was a member of the Club."

Dinosaur represented one of the first major battlegrounds in the modern environmental era. The Bureau of Reclamation withdrew and the national monument remained intact. The Sierra Club and other conservationists yielded, however, over the issue of Glen Canyon. It was the convenient thing to do, particularly since Glen Canyon lay outside of national park boundaries. It was a choice leading to regret, considering the magnificence of wilderness lost and the ultimate degrading influence on the Colorado River in the Grand Canyon. As Martin put it:

"If we hadn't believed in ourselves, we never would have stopped Dinosaur. If we had believed in ourselves enough, we would have stopped Glen Canyon Dam on the Colorado River. We just didn't think we had that kind of strength, and yet the snowball was already rolling. We had the public's confidence in us, and we had the nation on our side as the result of Dinosaur. We could have carried that momentum through the whole Colorado River system. I don't mean there wouldn't have been any pressures, but there wouldn't have been any dam once we got the great Escalante National Park. That's what they were going to call the entire region surrounding Glen Canyon. It was all on the maps in the forties as a park project, the whole blooming thing."

Now, in August 1981, it was another Glen Canyon crisis that

brought me to Lee's Ferry for the start of what Martin called the Grand Canyon Invitational Study Tour. It was a joint venture between the American Wilderness Alliance, which gave mostly its name, and Martin Litton's Grand Canyon Dories, which provided the trip without cost to a variety of people presumably of influence "in the hope that first-hand observation will lead to better understanding of the Grand Canyon and the issues related to it." As the printed invitation stated, "The trip is designed for fun and good fellowship as well as to provide a degree of exposure to human and natural history, hydrology, and the political and environmental choices ahead."

Lee's Ferry hardly suggested anything of its past. It was named for the ferry operated in the 1880s by John Doyle Lee, a lusty Mormon, then a fugitive for having commanded the massacre of 123 westbound emigrants in southwest Utah. The evidences are long gone, Lee's Ferry itself having been replaced in 1929 by Navajo Bridge, four miles downstream. Lee's Ferry suggested to me some busy marina in a state of disarray. Besides our boats, there must have been at least a dozen others, all readying to travel over the same route, the boatmen loading gear and acting knowing and efficient, and their paying guests acting helpful and outdoorsy.

People are drawn by what is called "the longest, wildest, grandest white-water route in the world," a true statement as far as it goes, but as we traveled I would continually refer to Major Powell's report, written in diary form, and try to note differences. The most important was that everything he did was deliberate, without diversion, and thus, totally absorbing and uplifting.

The Grand Canyon even now merits that kind of attention. My son, while in his early twenties, worked three summers in the national parks, after which he concluded, "People ought to be required to take a test before they are allowed to make a visit." The idea may not be feasible, considering the sheer commerce generated by national parks and the demands of democracy being what they are, but there is something to it. For it takes time and patience to see the Grand Canyon, or any national park, to feel it, to allow messages to filter through one's outer defenses and touch the inner spirit. Even the thought of the Grand Canyon, wherever I may be, evokes mental pictures of being with Powell.

As on August 14, 1869, when he entered Granite Gorge and wrote: "Down in these grand gloomy depths we glide, ever listening, ever watching."

And three days later on August 17: "It is especially cold in the rain tonight. The little canvas we have is rotten and useless; the rubber ponchos have all been lost; we have not a blanket apiece. So we build a fire; but the rain, coming down in torrents, extinguishes it, and we sit up all night on the rocks, shivering, and are more exhausted by the night's discomfort than by the day's toil."

River tourists are exposed at least to sandstorms, rainstorms, and chills after everyone gets soaked going through the rapids. But picture James G. Watt, the nature-destroying Secretary of the Interior under President Ronald Reagan, who traveled on the river a few months before Martin's invitational study tour. On completion he complained as follows: "The first day was spectacular. The second day started to get a little tedious, but the third day I wanted even bigger motors to move the raft out. On the fourth day we were praying for helicopters, and they came." This led some wag to quip that if Watt had his druthers he'd go down the Colorado River in a hovercraft—which may not be so unlikely. I recollect on an earlier visit standing at the South Rim when members of a group arrived for a glimpse of one of the greatest vistas on earth, but only a quickie. They had arrived on the scenic flight package tour from Las Vegas, with time for lunch, souvenir shopping, and a few minutes of sightseeing before heading back for the gambling and night spots.

I brought my friend Jane, the kind of person I knew would absorb herself fully in the Grand Canyon. Martin gave members of the tour the option of taking various segments on the trip, ranging from four days to the full eighteen. We opted to do it all, that is, from Lee's Ferry to Lake Mead, or to state it otherwise, from Mile 0 to Mile 277. One of our companions said that he was too busy to allow more than a week, which only made me think again of John Wesley Powell and his tribulations.

The immediate issue that led Martin to conduct the trip was a proposal of the Bureau of Reclamation to furnish "peaking" power from Glen Canyon Dam for distant cities. It would enhance the generators in Phoenix, Grand Junction, Salt Lake City, Cheyenne, Santa Fe, and elsewhere in late afternoon, when air conditioners and electric ranges work harder. However, as the gates of the dam open and close to meet changing power demands, the flow of water would be altered, jeopardizing float trips for rafts and dories. The same effect is evident in one sense or another at man-made reservoirs everywhere: Drawdown leaves boat ramps high and dry and exposes wide bands of dusty flats and muddy shorelines.

Before the age of the dam-builder, the Colorado River would rise gradually to high flows in June and July, then recede gradually to low flows in winter. It doesn't do that anymore. Now it rises and falls in severe fluctuations every twenty-four hours, as controlled flows are released through Glen Canyon's penstocks. The daily differences in height in summer amount to as much as ten feet, all of which result in severe impacts on the river-life community, including plants, wildlife, beaches, and the unending shaping of the great canyon itself.

We could see this as we floated downstream. Cool green reflections sparkled from the waters of the Colorado, in contrast to times past. "Too thick to drink and too thin to plow," said oldtimers of a river that seemed more mud than water, carrying endless tons of silt from upstream sources in Wyoming, Colorado, and New Mexico—the silt that gave the river tools for scouring and gouging, widening and deepening the Grand Canyon. Since construction of Glen Canyon Dam, the silt is blocked; there is little of it, except for flooding by tributaries and occasional rains and thundershowers.

Still, the river is a marvelous, roaring, living presence. I would listen to thunderous vibrations of white water crashing downstream like a freight train on a steel trestle. The roar would grow, then I'd look ahead into a maelstrom of standing waves, yawning holes, whirlpools, and rushing eddies, and hold tight as we plunged through, soaked and chilled with icy water. At Badger Creek we clambered ashore to make camp for our first night on the river. It was just above here, on entering Marble Gorge, that Powell recorded in his diary: "We have learned to observe closely the texture of the rock. In softer strata we have a quiet river, in harder we find rapids and falls. Below us are the limestones and hard sandstones which we found in Cataract Canyon. This bodes toil and

31

danger." Badger Creek actually creates the first of the Grand Canyon's ninety-six rapids. At the confluence, the river seemed to drop off into space.

Each day we plunged through soaking waves, bailed the boat, gazed at towering walls two thousand feet high, alternately burned under the sun and chilled by the shade of the walls. I watched chapters of earth history emerge from the river, forming higher and higher cliffs. I perceived a different Grand Canyon than I had known from earlier visits to the rim, or from hikes down to the river: an endless composition of alcoves and amphitheaters, columns and cornices, horizontal slabs, black marble sculptures polished by flowing water, grottoes, side canyons, springs and seeps, and thousand-foot waterfalls.

The Canyon continually deepened as we floated southwestward at the rate of about one hundred feet to the mile for twenty-five miles into the gradual rise of the East Kaibab Monocline. The river seemed to take on a reddish-orange color from redwall cliffs vivid against the sky, while the rims were far away in the stairstep succession of cliffs, and the world outside further still, distant and trivial.

We didn't wear much clothing and slept out in semiprivate nooks and crannies among tamarisk trees or on the rocks. Food supplies and personal belongings were packed in watertight compartments fitted in the sides of the dories. Cameras and small personal gear were carried in watertight surplus ammunition cans.

I noticed that Martin's boats have a touch of melancholy in their names: *Peace River*, for a stream dammed in Canada; *Vale of Rhondda*, a ravaged coalfield in Wales; *Moqui Steps* and *Music Temple*, sites buried beneath Lake Powell. They were beautiful craft, about seventeen feet long and seven feet wide, brightly colored—red, white, blue, and yellow—variously built of wood, aluminum, or fiber glass, each carrying a boatman and four or five passengers. Fiber glass is the strongest, most damage resistant, and easier to repair in the field (with epoxy glue and tape). A dory, as I learned, costs more to build, maintain, and transport than a rubber raft. Rubber boats usually bounce off the boulders, compared with dories, which split or crack. But dories don't bend or buckle in the waves, they ride slower, higher, and drier on the waves. I loved the dories for their rakish design, based on the Mackenzie River boat, derived from the traditional Portuguese fishing boat, in turn from the older African.

At Redwall Cavern, Mile 33, we lunched on sandwiches and lemonade in a huge chamber carved by the river out of limestone. Powell thought it large enough to contain an assemblage of fifty thousand persons. Whether or not that is possible, it *was* adequate in size for a group that had arrived just before us to set up a volleyball game. This stimulated some of our cohorts to debate the propriety of it. I remained open but checked Powell's diary. On the opposite side of the Colorado lay Vasey's Paradise, about which the explorer wrote as follows:

"The river turns sharply to the east and seems inclosed by a wall set with a million brilliant gems. On coming nearer we find fountains bursting from the rock high overhead, and the spray in the sunshine forms the gems which bedeck the wall. The rocks are covered with mosses and ferns and many beautiful flowering plants. We name it Vasey's Paradise, in honor of the botanist who traveled with us last year."

This led me to pay more attention to life along the river—the great blue herons flapping their way downstream, ravens, canyon wrens breaking the stillness, and red, blue, and purple dragonflies hovering above the water beneath a canopy of cottonwood and box elder.

We weren't completely a dory party, actually seven or eight dories plus three or four oar-powered rubber rafts, all put to use in accommodating a sizable group of forty. In one sense the numbers defeated the pursuit of solitude, yet brought together interested and interesting people.

At the first campsite, Tim, the trip leader, briefed us on some of the essentials: how drinking water is taken from the river and chemically purified; what to do if a boat tips over; about cactus, scorpions, centipedes, tarantulas, rattlesnakes, and whirlpools. And about "the unit," the portable chemical toilet that must be unloaded and reloaded at every campsite. Every party is required to have one—it's the answer, or attempted answer, to problems of pollution, sanitation, and public health.

We weren't alone on the river. There was plenty of company. Large motorized rubber rafts, "baloney boats," each carrying twenty passengers or so, would come by in flotillas of three, traveling much faster, of course. The motorized baloney boats would average thirty to forty miles per day, while we averaged ten. They cover the whole route in a week or eight days, where it takes the oar-powered dories eighteen to twenty days. We met a baloney boat party carrying members of a French canoe club who were thoroughly envious. Anyway, there was lots of togetherness as boatmen raced for the choice campsites, with losers taking the nearby leftovers.

Most boatmen knew each other. They shared a camaraderie born of river-love transcending the rivalry of their employers. In our party they were virtually all volunteers, with the exception, I think, of Tim, the trip leader, and Lori, the cook and Tim's girlfriend (later to be his wife), a handsome, self-reliant, and thoroughly competent young woman who fulfilled her duties of keeping everyone fed and then handled her raft on the river adeptly, a striking figure, as well as any man. The others weren't getting paid, but it was the fun of the river and the fight to save it that brought them out. I had met only one of them, Bruce, before, and poor Bruce showed up too late. I had traveled with Bruce in the Sea of Cortez aboard the *Baja Explorador*, a marvelous wooden schooner that, in its earlier life as the *Brown Bear*, had carried Olaus Murie and Victor Scheffer, two noted biologists, on their expedition to the Aleutians in the mid-thirties. Bruce was slow in volunteering for the trip and in getting back from Mexico, but he came to Lee's Ferry anyway, if only to see his friends and to cheer the party on its way.

The boatmen were all vigorous people. Nels was a distance runner; he told me of the thrills of floating the Colorado in midwinter, facing harsh weather, yet enjoying the solitude. Jon, handsome, quiet, had been forced by arthritis to quit a promising professional football career, though he embodied gracefulness and concentration in plunging through the big rapids. Wally, a former schoolteacher, was an independent spirit whom Martin had fired for being *too* independent, yet I found him sensitive and searching. Sam had worked as a commercial boatman for a number of years, but now was a river ranger on the staff of the national park; actually, he'd been boating one way or another all his life, including rowing on the crew at the University of Washington. Sam wore a full red beard that fit more with his religion, Buddhism, and his meditation than with his employment by a federal agency that normally requires "proper" dress and grooming.

Three of the boatmen could have been invited without rowing—that is, they had other credentials. Roderick Nash was the best known, a history professor at the University of California at Santa Barbara, who had written a well-recognized work, *Wilderness and the American Mind*. I had known him casually for years. A good-looking, well-spoken outdoorsman in his early forties, Rod brought his own raft and seemed to have all the right camping equipment. He was a different species than the other boatmen, more intellectual or cultivated perhaps, or more elevated; for whatever reason, he evidently had earned the reputation as "Rod the River God," or simply "Rod God." Robert Jones, an environmental reporter for the *Los Angeles Times*, also brought his own raft; he was clearly not an expert (though he may have become one since), but managed. And there was Mark Dubois, in his early thirties, as tall as Abraham Lincoln and as self-effacing as I fancy Lincoln to have been. Mark didn't talk much about the meaning of nature, or humility, or sacrifice, or doing without, but clearly he understood and lived his own defined role. As a boy in Sacramento, he became a spelunker, exploring the caverns honeycombing the canyon of the Stanislaus River in the foothills of the Sierra Nevada. Then he became a commercial river guide on the Stanislaus, a proficient white-water raftsman, who could also kayak without a paddle, using only his hands and the shift of his body weight to guide himself through the rapids. Mark had been to college without graduating, but he had lots of learning in him. He was rather a celebrity in his own right, well publicized for having chained himself to a rock in the Stanislaus, threatening to give his life if the Corps of Engineers insisted on flooding the canyon as part of a dam-and-reservoir project. The Corps relented, but only for a while. Mark lost his battle, yet I venture he will always be a folk hero of nature-love. I picture him on the Colorado: smiling from his gangly height of six feet eight, greeting people with his bear hug, performing any and all chores as though each were a privilege, tender as a paper tiger with Sharon, his dark-haired, slender sweetheart, climbing the rocky side canyons with finesse, and barefoot yet, and diving fifteen or twenty feet into the pools.

As for the passengers, they included a clutch of journalists, Washington congressional staff people, representatives of environmental organizations, the park superintendent, and assorted others. When we first assembled—at a hotel in St. George, Utah—Jane and I sat at dinner with the congressional folks, whom I had known in Washington. "What in the world were they talking about?" she asked me later. It was all about procedures in politics, with a language of its own, filled with trivia and illusions of self-importance, when actual importance had only fleeting value at most. The group included John Oakes, retired editor of the editorial page of *The New York Times*, who over the span of years has probably written the most effective environmental columns in journalism; Bill Moyers, who had worked as a principal aide to President Lyndon Johnson in the White House and had become a television personality; Luna Leopold, geologist and hydrologist of some note, but more distinguished in my mind as the son who put together choice writings of his father, Aldo Leopold, into the conservation classic, *A Sand County Almanac*; and Wilbur Garrett, editor of the *National Geographic* magazine.

A trip of this nature is no place to take oneself seriously, and few did. After all, we were all getting soaked and baked together, and more or less depended on one another. Besides, it was impossible to measure status by clothing or lack of it. "I know who you are," some young girl said to me as though I really counted, then turned to a friend standing close by at the moment and asked, "But who are you?" It was Rupert Culter, basically modest, but more so in his early years before he had become a sub-Cabinet member in Washington. "*I* am senior vice-president of the National Audubon Society," said Rupert, as though it made a damn bit of difference on the Colorado River. John Oakes might have worn the pose of a gray eminence, but he was too absorbed in the environment and the issue. Bill Moyers did his best to get along like everybody else. Luna Leopold tended to be self-important, but with justification, considering the mantle of his father. Garrett, however, could never forget, or let anyone else forget, that he was editor of that scholarly, literary journal, the *National Geographic*.

His trouble was that he wasn't with us long enough. A wilderness trip involves sharing all kinds of things, from secrets to smells. I used to think that sharing booze counted, but the truth is it gets in the way. Garrett brought along a friend, a banker, who got smashed every night he was on the trip, which he could have done just as well at home. Wilderness provides a natural high. Or as the lady of means said on one trip or other, tearfully and laughingly, while deep in muck and misery, "It's amazing if you have enough money how much discomfort you can buy."

The trouble with our trip was that people were coming in for a few days and then leaving, barely getting dirty or working up a good body odor. Worst of all, most weren't even climbing out, but were being transported by helicopter. Martin would rationalize the rightness of the cause, but it didn't make sense to me to pose righteousness on one hand and then accept a special privilege the public is denied. Still, this system enabled me to meet W (no first name, no period) Mitchell, a paraplegic who could not have hiked in or out. At the time of this trip, Mitchell was mayor of Crested Butte, a little town in the Colorado Rockies, who had led a successful fight to prevent a large mining operation from despoiling a scenic mountain at the edge of town. Mitchell had survived two critical accidents. In the first he was burned over 60 percent of his body, his hands and face disfigured. In the second his back was broken. He didn't figure that life was over, but just beginning. And down the Colorado River he went, along with the rest of us.

On the morning of the fifth day, at Mile 77, we pulled ashore to study Hance Rapid. The river had meandered through the great inner canyon of exposed ancient rocks, angled and tilted, the Grand Canyon series, with intermittent powerful rapids. Now it entered the upper Granite Gorge. "You don't have a chance at Hance," the saying goes. The boatmen climbed a hill to check the water. Hance, a long curving stretch dropping thirty feet over its half-mile course, was a problem, with rocks hidden below the surface or barely sticking up. It would take a zigzag course. A minute or two apart, boats would zoom down the far side under a wall of black rock, yawning and pitching. I was riding that day with Wally. He stood up for a good look, then sat again, heading the dory into boiling waves. The bow dropped like the first car of a roller coaster beginning its run, then reared skyward. We passengers held tight to the lifeline and presently were through, riding choppy tailwaves.

At Mile 87 we passed under the Kaibab Suspension Bridge, the only crossing of the Colorado in 350 miles, part of the route hikers follow between the North Rim and South Rim, one of the superb do-it-yourself adventures of our national parks. Just below it we stopped at Phantom Ranch, a simple tourist hotel, civilization's only outpost in the canyon, where some of our party left and others joined. I took a few minutes to contemplate the Powell Report. He might have been describing that very day:

"Clouds are playing in the canyon today. Sometimes they roll down in great masses, filling the gorge with gloom; sometimes they hang aloft from wall to wall and cover the canyon with a roof of impending storm."

My theory before the trip had been that the boatmen did all the work and had the fun, while the passengers went along for the ride. But this was not quite true. They were more than willing to let us have our turn, and some of us got pretty good at it. I tried my hand several times and worked hard, but really wasn't too proficient. I suppose it's something that comes with practice, or perhaps the rekindled rhythm of an earlier activity. It demands a certain intuition to coordinate arms and oars with the flow of the current, and a sensitive eye to perceive the path to follow, the path to avoid. The idea is to row against the tide to gain better control and vision, and to make sure that if the boat must strike a rock, it won't strike as hard. The rapids, formed by rocks and gravel washed into the mainstream, are rated on a scale of 1 to 10. The big ones the boatmen would handle themselves.

We buckled life jackets in advance of Horn Creek Rapid (rated 7 to 9). The dory plunged into a hole, climbed a wave, heaved, and twisted. We ran along one wall, then split across river, slipping down the tongue of a deep twenty-foot trough, while huge rocks flashed by in the whirlpools. When I later found my notebook it was water-soaked, but then so was I. At Hermit Rapid (7 to 8), I gave my friends something to talk about when I flipped head over heels completely out of the dory. It happened so quickly I didn't have time to grow tense, and managed to hold tight to the lifeline. Wally praised the performance. "I'll give you a ten for that one!"

he exclaimed. Crystal, just three miles beyond, was even more hairy, with rocks on the right and a churning cauldron on the left. Here, passengers were directed to leave the boats and walk over the rocks. Sitting on boulders we watched the boatmen find the narrow slot, while the boats danced on waves. Even so, two dories were banged up in the holes.

It wasn't the excitement that I found most stimulating, but the tranquillity. People around me, like Martin, Luna, and Rod, would knowingly discuss rock formations I couldn't identify or comprehend, ranging from Kaibab limestone, 250 million years old, Hermit shale, Redwall limestone, Tapeats sandstone, to Brahma and Vishnu schist, 2 billion years old. I thought of, and sought to identify with, Joseph Wood Krutch, a literary personality who gave up one career in New York to pursue another in Arizona, studying and contemplating the meaning of ancient nature. If we do not permit the earth to produce beauty and joy, he wrote, in the end it will not produce food either. Or, stated otherwise, if we do not value the earth as being beautiful, as well as useful, it will ultimately cease to be even useful. Happily, in such places as the Grand Canyon, the individual can reach beyond himself to learn love and reverence for nature. Thus, I felt inspired and elevated while gliding through a section of river fittingly called the Jewels—passing Agate, Sapphire, Turquoise, Ruby, and Garnet Canyons—where mica in the rocks sparkled in the sunlight. Such moments rendered all discomforts insignificant.

We explored ashore, up steep side canyons to springs and gardens and ancient Indian stone structures. I contemplated the walls weathering, crumbling, tumbling shreds of sand, gravel, rock, and mud into the water. The natural silt load rebuilds the beaches each season, though they, the beaches, denied the loads from above Glen Canyon, are now only fragments of their former selves. Mark Dubois, climbing barefoot, covered more ground than anyone, yet all of us extended to the fullness of our limits. When and where in the world would I ever again see a natural handiwork like Elves Chasm, where pendulous waterfalls drop from one ferny grotto to the next clear pool below, like the falls in a Chinese painting?

But what a contradiction to be climbing the talus slopes to stare at handprints left on the walls by Anasazi Indians a thousand years

39

ago and then to hear the racket of a low-flying helicopter on a commercial sightseeing tour. With such exploitation, the Grand Canyon experience has been diluted and degraded. Is it the American way that prevents saving things worth saving? At Deer Creek Falls and Havasu Creek, lush oases, we merged with other parties into mob scenes overrunning wild beauty. The French canoe club members arrived topless in their baloney boat. An American woman drinking beer on a rock could hardly wait for her trip to end: Her rubber boat had crashed into a boulder, leaving her with a nasty cut over one eye.

As people flock to these white waters, problems grow. Congestion, competition for campsites, trampled vegetation, destruction of natural and archaeological features have been the side effects of popularity. Years ago, when there was more than enough to go around and a mere handful of takers, it didn't make any difference. But it does today. A river like the Colorado needs to be protected from people, as well as for people. The important point is to feel as part of the flow, the flow of a timeless river, the flow of history. That doesn't come easily, which is why continually reviewing Powell's record, with his expression of despair, discovery, and exultation, is especially valuable. As on August 24, when he wrote:

"How anxious we are to make our reckoning every time we stop, now that our diet is confined to plenty of coffee, a very little spoiled flour, and very few dried apples! It has come to a race for dinner. Still, we make such fine progress that all hands are in good cheer, but not a moment of daylight is lost."

In our own party there was slippage in sanitation. People were leaving litter and beer cans. They weren't following the procedures at "the unit." I discussed this with Wally, who was in charge of the portable toilet, including packaging the human waste to carry out. Wally, self-sufficient, independent minded, a master with the oars, would allow himself some time each day to walk, or hike, away from the group to be alone in the Grand Canyon. He was aware of the abundant regulations designed not to restrict, but to accommodate human use. They failed, he said, to address the basic question: "What are we doing here?"

W Mitchell, the paraplegic, wore a confident smile, transcending disability with poise that showed he knew exactly what *he* was doing in the Grand Canyon, living the experience to the fullest while begrudging no one who could do more physically. I imagine that he felt somewhat like Major Powell, the one-armed Civil War veteran, when he wrote on August 29, 1869: "When he who has been chained by wounds to a hospital cot . . . at last goes out into the open fields, what a world he sees! The first hour of convalescent freedom seems rich recompense for all pain and gloom and terror." At Havasu, Mitchell was denied the five-mile hike to the Shangri-la at Mooney Falls, where clear waters tumble over red limestone cliffs into a turquoise pool, yet he wasn't idle. He and Sam West, the red-bearded Buddhist ranger, swam together in a calm-water inlet where we had pulled our boats ashore. When I climbed down from the falls I watched them, sensing some magical communication between them and appreciating that limbs alone do not make a body whole.

The *Today* show people were with us as we approached Lava Falls, at Mile 179, the last major rapid, the most celebrated of all ninety-six, a final showdown. There were four of them. They surprised me, especially considering they had come from Los Angeles, that center of urbanity. They didn't demand extra attention or service, and they were good campers. Only the producer was nervous. They stayed four days, and when they helicoptered out, bid endless goodbyes. As it happened, I rode in the same dory through the falls with the *Today* reporter, Boyd Mattson, W Mitchell, and Sally Ranney, a tall, beautiful blond environmentalist from Denver. Lava, rated 8 to 10, drops thirty-seven feet in two hundred yards. Powell imagined the falls being formed by a river of molten rock running down into a river of melted snow, with a seething and boiling of waters, and a cloud of steam rolling into the heavens. It was an exciting run, which the TV cameraman shot from a helicopter, and then it was over.

We continued through lower Granite Gorge. The canyon opened into the Mohave Desert, landscaped with mesquite, ocotillo, prickly pear, and barrel cactus, and presently the river was lost under the waters of Lake Mead. The appearance of large motor cruisers told us the adventure was over. We camped one last night, miserably in a storm of blowing sand, and then it was over.

"Sometimes the only thing to do is to step back and take a fresh look at life and the world from the uncluttered vantage of the wilderness," according to the litany of that king of river rats, Martin Litton. "More and more, as wilderness grows less wild in the presence and under the pressures of society's products—including too many of us—we're learning that some of the most healing, most invigorating contact with the natural earth is achieved without leaving any marks at all—by floating with the currents of free-running rivers."

It isn't easy to avoid leaving marks; it isn't even possible. But I wish I could do that Grand Canyon trip again, with more time, and with Martin Litton, who surely must be the most determined, evocative, and flamboyant personality since John Wesley Powell. "I know nothing about public affairs reporting and I have nothing to say," he announced in his opening remarks to my class at the University of Idaho. Then he carried on for an hour and a half. I could have listened to him all night.

CHAPTER III

Seeking the Revelation That Came to John Muir in Glacier Bay

Terry McWilliams hooked a seal instead of a salmon. We were fishing in Glacier Bay when she felt a tug on her line, a heavy weight, but without the play or fight of a spirited fish. Bob Giersdorf scanned the waters and exclaimed, "You've caught a harbor seal—it's a pup!" Then he turned to Rick Kearns, factotum on the forty-two-foot cruiser *Ice Folly*, and said, "Reel it in and we'll net it." But Rick, in his early twenties, was slightly overwhelmed. "You mean, like a fish?"

My friend Giersdorf has an ingenious touch, devising, designing, improvising, and accomplishing what seems, at least to me, beyond doing. Perhaps it's an essential quality for survival in Alaska. He took the fishing rod and reeled in the pup, slowly and gently, and hauled it aboard the water-level platform, four or five feet below the deck. The seal weighed about thirty to thirty-five pounds and appeared numb with fright. The hook was stuck in its mouth, though no blood showed. While Rick held the seal, Bob deftly extracted the hook with a pair of pliers and headed the seal homeward.

Bob is one of my successful friends, who made good as an entrepreneur and marketer of tourism in Alaska. He was born in 1935 in Thompson Falls, Montana, where his father was working as a transient welder following the oil fields, before heading for the World War II shipyards in Portland. Bob made his first trip to Alaska as a teenager in 1951, driving a trailer up the Alaskan Highway and spending the summer earning high wages in construction. Home again, he enrolled at the University of Oregon, married in his sophomore year, and then decided that schooling was interfering with his opportunity to make it in Alaska.

Americans have been drawn north to the frontier for diverse reasons. The drive for business success in a growth environment is only one of them. Individualists crave the chance to escape the perils of social conformity, regulations, and bureaucracy. Some want only to escape. I recall an early trip of mine, when I went to St. Lawrence Island, a rocky, blustery outpost in the Bering Sea, forty miles from Siberia, where the Eskimo culture revolves around the walrus, as the Plains Indian culture revolved around the buffalo. I slept in a classroom at the schoolhouse and took my meals with the teacher and his family. They had come from Michigan following the tragic death of a child, which impelled the despondent mother, the teacher's wife, to flee everything familiar, for what she hoped would be the end of the earth.

Chuck and Sara Hornberger, friends of mine who live at the edge of wilderness in the Lake Clark region east of Anchorage, came north for other reasons. Chuck had been a diesel mechanic in the navy, and Sara, a teacher. They met and married in Arizona and moved to Idaho, while dreaming of living in Alaska, self-reliant and free of crowds. When Sara was offered a better teaching job at Naknek, a fishing community populated mostly by natives, they packed up their three small children and headed north. Chuck's first job was maintaining diesel engines for the power company, but ultimately they got what they wanted: the property on Lake Clark. It's not that they dislike people, except in heavy doses. They built a little resort, accommodating a few guests, but without straining to succeed in business. They serve fresh vegetables they grow themselves, which is no small feat. They get by very reasonably on their fruits and vegetables, varied with caribou, moose, and salmon. Most of their electric power comes from Chuck's ingenious windmill. Winters are quiet. They may go for a week or ten days without seeing another soul, but they like it that way and found what they came for.

The Hornbergers' friend, Dick Proenneke, migrated from Iowa. A former heavy-equipment operator and mechanic nearly blinded by a work accident, he vowed once he recovered to concentrate his focus on the earth's beauty. At the age of fifty, he withdrew to Twin Lakes and with care and craftsmanship built his own cabin. He aimed to spend his time hiking, climbing, canoeing, following wildlife, and keeping a journal. That journal would become an engrossing adventure story, published under the title *One Man's Wilderness*. On the opening page he recorded his goal:

"What was I capable of that I didn't know yet? What about my limits? Could I truly enjoy my own company for an entire year? Was I equal to everything this wild land could throw at me? I had seen its moods in late spring, summer and early fall, but what about winter? Would I love the isolation then with its bone-stabbing cold, its brooding ghostly silence, its forced confinement. At the age of 51 I intended to find out."

Celia Hunter came with much the same spirit. During World War II she and I were both stationed at the military air base at Long Beach, California, though I never knew her then. In those days I was navigating planes across the Pacific, while Celia was shuttling fighter planes across the continent. Women were stirring for liberation. Men conceded it might be ladylike to fly, but not to fly out of the country. Following the war, however, Celia and her partner, Virginia Hill, headed north in two beat-up warplanes. Grounded repeatedly by severe Arctic weather, it took them twenty-seven days to reach Fairbanks. Ultimately, they staked a claim on a blueberry-covered ridge above Moose Creek, just outside Mount McKinley National Park, dreaming of establishing a wilderness retreat where they could provide comfortable accommodations without destroying the beauty they beheld. Celia and Ginny became as self-reliant as any men in the bush. They devised their own systems of heat, water, and garbage disposal; they learned to endure bears, washouts, and park bureaucrats. The complex of tent cabins and rustic chalets called Camp Denali, endowed, from its perch above Wonder Lake, with a magnificent view of the tallest mountain on the continent, became the most famous hotel in Alaska without being a hotel at all. It was more of a house party for lovers of wilderness and the outdoors. So they ran it for twenty-five years, experiencing many moods of wild nature, until turning over the operation to others of younger age. Ginny became a wife for a time (married to a park ranger), a mother, and a landscape photographer. Celia, always handsome and vigorous, became a humanitarian and wilderness activist. Somewhere along the line she wrote these lines that I treasure:

"National security often is visualized in military terms, but true security and prosperity depend upon safeguarding the earth's natural systems. In a healthy land base there must be room for wild, untamed regions of substance and dimension. It's a question of survival, as well as aesthetics and enjoyment."

I mention these friends of mine to present a picture of ethical messengers to the Alaska wilderness, who want to give as well as take from it. Yet, they represent only a part of the tableau, the rest of which romantics like myself tend to overlook. I was reminded of the truth while reading the account of the Harriman Expedition of 1899, titled *Looking Far North*, by two historians, William H. Goetzemann and Kay Sloan. They recount the saga of Edward H. Harriman, the enlightened Union Pacific railroad mogul who steamed into Alaskan waters aboard his luxurious yacht, the *George W. Elder*, with a complement aboard of thirty of the nation's preeminent scientists, naturalists, artists, and photographers, including John Muir, John Burroughs, George Bird Grinnell, Edward S. Curtis, Louis Agassiz Fuertes, William Healey Dall, and C. Hart Merriam.

While cruising in Prince William Sound (as historians Goetzemann and Sloan disclose), a visitor approached the *Elder* in his small boat. He ran a fox farm on one of the many islands in the Sound, and he hoped the blue-hued pelts would bring a large profit when it came time to skin the animals. Perhaps, he suggested, the expedition might enjoy a tour of his enterprise. He had originally bought two pairs of blue foxes from the Alaska Commercial Company and now his farm contained forty, each of whose skins, he estimated, could bring from fifteen to thirty dollars. Entrepreneurship, it seemed, thoroughly pervaded Alaska's coasts, and even the smallest islands held men with business schemes. That is Alaska. The authors synthesize it so: "This had been Alaska's heritage from the very beginning, when the first Russian seal hunter descended upon its shores. A pristine wilderness that seemingly beckoned the man of nature, like John Muir, it had seen few such men. Rather, it had entertained for the most part ruthless exploiters from all nations—Russia, Britain, the United States, and even France. Alaska had always been a bonanza, a 'profit point', and rarely the romantic park that many members of the expedition seemed to think it was."

That statement is true, too true. Yet, I like to visualize my heroes and friends, the partisans of wilderness, as giving wholeness to Alaska, and giving meaning to it in the advancement of human culture.

"Denali and the Alaska Range suddenly burst into view ahead, apparently very near. I can never forget my sensations at the sight," wrote Charles Sheldon of the start of his monumental 1906 adventure in naturalism. Denali, the High One, or god of the great range, had only lately been named Mount McKinley by a young easterner (who had participated in an 1896 party). But Sheldon preferred the ancient name. He had already seen the mountains of the Alaska coast, the massive St. Elias Range, and those of the Yukon, yet he was overwhelmed by the mass and majesty of Denali, rising 20,320 feet and covered with glaciers 30 and 40 miles long.

Denali was the capstone of wilderness, a defiant giant that had never yet been climbed. Sheldon came to pursue his interests in wildlife. As a civil engineer he had made successful mining and railroad investments in Mexico, and had become fascinated by the desert bighorn sheep of that country. In 1903, at the age of thirty-six, he retired from business to explore and study the wild sheep of North America, following a path from Mexico to Arizona and north to the Canadian Rockies, the Yukon, and the northern slopes of the Alaska Range.

With the help of three packers he built a cabin on the bar of the Toklat River, living there for a year while hunting various species of animals for food, collecting and preparing specimens for the Smithsonian Institution, and keeping detailed notes for his book, *The Wilderness of Denali*. He lived mostly alone in the wilds, the packers having left after the cabin was built, and his guide and assistant, Henry P. Karstens, shuttling by dogsled to bring in supplies and take out specimens for shipment.

Sheldon saw the north country in the throes of growth and change. Miners coming out from Fairbanks were making devastating inroads in search of riches. Meat hunters prowled the slopes of Denali and its sister mountain, Foraker. Sheldon felt concern for the rich animal community: the barren-ground caribou, America's native reindeer, in huge herds, often in the thousands, advancing in migration across the tundra, living in harmony with wolves, wolverines, grizzly bears, moose, and Dall sheep. In an effort to save the wildlife, Sheldon proposed setting the area aside as a national park. It took time before Congress acted favorably to achieve this goal. Nonetheless, Sheldon was present at the White House on February 26, 1917, when President Woodrow Wilson signed into law the bill establishing Mount McKinley National Park and then turned and presented the pen to him. In due course Sheldon's aide in the wilds, Henry Karstens, would become first superintendent of the new park with a simple wooden hut sixty miles inside the park boundary and little more.

John Muir came to Alaska in pursuit of glaciers. Muir is one of the prime examples I cite to students on the values of self-education. He walked away from the University of Wisconsin to pursue studies in what he called the "University of the Wilderness." He conducted his now celebrated solo thousand-mile walk to the sea across Kentucky and down to the Florida coast, learning about nature from nature itself, free of hidebound textbooks and classroom formulas. Then he headed west for California, living during his years there more outdoors than indoors. He challenged the prevalent science of his time and proved the influence of glaciation in shaping the features of Yellowstone. Yet, Muir perceived the mountain landscape in terms of poetic imagery merged with science, as for example:

"Vapor from the sea; rain, snow and ice on the summits; glaciers and rivers—these form a wheel that grinds the mountains thin and sharp, sculptures deeply the flanks, and furrows them into ridge and canyon, and crushes the rocks into soils on which the forests and meadows and gardens and fruitful vine and tree and grain are growing."

In 1877, two years before his first visit to Glacier Bay, Muir went prowling in the wilds of the San Gabriel Mountains in southern California. His discovery was that even bears made their way through the sprawling tangle called chaparral only with difficulty. He was compelled to creep for miles on all fours, through thickets which had become wood-rat villages, his sole companionship coming from bears, wolves, foxes, and wildcats. It was solid training. For all the solitary travels of his lifetime, Muir probably never experienced loneliness or fear.

In Alaska Muir earned the name "Ice Chief" while spending summers exploring and learning. In 1879 he pushed his luck for an exploration of Glacier Bay. He went near the end of October—long past what we today call "the season"—when the mountains were mantled with fresh snow from the peaks and ridges of the Fairweather Range down to the level of the sea. Days were growing short. Winter with heavy storms was nearing; avalanches would boom down the long white slopes and all the land would be buried. Muir, like Thoreau, enjoyed storms; he considered them rather exuberant, kindly expressions of nature. Still, he reckoned the main inland channels would remain open and it would be easy to keep warm in camp along the forested shores. He traveled in a large dugout canoe with three Indians and a missionary named Young. The expedition was full of foreboding for the Indians, heading into storm, sleet, and darkness, and more than once they wanted to turn back.

My three companions, Terry, Bob, and Rick, and I carried with us a copy of Muir's account, published in *Century Magazine* some years following his trip. We took turns reading from it as we followed in his path, contemplating the contrast between our times, with its comfort and convenience, and his.

The Indians lost heart with the howling storms. One conjectured that Muir must be a witch "to seek knowledge in such a place as this, and in such miserable weather." Fearing that he would lose them, he sternly advised that for ten years he had been wandering alone among mountains and storms, but always in company with good fortune; that when they traveled with him they need fear nothing; that the storm would soon cease, and the sun again shine; that only the brave could look for Heaven's care.

While ashore, the Indians and missionary mostly stayed in camp, so Muir did a lot of walking alone on the mountain slopes, through rain, mud, and sludgy snow, crossing boulder-choked torrents, wading, jumping, wallowing. He found Glacier Bay a quiet complex of ice and snow and newborn rocks, freshly glaciated. On one hand he called it "dim, dreary, mysterious." However, when sunshine streamed through luminous fringes of the clouds, falling on the green waters of the fjord, the crystal bluffs of glaciers, and spreading fields of ice, Muir was overcome by what he called "icy wilderness unspeakably pure and sublime."

We followed his course from the tourist center at Bartlett Cove up the bay, passing the Marble Islands, rocky islets really, teeming with birds—cormorants, puffins, oyster catchers, guillemots, murres, and gulls—which we stopped to observe with binoculars, particulary the gulls busily warding off an eagle trying to invade their nesting area. While heading up Muir Inlet to Muir Glacier, we saw a humpback whale, a prize sight. It was black on top, and white bellied, playfully rolling on the surface, standing on its head and thrashing at the surface with its flukes, then bending in a graceful arc and plunging below. The waters of the fifty-mile-long bay were flecked with icebergs, great blocks of ice broken loose from the glacial mass when their time is come. Glaciers in every stage of development reached the water's edge at narrow, fjordlike inlets, often with cliffs at least one hundred feet high. We passed a kayak or two, seemingly small and slow, yet I admired (and envied) the kayaker's harmony with his environment.

Glacier Bay National Park covers roughly more than 3.3 million acres, which makes it as large as Yellowstone and half again. Happily, there is no way to reach it by car. Wilderness is able to speak more or less on its terms. Glacier Bay bisects the park, with two major branches, Muir Inlet, to the north, and Tarr Inlet, northwest; they join the bay near its midpoint, where it is ten miles across. Below this junction forested slopes comprise much of the shoreline; above it, subtidal rocks and small islands are slowly appearing.

The ebb and flow of its sixteen active tidewater glaciers in such a grandly proportioned theater reflect the rhythmic changes of the climate of the planet and the web of life. Once glaciers yield, the barrens are dotted with fireweed, horsetail, mosses, and other pioneer plants, providing the foundation for spruce and hemlock. Animals arrive: harbor seals on densely packed icebergs, as we saw at the face of Muir Glacier and Johns Hopkins Glacier; bears, otters, and mink, and mountain goats and hoary marmots in the alpine meadows, feeding on grasses, sedges, shrubs, and lichens.

When Captain George Vancouver sailed through the Icy Strait in 1794, Glacier Bay was only a dent in the shoreline. A towering wall of ice, more than four thousand feet deep in places, blocked the seaward outlet. John Muir noted the beginnings of the spruce-hemlock forest and calculated the glacier had retreated forty-eight miles. He studied and described the fjords and tributaries, resulting from glacial erosion, the imposing array of jagged glacial spires and pyramids and flat-topped towers of many shades of blue. His conclusion was simple:

"Glacier Bay is undoubtedly young as yet. Vancouver's chart, made only a century ago, shows no trace of it, though found admirably faithful in general. It seems probable, therefore, that even the entire bay was occupied by a glacier of which all those described above were only tributaries."

Blessed with the long day of an Alaskan summer, we hove to in late afternoon near the base of Muir Glacier to watch huge columns and figures of a thousand shapes tumble into the sea, creating heavy swells and rocking seals on the ice. This action is called calving, and the sound of it may carry ten miles or more. Or as Muir pictured it:

"When a large mass sinks from the upper fissured portion of the wall, there is first a keen, piercing crash, then a deep, deliberate, prolonged, thundering roar, which slowly subsides into a low, muttering growl, followed by numerous smaller, grating, clashing sounds from the agitated bergs that dance in the waves about the newcomer as if in welcome; and these again are followed by the splash and roar of the waves raised and hurled against the moraines."

Finally we anchored for the night in Blue Mouse Cove, below the Brady Icefield. There was little night or darkness. We fished

51

for our dinner of halibut and salmon in calm, sheltered waters, bronzed in the reflection of the sun hanging low over the silent white mountains, including Muir's favorite, 15,320 feet high, Mount Fairweather, which he described as "fashioned like a superb crown with delicately fluted sides." We were deep in wilderness, both subdued and uplifted by it, and also, I think, by the camaraderie and understanding among us.

Terry McWilliams was thirty-nine. She had been in Alaska for eight years. A graduate in political science of the University of California at Los Angeles, she had worked for the USO in the Pacific, then for the parks and recreation department at Spokane, Washington. At the age of twenty-eight she married a young man eight years her junior. It lasted one year. "I wanted to stay married, but it wasn't his thing," she told me. "He was a loner for the outdoors." Wilderness draws these people, restless, roaming, dreaming. Some have had half an education, which now and then they try to complete, but chances are it fails to yield fulfillment. Following Spokane, Terry had come north for a job with the Anchorage recreation and health program, which proved a step to becoming the director of state parks—evidently the first woman in the country to hold such a position. It lasted only three years, until 1980, with issues of politics and principle contributing to her departure.

Once Terry told me of how she crossed with her boss, the state director of natural resources, over a logging plan for the Bald Eagle Council Grounds in southeast Alaska. In this particular area along the Chilkat River (actually not far from Glacier Bay), eagles arrive in late fall, drawn by late salmon runs in unusual upswellings of warm water. This one section, seven or eight miles along the Chilkat, attracts the greatest concentration of eagles during fall and winter of any place on earth. At any given time there may be as many as three thousand, possibly more, grouped in masses of fifty to one hundred eagles per tree. It was here the department of natural resources, the agency responsible for managing state-owned lands, elected to promote a large-scale, long-term timber sale contract, principally to revive a sawmill at the town of Haines. The logging would be done by "clear-cutting," leveling vast tracts as the cheapest and easiest way to extract timber. Terry insisted the land-use plan denied consideration of other values and other resources, such as Chilkat State Park, 5,400 acres of scenic beauty. Her boss was a biologist, but also a politician. "There is nothing wrong with clear-cuts," he countered. "Well, I protest in behalf of my constituents," said she bravely, but in vain.

She quit her job for another reason: so that she could spend more time raising and racing sled dogs, seeing more of Alaska by kayak and on hiking trails. Even while directing the state park system, she was bent on travel, on seeing places and talking to people for herself. That was how I met Terry in the first place.

It was at the railroad station in Anchorage, a worn frontier vintage piece. Bob Giersdorf had invited me to join him, a potential business associate, a Forest Service official, and the director of state parks, for a three-day cruise in Prince William Sound, where he was interested in establishing a commercial tourist operation. Terry was dressed for the outdoors, neatly, unlike some outdoorsies I know who give the impression they've been sleeping in their clothes for a month (and sometimes smell like it). She greeted me with bright eyes bordered by dark hair and broad smile revealing a set of large white teeth, the kind of open expression men are apt to misconstrue, coming from such an attractive woman.

The trip was thoroughly enjoyable, riding the seedy Alaska Railroad to Whittier, then cruising Prince William Sound aboard the *Arctic Tramp*, a classy old motor schooner. It was for me as much a primitive wonderland as Glacier Bay, overwhelming with glaciers and fjords, Dall porpoises pacing the ship's bow, harbor seals on the icebergs, bald eagles perched on shoreline snags, sea lions congregating by the hundreds on wave-swept rocks, the occasional tall black dorsal fin of a killer whale, and the steamy spout of a humpback. Terry's interest was in island parks, which she discussed knowledgeably. She was one of the boys, as it were, but she slept in her own cabin, and that was it. Later she invited me to go with her to Wood-Tikchik State Park, in southwest Alaska, a wild complex of craggy cliffs, fast-flowing rivers, waterfalls, and marshly lowlands. We stayed at a rustic resort, 40 miles from the closest settlement and 250 miles west of the westernmost highway on the continent, one of several lodges catering to sport fishermen. We were there to observe the park. She gave no suggestive personal hint and neither did I, proving something about wasted opportunity, but I felt better not to have tried.

When Bob and I discussed sojourning in Glacier Bay, I suggested inviting Terry, the good sport and good companion, and he was for it. She arrived full of enthusiasm, brimming with news of her fiancé. He was thirty (and she, as mentioned, thirty-nine). Somehow it didn't surprise me when she wrote the following April, while in Kotzebue for a dog race: "My friend Bill and I are defunct. So much for the young ones. I guess I knew it was too good to be true."

My friend Giersdorf had his quota of entanglement, but put it behind him in the sixties to concentrate on Lori. He was married, living in Anchorage, and working for an airline when he met Lori, who was living in Fairbanks and working for another airline. After heavy shuttling and soul-searching, he proceeded on the course to marriage with Lori. The two of them are married to the business as well, living in a high-rise luxury condominium a few blocks from their office in Seattle. It wouldn't be my way, to be rooted in a city business and condominium, yet I don't feel it detracts anything from him—in ethical terms, I mean. The pursuit of business, as I see it, doesn't necessarily equate with moral corruption any more than poverty and protest equate with purity.

When he first came to Alaska, Bob worked in construction, which paid high wages. However, when a strike appeared imminent, he looked for a stopgap job and found it with one airline, starting at the bottom and doing something of everything, then advancing in position with another airline. He campaigned for statehood (which came in 1958), was active in the Jaycees, and bought a bowling alley at a shopping center. He ran for the state legislature as one of thirty-seven candidates in the Democratic primary, and won the primary and the election. The following year the governor appointed him to the Senate, but he was still only twenty-four, actually eighteen days under the legal requirement of twenty-five, and was exposed by a Republican newspaper. Though barred from the Senate, he served his term in the House, ran again, and lost. Nevertheless, by 1962 he was vice-president for marketing and sales of Alaska Airlines and moved to Seattle.

"We did exciting things to build a little airline. We did it with

54

mirrors, not money. We had few cash dollars to spend, but used innovation and imagination." I do, in fact, recall the stand-up bar and the movie shown from a projector in the middle of the aisle, at a time when larger airlines were toying with the idea of in-flight films. The Golden Nugget theme and gold rush decor were garish, except on an airplane flying to and from Alaska. Through Bob's influence the airline did some very nice things. It acquired and maintained the Wickersham House in Juneau, the home of Judge James Wickersham, Alaska's foremost pioneer. It aided the King Islanders at Nome through a cooperative to market their ivory and stone carvings and encouraged a revival of their native dancing.

Then there was the Russian adventure. Bob had dreamed of promoting his little airline with tourist flights to Siberia. It was a daring idea. Sitka was an old Russian capital in Alaska that still had a famed ikon collection, an Orthodox bishop, onion domes, and old Russian wooden architectures, the glimmerings of the imperial past. Lori had wanted to honeymoon in the U.S.S.R. because her father had been born in Odessa. Once in Moscow he arranged to meet ranking officials of Intourist and the civil aviation authority through what he calls his "impertinence and impetuosity." He smiled and they smiled. They all had a drink, then another. He laid out his maps and boldly asked for the airline rights to serve Siberia.

"But we ourselves have never been allowed to vist the U.S.A., as we would like," the Russians said. "Your government won't give us a visa."

"I can fix that. However, when you come will you visit Alaska for a week? We would be privileged to show you the landmarks of affinity with your heritage."

He did fix it, the Russians came and were handsomely received in Sitka. In 1969 the summer flights to Siberia began. The Golden Samovar theme replaced the Golden Nugget.

In 1972 control of the airline changed hands and Bob looked elsewhere for opportunity as a tour operator on his own. First he acquired the tour operation of his old airline at Nome, then he established a program at the Pribilof Islands, noted for birdlife and seal rookeries. He entered a marketing agreement with the concessioner at Glacier Bay, then acquired the failing concession. This consisted of Glacier Bay Lodge, which the government had built, a marina, and a cruise boat, *Thunder Bay*, used for day cruises. Presently he acquired a much larger boat that had been in service in the Bahamas. It could accommodate almost one hundred passengers in staterooms and allow for sightseeing either from the decks or from a lounge equipped with picture windows. He renamed it *Glacier Bay Explorer* and began cruises overnighting at the foot of a glacier far up the bay. In due course he acquired three other ships like it, built to his specifications. They change cruise routes with the seasons, ranging from Alaska and the San Juan Islands north of Seattle in summer to Baja, California, Panama, and Tahiti in winter. My friend, plainly, is the mogul of the mini-cruisers.

Bob has combined business success with appreciation of wilderness, in its own right and in his business. We shared a lot of dialogue in Glacier Bay, particularly before, during, and after that halibut and salmon dinner in Blue Mouse Cove. Bob is a little under six feet, his curly hair thinning, a manly type well put together but pale from being indoors too much and getting paunchy, a good listener, yet never at a loss for words. He began by recounting the disastrous encounter in the early 1960s with Jascha Heifetz, the imperious violin virtuoso, at Bell Island. I was acquainted with Bell Island, a rustic spot outside of Ketchikan, ideal for fishing, which Alaska Airlines leased and operated when Bob was one of its top officials. As he told it:

"I was enthused and excited to learn that Jascha Heifetz had booked a fishing package to Bell Island and was glad I had to be there on some other business when he arrived. But from the time he and his party stepped off the airplane we had trouble. They looked around and were in shock. They had been sold in their minds' eyes a resort—a *real* resort—and instead they found this quaint little backwoods kind of place. They shook their heads and decided to walk the long, long boardwalk to the lodge. There were two men and two women, none related. They hit the lodge and started a white-glove inspection.

"It was lunchtime. They sat down, looked over the menu, and said, 'We can have none of this! We want certain entrées,' et cetera. Right after the luncheon encounter, they checked into their rooms and came wheeling right back. 'This will never do. The place isn't clean.' The walls weren't even painted, they complained—but of course the walls were rustic wood. They couldn't cope with the odor of sulphur from the hot springs and thought we must have plumbing troubles.

"Within the first two or three hours it became clear they were in the wrong place. I had to talk to them. I suggested that a grave error had been made and we were sorry Bell Island didn't meet their expectations; we'd be glad to call an airplane and hoped they'd be able to make alternate arrangements more to their suiting. They said no, but hell no, they weren't going to leave. So they pursued the encounter session.

"Their next stop was Sitka. Because of the music festival and other things going on, Sitka was excited, really excited about having Heifetz and his friends. People turned out in costume to give them a VIP welcome. As they came off the plane, our representative greeted Heifetz. 'Well,' Heifetz said, 'I want to make a few arrangements with you now. We'll have shrimp . . .' and whatever they wanted. 'And we will do this and we will do that—,' giving orders to people trying to be good hosts. A couple of them wanted to take a picture. 'Absolutely not. I'm not on a concert tour. This is my own time.'

"They went from Sitka to Skagway. By this time they were ruthless. When they got on the ship at Skagway to take the southbound cruise to Vancouver, they started doing their number. The captain made an unscheduled stop at Juneau and put them off. 'This is one thing,' he told Heifetz and friends, 'we will not be subjected to, and we won't subject the rest of the passengers to it either.' They were tearing everything to shreds and everything anyone tried to do for them."

All of which suggests there's some effort to being a guest in the backcountry, a place to take as it comes or to avoid. Presently we shifted gears to talk of the day in Glacier Bay. As he recounted:

"The traffic was real tough. We passed exactly two boats. One thing I enjoyed was getting up Adams Inlet, taking the time to see a new area, a new arm. The values preserved here are not only the marine life and scenic wonders, but quality of experience. Glacier Bay is one area where you can get out and experience absolutely uninterrupted wilderness. It's the only national park that encompasses this type of body of water. Instead of highways or any other form of transportation, waterways become the access to allow an absolutely pristine area to be viewed from the platforms of a vessel, where all the perspectives are at arm's length.

"The whole thought of Glacier Bay from the time Vancouver saw it at Icy Strait is overwhelming. To realize that not many years have gone by since Muir was here, barely more than a century, makes you aware that you're in a dynamic, changing area; I know of no region on the face of the globe where the face of geography is changing at such a rate and in such an expanse actually visible from year to year.

"This is what hooks people on Glacier Bay—an area locked in a time warp. In sixty miles you can, as we did today, travel past everything from a climax forest to Muir Glacier down to virtually barren rock. You see the glacier receding. These weren't historic fishing streams, but accidental ones, new streams that open to spawning after the ice gives way to new tributaries. Whales, birds, porpoises, and all the animals come in and adopt an area. Likewise, the glaciers themselves, some receding, some advancing, the mystery of all that—when you look at that mass, the tremendous mass of weight, locked up for centuries, you can sit and hear the rebirth of something very old, as the glaciers move and churn and open for the first time, yielding wedges of calving ice, suddenly exposed to this environment."

Yes, I said, but I've always wondered about the passengers seeing Glacier Bay from a cruise ship. When one of those floating pleasure palaces reaches Sitka, only 60 percent of them go ashore. Others stay aboard playing bridge. A park naturalist told me of how he boarded a cruise ship to give a guided lecture of Glacier Bay and passengers were too preoccupied playing the slot machines to pay any heed. They look out the window and could almost care less where they are.

Bob's answer was that the cruise ships embody a resort atmosphere, while the concession boats, which he operates, attract a clientele committed to Glacier Bay. "I've had many people describe it as a highly emotional personal experience, like going behind the altar of a temple."

Are these the words of a missionary or a merchandiser? I like to think of my friend as an entrepreneur with a conscience, and with a commitment to the preservation of wilderness. He explained his feelings as follows:

"Of course, we in the travel industry must share the responsibility to protect a pristine environment. I used to enjoy Mount McKinley National Park, but I watched the effects of growing traffic density on the one road through the park, driving wildlife away, degrading the entire scene. Controls make sense, for all land has a certain limit, a ceiling in carrying capacity.

"Still, it should be possible to view and enjoy, as well as to protect; to share the wonders of Alaska with the American people, and not simply those with ability and agility. I agree with wilderness and the idea of sanctuary for backpackers and campers, and for kayakers and sailors, free of noise and mechanical intrusions, but there should be a place for motor-powered boats and motor coaches. For one thing, most visitors come to Alaska in their later years, because of the cost, distance, and time involved. For another, these vehicles contribute to conservation, too, through energy efficiency and controlled access. The real estate in Alaska is large enough to do things right, providing, first, there is adequate planning for the parks, and, second, that we in the industry discipline ourselves to accept proper types of visitation and a limit to numbers based on carrying capacity."

Glacier Bay has been a testing ground of the carrying capacity concept. One of its principal attractions, particularly for the cruise vessels, has been the occasional spectacle of humpback whales. These wide-ranging mammals come north for a few weeks in summer to feed on shrimp and small organisms. But the number of whales declined sharply during the late seventies. The blame was placed on increasing human disturbance; preliminary studies indicated whales were avoiding the bay because of rising cruise traffic and because of small pleasure and charter boats traveling erratic courses. As a result of findings and recommendations, Bob made extensive noise-reduction modifications on the two concession-operated tour boats, *Glacier Bay Explorer* and *Thunder Bay*. The National Park Service instituted regulations restricting the number and movement of cruise liners. But in the summer of 1982, when we made our little cruise on the *Ice Folly*, numbers of whales were up, with the highest density in Bartlett Cove, where ship and boat traffic is most common. All of which reveals how little we know about whales, and how much more we need to learn to give them a chance for survival.

It troubles me when access to wilderness is rendered simple, then justified on the grounds that wilderness is being protected by so doing. It troubles me when I do it the easy way. Not simply that I may be cheating, but that I'm not deriving the full benefit that comes with effort. What, I wonder, would John Muir say? And Charles Sheldon?

As I mentioned, when Sheldon made his first visit, Denali had not yet been scaled. James Wickersham, the Alaska territory's delegate to Congress, in 1903 had been the first known man to try it. The first successful attempt, however, was made in 1910 by an adventurous quartet of prospectors known as the Sourdoughs. Without any special equipment, but with grit and good luck, they chose the right route along Muldrow Glacier and made it to North Peak, where they planted a fifteen-foot pole, hoping it would be visible from Fairbanks. But it was not; their achievement went unrecognized for three years until another party went on to the higher South Peak, from which they identified the Sourdoughs' spruce pole clearly outlined against the sky.

Denali has been climbed many times since, by more than one thousand mountaineers, over three fourths of this number since 1970. Now they fly in light planes with the latest in equipment to a landing camp at 7,784 feet, proceed to base camp at 10,826 feet, and from there to South Peak. I don't deny that climbing remains a serious, hazardous challenge, but that's the point. Forty climbers have died on the mountain, ten during 1976 alone. Above 15,000 feet weather is tough, tougher than terrain, with fierce, sudden storms during the peak climbing months of May, June, and July. Climbers ascend too fast for proper acclimatization. This would have been impossible in the early days, when the untracked country tested skills and endurance of mountaineers.

John Muir punished himself, by all standards of normalcy. Who in his right mind would venture into Glacier Bay at the end of October? On the other hand, he's not the only fool recorded in history. Jesus Christ was another. Once he and three disciples undertook to visit a high mountain, likely Mount Hermon; it was a deliberately planned experience, avoiding shortcuts, in the expectation of rising above hazards and finding unlimited good. Revelation derives from effort, as evidence in Muir's description of the Fairweather Mountains:

"The white, rayless light of the morning, seen when I was alone amid the silent peaks of the Sierra, had always seemed to me the most telling of the terrestrial manifestations of God. But here the mountains themselves were made divine, and delivered his glory in terms still more impressive."

Because he sought to meet the harsh country on its terms, Muir was able to evoke lofty images. When he and his canoe party were driven wildly up the fjord, it was as though the storm wind were warning them: "Go, then, if you will, into my icy chamber; but you shall stay until I am ready to let you out."

I weighed such thoughts and proposed that we spend most of the next day ashore. I needed it and wanted to see what my friends would do. After passing Reid Glacier, Rick put us ashore at the edge of Lamplugh Glacier. Terry and I started scrambling over rocks, with Bob, loaded with assorted camera gear, bringing up the rear.

Terry climbed lightly and gracefully. We would reach what appeared to be the summit, but it yielded to another behind and above it. At each plateau we rested, listening to the flow of water in crevasses of the glacier. Humble plants covered the rocks, principally the pioneers, forming mats on sands and gravels and building soils for other species to follow. Muir at heights of two thousand to three thousand feet found alder bushes and a profusion of flowering plants, with a few grasses and ferns. "Comes this delicate life and beauty," he wrote of his Alaska glacier garden, "to teach us what we in our faithless ignorance and fear call destruction is creation."

From each succeeding vantage new perspectives opened, of mountains, ice masses, and deep fjords. The day was unusually warm and bright for southeast Alaska, often shrouded in cloudy gloom. A cruise ship advanced into the northwest arm of the bay, two thousand feet below us, then turned as the land narrowed and headed out. We watched it, the three of us, thoroughly refreshed. Bob had never wavered, clambering the steep slopes with cameras jangling from his sides. With such clarity and elevation, it was a choice day for photography. By any measure, the day was choice.

CHAPTER IV

The Cost of Convenience at Lake Clark

Chuck Hornberger darned near skipped his youngest daughter's wedding, even though she wanted him to give her away, like the father of the bride is supposed to. She told him he would have to wear a tux and that set him off.

"I said, 'Forget it.' She said, 'Well, you're going to have to dress up.' I said, 'I'll wear something clean and neat and if that's not good enough you can go someplace else.' So I wore a pair of wool trousers and a neat cotton shirt and I was comfortable. I was the only one in the wedding that didn't have on a suit and it didn't bother me. I just don't see all that put-on.

"Clothing is expensive when you buy it; when you don't see a lot of cash in a year it's not something you absolutely have to have, but with judicious wear and maintenance it will last. We wear a lot of wool; you get it wet and it's still warm. In winter I wear wool pants, wool shirts, and long underwear. Down is nice, but when you get wet you're cold."

I had asked Chuck if he owned a suit of clothes. Clearly he's given up on that sort of thing, not that he was ever into it. We were drifting downstream on the Chulitna River in his small boat, ideal for this kind of trip, heading for Long Lake, without anything special to do, but seeing what we might see, and talking about life at the edge of wilderness, with a chance to fish for grayling along the way. Chuck said it was a good day, that we might easily cross the trails of moose, caribou, deer, otter, possibly bear, as well as waterfowl—ducks, swans, and Canada geese—and eagles, falcons, and songbirds.

"How about porcupines?" I asked.

"Yes, porcupines too."

We had just had an encounter with a porcupine at the lodge, not exactly a pleasant one. Chuck shot it with a rifle and disposed of the remains in the brush. I asked if he couldn't as easily have chased the animal off. His answer was simple. Porcupines invade gardens, devouring strawberries, cabbage, and cauliflower; they have no natural enemies, except for the lynx and fisher, and there are no fishers in the neighborhood. Moreover, porcupines are prolific reproducers and abundantly evident. He made me realize that if I were trying to keep a home in this setting, I would probably dispatch troublesome porcupines in like fashion; there might be a more considerate approach, but this would be the most direct.

Chuck and his wife, Sara, own Koksetna Lodge on the northwest edge of Lake Clark. They built it with their own hands, a small and simple facility, which is not to say unsophisticated. Their little property is cradled by the kind of expansive and exuberant nature that renders painters, poets, and philosophers humble and hopeless. They themselves are fitting to the setting, sensitive, hospitable and expressive, in his and her own ways. Having been to college and taught school, Sara is versed in wordly themes. Chuck has a native widsom that tells him to be frugal with words, but to make them mean something when he speaks. When I arrived in mid-August (on my second visit there in three years) I was the only guest. To think of those tourist groups traipsing around looking for Alaska and missing what I would consider the soul of it—yet I was the beneficiary, since I was quartered in the cabin closest to the sparkling waters of Lake Clark, with an unbroken vista of the peaks across the lake. Thoroughly inspirational and romantic, the ideal honeymoon spot if I should ever again . . .

The name Lake Clark sounds scarcely tinged with romance, mystery, or challenge, unlike other national parks in Alaska. Denali, Gates of the Arctic, Katmai, Kenai Fjords, Glacier Bay, and the Wrangells are all names that conjure Alaskan images, while Lake Clark could as easily be in Kentucky or Kansas. It was, until the epochal 1980 congressional legislation establishing new national parks and national wildlife refuges, unknown territory except to those in the immediate area, and to a large extent remains so today. Yet Lake Clark National Park encompasses four million acres of land and water, most of it wilderness. The legislation told a little about the nature of the wilderness when it specified the purposes of the park: "to protect the watershed necessary for the perpetuation of the red salmon fishery in Bristol Bay; to maintain unimpaired the scenic beauty and quality of portions of the Alaska Range and the Aleutian Range, including active volcanoes, glaciers, wild rivers, lakes, waterfalls, and alpine meadows in their natural state and to protect habitats for and populations of fish and wildlife including but not limited to caribou, Dall sheep, brown/ grizzly bears, bald eagles, and peregrine falcons."

I had flown this way for the first time in 1965, while en route to Cold Bay at the edge of the Aleutians, knowing nothing about the region but struck by the spectacle of smoky volcanoes with glaciers flowing down their flanks, and by the deep, clear lakes and glistening rivers in the valleys, hoping that some day I could see more of it at close range. Several times since then I've flown this way again, eye level with the two principal volcanoes, Iliamna and Redoubt, in the Chigmit Mountains, the meeting ground of the Alaska and Aleutian ranges, jagged mountain waves that dominate the southern half of Alaska. Of the lakes, Clark is the largest, sixty miles long and up to ten miles across, but not the wildest, as compared with Twin Lakes, Dick Proenneke's sanctuary, or Turquoise, or Telaquana, or Two Lakes, which are higher and more remote still.

The rivers, glacier fed, wind through rolling foothills and high plains, with scrubby spruce woodlands and tundra specked with spongy, boggy ponds, the kind of terrain that calls to my mind the picture of a moose feeding alone, luxuriating in the sheer quiet. The only way for humans to reach Lake Clark is by light plane, either 150 miles from Anchorage or 40 miles from Iliamna. People do come, a few to hike and camp and float the Chilakadrotna and Mulchatna rivers, but most of them to fish. They stay at small resorts and lodges scattered around Lake Clark and are flown in float planes to the choice spots. Having written for years about the fishing environment (rather than the fishing itself), my feeling is that this is fine for the true sportsman, who, like the moose, treasures solitude and patience, but too many with rod and reel are as jumpy in the wilderness as they are in town; and if they don't catch fish the whole trip is a waste.

Such people would be lost at Koksetna. Chuck Hornberger is too deliberate; he and Sara are too much in tune with the rhythms of life around them, too self-reliant and independent to cater to any tastes but their own and those of people like them. Fishing is not the big thing, as compared with being in this country and getting some small feel of what it's about.

In the first hour we covered all of eight miles on the Chulitna River. We saw a cow moose with twin calves, a roosting bald eagle, nesting mallards and mergansers with their young, taking to the water for the first time. We pulled ashore at the ruins of an old cabin. "Charlie Wolf's place," said Chuck as though Charlie now lived somewhere down the road. It was vintage 1930s, pretty well collapsed with moss and birch growing out of the roof. I asked Chuck how those lonely trappers felt about civilization and wilderness.

"I think they wanted to get away from it all to do their own thing, following a subsistence way of life. They weren't interested in getting rich and were exploited by those who bought their furs. Actually, this country has been covered by white men ever since the gold rush and before—there's historical evidence, places named after gold miners. One placer miner did a lot of discovery, found copper, silver, and gold occasionally.

"Those trappers probably all tried to catch as much as they could, without an eye to maintaining the species. But it was tough to get around in this environment and steel traps were tough to carry. That's why we have a lot of fur today. Even now, some people love to get out in the woods, set up a trapper's life-style, and get away from it all.

"This river, the Chulitna, has been a subsistence area for native Athabascans over the years. They migrated in narrow skin boats, ten or eleven feet long, lined with willow or birch, letting their dogs run on the banks. It worked pretty good. In spring they would trap beaver and muskrat, then cross Lake Clark to Nondalton to fish for salmon. Near mid-July they would put up the salmon as food for themselves and their dogs.

"Under the federal legislation that gives natives the right to select land for permanent ownership, they have selected all the land up the Chulitna River for about twenty miles—primarily because they have hunted and trapped here for a long time and it is a good source of game. But subsistence is no more. That's only my opinion. There *is* a lot of use of the natural resources as far as meat goes, but it's more of a traditional thing, been done over the years and passed down, but now people locally do not truly rely on game for their food.

"Outboard motors and snow machines make it easier to get around. It opens a new concept of subsistence life-style. It also gives people a lot more leisure time for hunting: getting theirs and getting home quicker. They can live in villages, go upriver and shoot a moose and be back that night. They're *partially* subsisting on wild game, but they still have to earn money somewhere to buy this machinery and gasoline to run it, so the basic concept of living off the land like a hundred years ago has gone out the window.

"On one hand you can't go from a bow-and-arrow environment to high-powered rifle without creating stress on the game animals, but I've never seen local natives taking any game where it was wasted. They've always used everything, right down to the hooves. Anything shot out of season is used. They haul it down to the village; since there is no refrigeration, it is passed out to folks. As long as it's used I feel it's not all that bad, as long as it's not taken to extremes."

I've always felt the same way: that a little local poaching for food is on the harmless side and maybe beneficially thins a herd. Killing out of season for the sake of killing, or for the horns, is something else. But a good poacher wisely avoids taking more than he needs. So goes the unwritten law.

We talked about gardening in the bush country, which is no mean feat. Sara had told me of some of the problems: cold soil, often acidic and sterile, prevalence of cloudy days, short growing season, frost danger during the full moon days of July and August, root maggots in plants of the cabbage family as well as in radishes and turnips. Yet they managed, hanging cucumbers from the rafters, building frames of poles and lathes, composting above steer manure and using rabbit manure through compost to speed decomposition. Their greenhouse, glassed with windows from an old salmon cannery, was warmed by a homemade wood-burning stove. Out of it all come not only vegetables, but cheery nasturtiums, snapdragons, and dahlias.

"The old boy we bought from, Frank Bell, was quite a gardener [said Chuck]. He was the second white owner. The original owner was a World War One veteran named Sam Turner, who came back in the twenties and died here. Even before coming to Lake Clark, Sara and I were out in the woods, gardening, following the outdoors type of life. We like gardening, and it yields good food. We plant most of our stuff in flats inside the house and set it in the garden around the first of June. We also plant lettuce in the garden by itself. In a good warm year we'll have fresh produce out of the garden by the first of July, or mid-July. Also, we have strawberries and raspberries. Potatoes do real well.

"We have a large greenhouse where we raise squash, cukes, and tomatoes. We start tomatoes in the house in January. Usually by March they're blooming and we plant them in beds in the greenhouse. We'll have tomatoes by the first of June. It's a lot of work. In February and March the house looks like a jungle! But it's worth it. We both love tomatoes. If we didn't raise tomatoes, we'd have to buy them. All sorts of root crops grow well—cabbage, carrots, radishes, celery, turnips, kohlrabi—we have a lot of that. We generally use the greenhouse March first to mid-October; then we let it freeze up, which kills a lot of bugs.

"Sara and I get by very reasonably on food. I shoot a moose in the fall and we eat that, or caribou. Our biggest cash outlay is for mechanical contrivances, gasoline and oil."

I contrasted my Alaskan friends, Bob Giersdorf and Chuck Hornberger, both about the same age, forty-seven or forty-eight at the time of this writing, unlike as two men could be. One is rooted in simplicity, without much cash or concern for it, the other in complexity, playing for high stakes in business, flying to Panama or Tahiti the way Chuck makes it to Anchorage, or maybe to Iliamna, and yet much alike in their origins and self-reliance. Bob was born in Montana, Chuck in Wyoming, both on itinerant trails.

Chuck's father was a homesteader who didn't make it and sold out to the government as part of the resettlement program of the 1930s. The family moved to western Washington for a time, then to north Idaho, where his father worked in the World War II wheat harvest. When both parents became ill in 1946, the family headed for Arizona, two adults and five kids in a canvas-topped Jeep. In 1954, two years out of high school, Chuck enlisted for four years in the navy, serving as a diesel-engine mechanic on submarines, but also learning hydraulics, air systems, and other things mechanical. Following his hitch he returned to Arizona to marry Sara, the preacher's daughter, who was teaching at a one-room schoolhouse (housing eight grades) in a ranching community in the sticks.

Work wasn't plentiful, so Chuck rejoined the navy, this time in the nuclear submarine force. When he was assigned to the nuclear development center at Arco, Idaho, they bought a home and Sara got a teaching job. But he was transferred to the Pacific and for two years spent only thirty days at home annually. Teaching wages in Idaho then (and long thereafter) were low, which in 1963 led them to Naknek, Alaska.

"Sara's salary as a teacher looked good and we had always wanted to come north. I got a job operating diesel engines in the electric company, which was kind of down my line. Then I got a chance to buy a business, a gasoline station and freight hauling service between Naknek and King Salmon, fifteen miles away. It was a real good deal, no money down and pretty good terms. We never would have got a chance like this anywhere else and I ran that business until 1972.

"About 1965, like many others in Alaska, I bought an airplane and learned to fly it. It would sure come in handy. We got acquainted with Jay Hammond (later governor of Alaska), who told us about Lake Clark, how pretty it is. We filed on five acres of federal land, which was still possible then, and put up a small cabin. Then I met the old-timer who lived here. He was in his high sixties, having a hard time, especially since his wife didn't like the remoteness. When I first saw it, I said, 'This is the spot.' I would stop in to visit over the next two years. When he decided to sell, luckily he wrote us a letter and said, 'I want X dollars for it.'

Next day I hopped in an airplane, flew to Lake Clark, and bought the property.

"That was in 1970. Sara was still teaching at Naknek. She would go back there to teach school every August. I would go back and forth all winter long, hauling freight and gear. I would get in the airplane and say, 'Lake Clark' or 'Naknek,' and it would go. Sara taught school through the spring of '74, then took a leave of absence to spend the winter here. Finally, she wrote them, 'I'm not coming back to teach.'"

On the way back from Long Lake we took time to fish for grayling in a shallow, clear pool. It was so easy that Chuck let me catch most of the fish. I cast about ten times and hooked and reeled in seven fish, barely a minute or so for each. Those fish were incredibly naïve to be attracted by a little piece of glittering metal. The exercise couldn't be called sport, but at least the fish would go well for dinner.

I rested and read at my cabin. It was neat and spacious, with two bedrooms designed to sleep a total of six comfortably, and a living room, with a lot of nature books on the coffee tables and shelves. This was the largest of four guest cabins, all of which together provide nineteen bunks. But that's "an awful load," as Chuck would say, and he prefers to have no more than ten guests at a time.

He built the cabins himself, cutting and hauling spruce logs, then squaring them on three sides with his own simple chain-operated sawmill; however, he did have to purchase and fly in a certain amount of material for roofing, windows, and doors. His newest additions were the bathhouses, a touch of convenience and comfort, replacing the old outhouses and community shower. He's the kind of mechanically creative person who always has one construction project under way and the next one planned. Next on Chuck's agenda was an airplane hangar so he could work inside, when need be, on his two and a half airplanes. These include the old Stinson he bought in 1965 and a Cessna 180, the workhorse of the bush. He normally would fly to Iliamna for the mail, at least once weekly, more often during summer, and to Anchorage four or five times yearly to take care of business and pick up supplies.

"Flying is not the cheap way to go, but it's the only way," he had told me. "It's hard to come out in the woods and subsist. It don't work without a monetary income and still have the conveniences. Whenever you want something you pay for it through the nose out here. That's progress and civilization. Yet people have managed to do without. We've managed without a lot of conveniences, like a flush toilet, radio, and telephone. A couple of items Sara would like to have. One is a piano. It would be great. I could fly it in, but it's still down the road before we get one. We use the radio patch phone. It's handy to get messages, but dicey at times, especially when a thousand people listen in."

When I came over to the lodge, a few minutes before dinner, Sara offered me a glass of wine the Hornbergers themselves had made. It wasn't strong, but tasty. The lodge, the largest log structure on the property, served as combination kitchen, dining room, living room (or lounge, if you want to call it that), office, and Hornberger living quarters. There was lots of reading matter, the Hornbergers' own, plus inevitable paperbacks and magazines that visitors leave. This reminds me of the American I met in the Galapagos. As a successful engineer in southern California, he had earned enough money to buy a yacht. This had led him to bid farewell to business and wife and to sail to the Galapagos, where he built a small hotel. When I was there, I asked this erstwhile southern Californian how he kept up with world news. "Well," he said with a nonchalant shrug, "once or twice a year I'll tune in the high frequency to BBC. Now and then someone drops off a copy of *Time* magazine. The news doesn't seem to change very much. Anyway, I stay busy."

Sara likes to keep up with current readings and events, as evidenced during the dinner conversation. The food at dinner was fresh: fruits and vegetables from greenhouse and garden and the fish barely out of the river.

After dinner I asked Chuck to explain the operation of his wind-powered generator, and so he did:

"I spent so many years working in the diesel engine room of a submarine that I hate the sound of a diesel engine. Anyplace you go in bush Alaska you hear the racket of a diesel making electricity. We didn't want that here. At first we used all kerosene and gasoline to operate the lighting. When we needed electricity to wash clothes or something like that we'd start our gasoline generator.

"I'd been interested in wind power for years. Finally, in 1975 I came up with enough cash to buy a rebuilt wind generator. I built the tower for the windmill on the hill, bought the batteries, and completed this one-hundred-and-twenty-volt electricity system. The windmill keeps our batteries charged so we can have quiet electricity anytime of day or night without running the generator.

"The windmill functions as the fan on the end of a direct current generator, pumping electricity into the batteries. The electricity we use, in turn, comes right out of the batteries. Or if the wind is blowing, it comes from the generator, depending on the demand. There's a little bit of maintenance on the tower, climbing to the top and tightening fittings periodically, but it's worked out real good. Certainly it's a different kind of system, and a great one for here. I've had it going six years and my only complaint is that the wind doesn't blow enough. We have enough electricity when Sara and I are here alone because we're careful with it. We've gone for six weeks and no wind and we've had electricity.

"I do have a diesel generator, even after what I said about diesel. I got it this year. We use it for washing clothing in the washing machine. Gasoline is awful expensive for a gas generator and this year I've had to charge my batteries about six times, running the diesel generator about six or eight hours a day to charge enough electricity into the batteries to maintain the charge. The main reason for this is to provide for electrical conveniences. We've installed a pressurized water system and a new freezer; and we use it to run kitchen appliances, most of my shop tools, and all our lighting on electricity. Still, it's proved itself. Even if we didn't have wind, I could run that diesel generator six to eight hours about once every three days and have electricity all day and all night. It's worked out real good."

Next morning the superintendent of Lake Clark National Park, Paul Haertel, flew over to Koksetna from park headquarters at Nondalton across the lake. With a float plane, landing fields are everywhere; he waded ashore from his plane a few feet from my cabin. Paul was about forty, I'd say, and had learned to fly within the past five years. Many government people in Alaska, like him, are pilots—it helps them cover their territories and adds a little to their stature among the Alaskans. I had never met Paul; yet, because of my years of study and writing about national parks, individuals in the agency, such as Paul, and I have developed some common bond. It's like they know that I know (whatever the secret may be) without their telling, and they can feel secure because *I* won't tell that they know. Paul was headed on a patrol flight with a stop to visit Dick Proenneke at Twin Lakes and invited me along, a choice opportunity that I promptly accepted. While Sara and Chuck busied themselves preparing a package of fresh bread, veggies, and other goodies to send to their friend Proenneke, Paul showed me several maps and reports covering the national park.

Of the 4 million acres within the park boundary, 2.47 million acres already were classified as wilderness. But substantially more than 1 million acres were privately owned or subject to legitimate application for ownership, including large portions of the shore of Lake Clark. As one report warned:

"Current high land values are encouraging the subdivision and sale of private lands, and many persons from Anchorage and communities on the Kenai Peninsula are purchasing lots in the area. Construction of cabins and lodges on private lands will increase the local population (especially in the summer) and lead to an increased need of support activities, including supply of construction materials, equipment, fuel, retail goods, and other materials."

Even in Alaska! Despite its impressive dimensions, wilderness cannot be preserved whole. Then again, it's part of America and why should Alaska be treated or developed any differently than the rest of the country?

The weather was ideal for flying, with clear skies and smooth air. We observed a fragment of God's earth free of any trace of man's work, a land where the child might be considered worthy of the father, though one might wonder for how long. At least here in Alaska man's hope has not yet been overtaken by man's fate.

The Twin Lakes mirrored mountains and snow as we descended, passing Proenneke on the water heading home in his canoe. I had visited him three years before and found him well read and well informed for all his isolation. He was from Primrose, Iowa, and had worked as a navy carpenter during World War II.

Though stricken with rheumatic fever, he rose above it and headed for Alaska in the 1950s. He worked variously in construction, salmon fishing, and ranching before heading for Twin Lakes in 1967, at the age of fifty, to build his own cabin and a new life. *One Man's Wilderness, An Alaskan Odyssey*, prepared from his journals and photo collection, has become an Alaskan classic. He wrote of learning to live with bears, planting a garden, dining on cuisine of lake trout, Dall sheep, caribou, burned biscuits, and salads of fireweed spiced with green onions, experimental living in winter cold, and of his canoe trips:

"After the long paddle the cabin's gleam on the beach was a comfort. The more I see it the more I love it. Surely there is no stretch on the lake shore as sheltered as mine.

"After a supper of navy beans, I sat on my threshold and gazed off towards the volcanic mountains. I had been close to them today. The Chilakadrotna River showed me the beautiful fish and I returned them to her. I thought of the sights I had seen. The price was a physical toll. Money does little good back here. I could not buy the fit feeling that surged through my arms and shoulders. It could not buy the feeling of accomplishment. I had been my own tour guide, and my own power had been my transportation. This great big country was my playground, and I could afford the price it demanded."

His cabin was neat and well ordered. On one wall he had an inscription of his own design and composition: "Is it proper that the wilderness and its creatures suffer because we came?" We had arrived at the cabin a few minutes before Dick. After he returned and we exchanged greetings, I asked him the source of his inscription. He recollected once stopping at a trapper's cabin, finding a pile of carcasses, mostly foxes, and the place littered and strewn with animal parts. Soon after he encountered a fox that had one foot missing; that part was obviously left in a trap somewhere. Animals have been known to chew themselves free, sacrificing one limb to save their lives. "I thought about animals crippled and killed," said Dick. "It shouldn't be that way." Yet he was positive about things, citing improvement at Twin Lakes. One hundred river floaters and hikers had already been by during the summer, leaving not a single can, nor scrap of paper, nor litter of any kind.

Proenneke was wiry and weathered, in his late sixties, yet gung ho for living according to his own elemental pattern. There was, however, something different about him, as compared with my previous visit. He was conscious of being a celebrity. Did I know his book was in its seventh printing? Had I seen the article in such-and-such a publication, a clipping of which he happened to have at hand? It happens to the best of us.

Once back at Koksetna, I talked with Chuck about the oncoming changes in the Lake Clark environment. I learned to appreciate him as a conservative person, antigovernment and antiregulation by nature, a conservationist in his life on the land, but not one according to the standard definition. He fathoms wilderness by living next to it and reaching independent conclusions based on his studied judgment. That's why I listen closely and value his words:

"My term of wilderness is not where we live, though we're a long way from modern convenience. I haven't been down the lower forty-eight enough. Everybody says wilderness and parks there are overcrowded. I can see the spillover coming in this area. As for visitors, I'm in favor of them. That's how we make our living and I love to show this country.

"But too many people want to come here and kill something, whether animal or fish, rather than just enjoy the scenery. I love to drift down the river, as we did, and enjoy the quiet and the ducks and whatever else shows up. Until one gets used to quiet it's hard to understand.

"The trouble is that use has increased drastically in the past five years. The impact on the land is probably critical. It's a fragile system, tundra and bush have a short growing season of only three months over the summer. Much walking or use kills it. You saw trails over the tundra the natives used over the years that are now two feet deep. Game follows the path of least resistance. Some trails are a foot wide and a foot deep. You can imagine what it would be like with hundreds of people coming and going, especially over a small area in campgrounds.

"I'm independent enough myself to want to do what I want to do without anybody telling me yea or nay. Yet if it isn't regulated, or whatever, it's going to be grossly exploited as it has other places. So we go from there, trying to keep a good natural experience as simple as we can without doing any more damage than we absolutely have to. . . .

"I don't know what to say about the wilderness issue. Definitely it is something that is diminishing, decreasing in size. My idea of wilderness is a place where no one is. The more people use it, by my definition it's not a wilderness. People come here from down the lower forty-eight, spend time with us, and here we are in a nice comfortable place and to them this is wilderness. And yet I'm so used to it it's kind of a way of life with me.

"Definitely large areas should be set aside. I think it's a great heritage, if nothing else, something from which future generations can get an idea of what it was like, however small an idea. It's a great country and while we still have it it's a great idea to try to maintain some of it like it was. Down in the Midwest there is all that development, farms and big cities. Figure that two hundred years ago that was great forests and prairie. All it is now is blacktop pavement, shopping centers, and factories, and a few farms to support the commercialization of America and the world. Let's hope it don't happen here."

Before I left Koksetna, Sara and I talked about my coming back for a touch of winter. Chuck explained what it would be like and how he views that other, the out-of-season, season:

"Winter is quiet and stormy, but we really like it. We don't talk a lot between the two of us. Until one gets used to quiet it's hard to understand. We go for a week or ten days and never see a soul. Suddenly we get a good day in the weather and as many as five planes land to visit. It's a great place to get out and travel around. The lake is frozen. We get out on skis or snowshoes and fish through the ice. I haul in wood so I can burn it next year.

"It's a good life out here. In mid-winter I think it would be nice to be down in Arizona, if it was like when we moved there in 1947 or '48, but it's not and never will be again. So the best thing to do is throw another log on the fire and enjoy it."

CHAPTER V

The Maine Woods: Thoreau, the Essential Guide, Now As in His Own Time

One evening at dusk my companion, Morris Wing, and I had gone paddling and fishing on Lake Umsaskis, about midway down the Allagash Waterway in the North Woods of Maine. The fading sun streaked the dark water reddish gold. For a moment I watched a muskrat scurry through moist sphagnum moss along the near bank and dive into a little brook. Then Morris pointed quietly to a moose across the lake, feeding in a bogan, a slack-water cove in a bend of the river, where underwater plants obviously were to its liking. Along the Allagash the "lordly moose" is aptly named. It is master of the woods. In a fight between bear and moose the moose usually prevails, even capable of breaking the bear's back with its forefeet.

Instinctively, I thought of the words of Henry David Thoreau. "It is all mossy and moosey." I love that line, so simple and yet a stimulant to imagination, and the descriptive lines that follow: "In some of those dense fir and spruce woods there is hardly room for the smoke to go up. The trees are a standing night and the general stillness is more impressive than any sound, but occasionally you hear the note of an owl farther or nearer in the woods and, if near a lake, the semi-human cry of the loons at their unearthly revels."

That trip to the Allagash with Morris was in the 1960s. It was not my first visit to the cool Maine woods; I had been there twenty years before, during World War II. Nor would it be my last to this large natural frontier of the Northeast, where spring arrives weeks behind the rest of the country and winter well before it, and where moose, deer, and bear outnumber people. Whatever it is that calls me back I can't quite say. Certainly part of it involves pursuing the spirit of Thoreau. I was astonished that the scene of the sixties should parallel so closely his description of more than a century earlier. "What is most striking about the Maine wilderness," he wrote, "is the continuousness of the forest, with fewer open intervals or glades than you had imagined."

Such was my impression in the deeper recesses of the Allagash, the most celebrated canoe stream in a state celebrated for its canoeing, and in nearby Baxter State Park, surrounding Katahdin, the gray granite monolith that is Maine's highest mountain. Ten million acres of wild forest land, flecked with hundreds of gleaming lakes, without towns or local government and, in the sixties at least, still with very few roads, comprise the North Woods. As cities grow and megalopolis spreads, surely this Thoreau sanctuary becomes a more valuable treasure to both Maine and the nation.

The Allagash is properly called a waterway. On its one-hundred-mile northward course from Telos Lake, at the foot of Katahdin, to join the St. John River at the Canadian border, the waterway is composed of lakes (about three fifths) and the river (about two fifths). The Allagash variously roars, tumbles, cascades, and shapes deep, dark pools, such as those in which we fished. The hills surrounding Lake Umsaskis were round and low, a few hundred feet high, lightened by the foliage of the birch, beech, and aspen (locally called popple) and darkened by streams of spruce and pine, a rhythm of rolling country, before the background of a far ridge reaching two thousand feet. The interwoven complex of forest and water provides for a richness of wildlife— heron, gulls, ducks, loons, eagles, muskrat, beaver, bear, deer, moose, otter, mink, and choice fishing for trout.

Morris Wing reminded me of the relation between a sustained forest and the abundant wildlife. I had headed north through Bangor into Aroostook County, a single county that matches the combined size of Rhode Island and Connecticut, and most of it owned by large pulp and paper companies. From the town of Presque Isle I had flown into the woods in company with Morris, who managed one million acres for the International Paper Company. For fifty miles the forest underneath our little plane was virtually unbroken, except for an occasional lake shimmering in the sunlight, and now and then a sawmill sending up lazy flumes of smoke. In the bosom of these woodlands we arrived at our destination, Lake Umsaskis. During the time we spent together, Morris showed that he was clearly a master of the paddle. Lean and youthful as an outdoorsman, yet mature as a woods manager, he learned his way on the water routes of Maine while still a schoolboy. Many times he had covered the entire length of the Allagash, poling over rocky waters, portaging around waterfalls, and paddling across the broad lakes. But he also showed much about himself and the country.

"Don't forget that I feel as proud of the wild land as anyone," he said while we canoed and fished. "You can see for yourself that we manage it not only for pulpwood and timber, but to conserve wildlife, and to conserve solitude for sportsmen and canoers."

I was impressed by that testimony. After all, more than 80 percent, possibly 85 percent of Maine was still covered with forest. No other state possessed so great a proportion. The towering white pines, three centuries old and standing as high as 240 feet, were long gone, though even they would return in time, given human wisdom and appropriate self-restraint.

Just then we came abreast of an old timber dam and logging camp, ghostly relics of lusty river drives. Early loggers cared little about resources around them. Their harvesting practices were wasteful. In colonial times Maine pines were so immense twenty oxen were required to move a single tree from stump to wharf. For a full century Bangor was the world's largest lumber market and port. The harbor was clogged with wastage that would be classed as first-rate timber today. After the accessible woodlands were stripped, men and axes moved deeper inland. They disturbed the wilderness river, cutting a canal so that logs would flow south, instead of north. Fires were frequent. That was long before the days of management by trained foresters. "Although it is often condemned as such, logging is not necessarily destructive to wilderness," wrote William O. Douglas in *A Wilderness Bill of Rights*. "Where trees are harvested on a selective-cutting basis, there is always a forest remaining. The forest as a wildlife habitat is usually not disturbed and may even be improved, while the forest as watershed protection remains inviolate."

On visiting the Allagash in the sixties I felt the same way; perhaps, however, both Justice Douglas and I were imbued more with optimism than realism. Or possibly we are all conditioned to rationalize the realities of a structured society—including the hard facts of private ownership of forest land and the public demand for its products. Henry David Thoreau felt no such constraints. He rose above the rules of life as mortals live it to experience and express the wonders of nature on its own level, yet in a way to uplift his own kind and give us new self-respect. He exulted, for example, in the daring notion that the Maine woods were fit for heathenism and superstitious rites, adding:

"Nature was here something savage and awful, though beautiful. I looked with awe at the ground I trod upon, to see what the Powers had made there, the form and fashion and material of their work. This was the Earth of which we had heard, made out of Chaos and Old Night. Here was no man's garden, but the unhanselled globe. It was not lawn, nor pasture, nor mead, nor woodland, nor lea, nor arable, nor wasteland. It was the fresh and natural surface of the planet Earth, as it was made forever and ever—to be the dwelling of man, we say—so Nature made it and man may use it if he can."

Thoreau during his lifetime published only two books (*A Week on the Concord and Merrimack Rivers* and *Walden*), but his collected works, or daybook, run to twenty volumes, a mine of observations and discoveries about great and small things. He held neither dream, hope, nor design that his works would ever be recognized for what they are: classics of ageless prose that speak simply, directly, and upliftingly. "He illuminates the humblest of subjects by intense scrutiny and faithful reporting," writes Joseph Moldenhauer, editor of the authoritative edition of *The Maine Woods*, a faithful restoration of the original, published in 1864, two years after Thoreau's death. "He asks the reader to take nothing for granted, nothing on authority or on second hand—but to look closely and independently at what is to be seen."

Generous misinterpretation notwithstanding, Thoreau had no quarrel with civilization. He defined wilderness as a necessary component, warning against having "every part of man cultivated," which must ultimately barbarize him. "In wildness," he believed, "is preservation of the world." Thoreau dealt not in ecology, but in holism based on humanist values. Saddened at extermination of creatures of the wild, such as the panther, lynx, wolverine, bear, beaver, and turkey, he wrote on March 23, 1856:

"I seek acquaintance with Nature—to know her moods and manners. Primitive Nature is the most interesting to me. I take infinite pains to know all the phenomena, . . . for instance, thinking that I have here the entire poem, and then, to my chagrin, I hear that it is but an imperfect copy that I possess and have read, that my ancestors have torn out many of the first leaves and grandest passages, and mutilated it in many places. I should not like to think that some demigod has come before me and picked out some of the best stars. I wish to know an entire heaven and an entire earth."

Neighbors in his hometown, Concord, Massachusetts, considered him the local hippie. They were baffled by his failure to pursue "practical" activities and by his inclination to spend an hour in the rain, lost in introspection over the sight of wild ducks on a pond. They couldn't fathom his desire to keep life simple, flexible, and immediate, his unwillingness to collect possessions that might soon possess the possessor. His standards, however, were clear and consistent: "If a man walks in the woods for the love of them half of each day, he is in danger of being regarded as a loafer, but if he spends his whole day as a speculator, shearing off those woods and making the earth bald before her time, he is esteemed as an industrious and enterprising citizen."

Thoreau was industrious at his own calling, and optimistic and tolerant besides. His hopefulness and positivism are spread across pages of *The Maine Woods*. "What a place to live, what a place to die and be buried in! There certainly men would live forever, and laugh at death and the grave." So he enthused following his exploration of Katahdin. The idea was plainly not to hoard the treasures but to share them. Thus, in the appendix he advised the potential tourist of his day on what to wear, carry (in the way of compass, axe, pocket map and the like), the necessary provisions, the fee of an Indian guide, and the cost of the twelve-day excursion starting from Moosehead Lake.

Thoreau is the essential guide to wilderness, wherever it may be. The North Woods of Maine are not only a place, but a symbol, a fragment of universality with calling and meaning to people everywhere. It isn't necessary to be there to absorb the sense of the Allagash, to travel with Thoreau in the summer of 1857, accompanied by his cousin, Edward Hoar, and Joe Polis, the trusted Indian guide, master of the woods and woodcraft. They journeyed in a slender canoe of birchbark sewn with thread of black spruce, experiencing the same kind of adventure and hazard that canoers have known before and since their time. In paddling from Telos Lake to Chamberlain Lake, stiff winds out of the northwest produce waves that can be dangerous. So it was in Thoreau's day, too. "After reaching the middle of the lake," he wrote, "we found the waves as usual pretty high, and the Indian warned my companion, who was nodding, that he must not allow himself to fall asleep in the canoe lest he should upset us, adding that when Indians want to sleep in a canoe, they lie down straight on the bottom."

Each Allagash traveler finds his own image to record: rolling out before sunup, perhaps to be greeted by a thousand stars still bright in an endless heaven; then paddling and peering ahead through steaming fog, so dense that the nearest shoreline is difficult to see; and finally emerging into a sunlight that bathes fir, spruce, and white birch with brilliant tints of red and orange. Yet the images evoked by Thoreau speak for all. Such as this: "The lakes are something you are unprepared for: They lie up so high, exposed to the light, and the forest is diminished to a fine fringe on their edges, with here and there a blue mountain, like an amethyst jewel of the first water."

Thoreau failed to go all the way down the Allagash to its rendezvous with the St. John. He pitched his northermost camp on

Pillsbury Island in Eagle Lake, turning back from there to Bangor via the east branch of the Penobscot. "Somebody had camped there not long before," he noted with displeasure, "and left the frame on which they stretched a moosehide, which our Indian criticized severely, thinking it showed but little woodcraft." And what would Thoreau say about outdoor practices today, when there is such little woodcraft?

Thoreau personifies independence and personal freedom. In 1849 he refused to pay his taxes as a means of protesting the unjust United States war against Mexico. For his act of civil disobedience he was jailed. Ralph Waldo Emerson, his close friend, wanted to pay his taxes for him, but Thoreau refused. The frustrated Emerson came to visit him in prison. "Henry," he demanded, "what are you doing in there?" To which Thoreau calmly replied, "What are *you* doing out there?" But then Thoreau followed a simple creed: "The only obligation which I have a right to assume is to do at any time what I think right."

There must be some little something of Thoreau in all of us, an urge or desire or dream to be as proud and free, unfettered by convention, as he was. I can't say when and how I first became consciously aware of Thoreau, though I like to think he has been with me always. With Thoreau as companion, there is never room for loneliness, only challenge to rise above the mediocre.

Possibly I became aware of Thoreau on my first visit to Maine. I spent an enriching winter in 1944–45 at the edge of the North Woods. World War II was underway. I was stationed as a navigator with the Second Foreign Transport Group at an airbase at Presque Isle, about as far north and east as one could get and still be in the United States, but strategically located for missions to Europe (on which we would transport priority supplies overseas and bring planeloads of wounded home). Planes were much slower in those days and my crewmates and I would be aloft for many hours, sometimes groping through heavy blizzards that characterize the wintry North Atlantic. But then there was the return to Presque Isle, touching down at the end of a fierce night, secure at the sight of the friendly clear morning sky and familiar white hillsides massed with snow. It was more than home base, but home. "We never came home from an absence," wrote Mark Twain of that elegant steamboat house he built at Hartford, "that its face did not light up and speak out its eloquent welcome—and we could not enter it unmoved." So it was in returning to Maine, despite its cool climate and cool temperament.

I took long walks, dressed in parka, boots, and mittens. The air was clear and dry and I felt at times as though a part of a Rockwell Kent painting come alive, touching the golden sunlight on a snowbank in one of his thoroughly natural and undisturbed settings. In recent years I've been asked to explain the source of my interest in wild places and concern for them. It's been difficult to answer, but my experiences in Maine contributed, I'm sure.

So did navigation on those long overwater transport missions. Flying overland a pilot normally can rely on his radio compass, transmitting signals from checkpoints below. Combat navigators flew rugged missions from England to Germany, or beyond, but they would follow rivers, railroads, and cities, or they were guided by radar; they rarely used the celestial system. Overwater, however, a thousand miles from anywhere, the sole checkpoints were the stars visible through the lens of the navigator's octant. My geography was in the big heavens, glimpsing the infinite through the vacuum bubble of an octant, the artificial horizon, and unraveling a romantic mystery of time and space, of earthly rotation and revolution, riding with the stars in *their* latitudes and longitudes. I would measure celestial distances in terms of time and angles, then transpose them to the finite on a Mercator projection, the kind of map by which navigators have guided vessels since the age of Henry the Navigator. Everything has changed since my time; navigation is now done by pushing buttons in a computer, not by "shooting" celestial lines and fixes. I could feel some kinship, however, with all the navigators before me, back to the Portuguese and to the Polynesians before them, who first made their way by following the currents, and then the stars, adapting shells dug from the sand as their sextants.

In the Air Transport Command we didn't have to kill and rarely were subject to combat conditions, but there was always the element of risk and danger, which sparked the glow of anticipation, somewhat like mountain climbers experience. Ice dragged some down on the North Atlantic. Others crashed into mountains they never knew were there. On one mission to England my crewmates and I stopped at Goose Bay, Labrador. Almost immediately on takeoff from there on our next leg, the plane was enveloped in a blizzard. Clouds and snow were so dense the crew couldn't see out the windows to the wing tips. The stars were hidden, navigation impossible; the best I could do was dead reckoning, based on pre-flight data. The plane rose and fell, buffeted in the sky like a Conrad schooner in a typhoon sea. Streaks of ice glazed the wings. When ice formed on the propeller blades, the pilot pressed the throttles forward and then quickly pulled them back, creating an eerie whining sound while tearing off chunks of ice that thudded ominously against the fuselage. We plunged onward through the long Atlantic night, five young men isolated and alone. The cabin was in darkness except for the luminous green of the instrument panel, and we hardly spoke. The storm seemed endless. During one period both pilots were forced to grip the controls tightly as the plane rocked through the turbulence. As a consequence of icing, our airspeed dropped, but the pilots successfully maintained altitude. Crossing Greenland the sun cast faint light shadows at the horizon. Through holes in the clouds we saw the mountain of ice that caps most of Greenland, two thousand feet below. The worst was over.

Through such experiences I learned to respect weather and the elements. Navigation taught me the harmonious pattern of the universe, the lesson of cosmic unity. Pilots, too, are moved by the freedom and depth of skies to find new dimensions in their thinking. "In wildness I sense the miracle of life, and beside it our scientific accomplishments fade to trivia," wrote Charles A. Lindbergh.

Once back at Presque Isle I would share my encounters and observations with Harriett, often on those long walks. Harriett, a native of upper New York and a Cornell graduate, was a Red Cross worker at the airbase, quite different from many of the women to whom we were normally exposed. It was a time when my peers and I lived as though there were no tomorrow. We transport pilots and navigators were mostly in our early twenties and yet suddenly worldly. On one continent we would hear this line: "No momma, no poppa, no per diem. Baksheesh, Sahib." And on another: "How would you like to sleep with my sister? She's fourteen years old, plenty good!" On returning to the States, many headed for dim little bars and hotel rooms for two (at times with somebody else's wife) for sex, or romance, before the next mission overseas.

I was no different from the rest, but Harriett was. While my colleagues were rooted in the barracks card games or downtown beer parlors, I had the pleasure of her company. On evening walks we often had a specific destination—the compound of Siberian Huskies and Malamutes and Saint Bernards used on search-and-rescue missions, tended by Sergeant George Esslinger, a wilderness man.

There were twenty or thirty dogs, to the best of my recollection. Each had its own doghouse, yet all slept out, either on loose snow or on the rooftops of their houses. They were not unfriendly as we approached, one howling, then another and another, chanting some strange harmony that broke the stillness of a cold northern night.

"They howl because they're contented," George explained while serving us coffee, which he obviously enjoyed doing. "They're willing to serve their master more so than any other dog, except maybe the hunting dog. I never have to force my dogs— like cracking a whip—to make them work.

"The characteristic of the sled dog is that it won't let you down. When we were out on the trail on a search-and-rescue mission in Newfoundland, the weather was so bad the plane servicing us couldn't drop any food because they couldn't see us. We went for three days working out there and the dogs were still holding their own without complaining."

George came from International Falls, Minnesota, on the Canadian border but half a continent away. He and his family operated a resort at the edge of a wilderness of forest and lakes, where he guided fishermen and hunters. In fall and winter he ran a team of sled dogs, taking in hunters and bringing out deer they had killed, as well as hauling ice and wood to the resort. For sheer fun he and other drivers would stage endurance races of seventeen to twenty miles across the frozen surface of Lake Kabetogama. It was a routine that demands conditioning, but George was up for it. He was about thirty, medium height, heavy boned and low slung, plainly quick reflexed, and without an ounce of excess fat. He was soft-spoken and gentle. His education had taken him only through high school, but he imparted a sense of poise, confidence, and expertise in what he was about.

"I was surprised when they called my dogs and me to the service. Where in the hell would they use dog teams? Airplanes and jeeps move faster, but they wanted us for Arctic search-and-rescue, and machinery doesn't work in that cold weather and snow. You've got to have the old man on skis and snowshoes and the dogs to do it.

"First they gathered us in Montana. We had a select group of officers and enlisted men: Arctic explorers, a champion skier from Norway, the dog driver for Admiral Byrd, a professional parachutist, a tiger-hunting guide in the Yucatan. I was there five months, teaching new dogs with my team in wild country on the Continental Divide outside Helena. A dog learns quicker from another dog than from a man, so we matched up a young dog with an old dog on the sled."

Then he came to Presque Isle, the starting point for establishing bases with dogs and drivers in the remote reaches of northern Canada and Greenland. George would spend three or four months at Presque Isle, then go north to help at other bases. The small Siberian Huskies, weighing about forty-five to fifty pounds, were the lead team in getting into a plane crash because they were the fastest. The larger Malamutes would come up later with equipment, such as tents and wicker baskets for casualties. Saint Bernards and Newfoundlands were used for packwork where trails were sheer rock that a man couldn't manage.

George went on rescue missions in the wilderness with his dogs in winter and without them in summer. Few men were brought out alive. If they were still living when they crashed, the odds were they would perish from shock or exposure; the rescue teams would find them frozen to death. There were crashes on the slopes of Katahdin, in the North Woods near Millinocket, and in the Green Mountains of Vermont, as well as farther north. It was tough going in the Arctic in any season. Once during summer George tramped two and a half days through black flies and mosquitoes. Even netting over his face couldn't keep them away; and the insects were as bad at night as in the daytime.

There was always a lighter side to life. Like the time fifteen or twenty of the flight nurses piled into a single jeep and George hooked up a sled. Then he hauled them around the base. The nurses squealed, screamed, and laughed—before George gave the starting signal they couldn't believe a team of dogs could muster so much power, but there was no doubt about it before they were through.

When I returned on later visits the people I'd known and the wartime excitement were shadows of the past. Some of the hangars and frame buildings of the airbase were still standing, adapted to other uses of one kind and another, but I couldn't find the dog compound or even determine where it had been.

The North Woods, nevertheless, seemed to approximate the settings that Thoreau had described. During the 1960s the proposal to designate the Allagash as a national river to be administered by the National Park Service was a matter of active public interest and controversy. The Park Service declared that the area "had preserved its wilderness characteristics to a remarkable degree."

So it appeared when I traveled with Morris Wing, and another time when I went north again, through some of the holdings of the Great Northern Paper Company, the largest landholder in the state. That company controlled more than two million acres, but, as I observed, not solely to feed cellulose to its mills. It protected on its property thirty-eight miles of the Appalachian Trail (for which it received a commendation from the Wilderness Society). A Great Northern brochure of those days, titled *Recreation in Northern Maine*, was filled with references to the need of "preserving the wild beauty of forest land . . ."; "preservation of plenty of natural forest where animals and birds can find food and breeding grounds . . ."; and "doing everything possible to preserve and protect Maine's forests." A vice-president told me: "Our viewpoint is that land is more than ownership, but a trust."

The large companies resisted the national park proposal and had some powerful arguments on their side. "If, as conceded, wilderness characteristics have been preserved," they demanded, "why not leave things be?" The national park idea indeed was rejected; instead, Maine voters in 1966 approved a $1.5 million bond issue to establish the state-administered Allagash Wilderness Waterway "to protect and enhance the natural beauty, character and habitat of a unique area." That in itself was a revolutionary advance for a citizenry rooted in frugality and the feeling that least government controls make for best government. Great Northern, for its part, sold twenty thousand acres to the Maine Park and Recreation Authority as the core of the new state area and, for an extra show of good faith, presented seven hundred acres, including the Allagash Falls, the scenic climax of the entire trip, for public ownership.

In 1983 I returned to Maine. Morris Wing was retired, but his company, International Paper, was hospitable. Call it part of the process of public relations, or corporate communications, or whatever, but over the years I've welcomed chances to examine the way such firms meet their obligations and opportunities of forest trusteeship. Thus, I spent a couple of days in the woods with Ron, a forester, and Paula, a public relations person, both capable people, though plainly company people. Ron was in his mid-thirties, an outdoors person since Boy Scout days, who fished and canoed and delighted in photographing moose, which we luckily observed at unusually close range (of possibly only twenty or thirty feet). He knew the woods, but wasn't of the woods. To Ron it was the pioneering American way to get out the logs, difficult, inaccessible terrain notwithstanding, rather than to leave them be as documents of unscarred America. Paula, in her early thirties, was an attractive brunette, a pert little package of energy and enthusiasm, ever consistent in commitment to the rightness of her employer's cause.

Both appreciated and enjoyed unspoiled nature, I don't mean to say they didn't. "What *is* wilderness?" Paula would ask me while we stood at a lakeshore, to which we had driven, admiring a moose as the centerpiece of a serene panorama. For Paula that was wilderness; she felt she was in the middle of it. I said nothing to disabuse or contradict her. Perhaps the values of wilderness should be left for subjective perception; although, as in the pursuit of higher consciousness, through yoga or any physical or mental exercise, the more one knows of it the deeper and more fulfilling it becomes. Opening the door to one secret only leads to more passageways in approaching the sanctum of nature.

We drove through the woods to overnight at an old International Paper patrol cabin in a wild setting on St. Francis Lake. From there we canoed and fished till dark. Ron was an excellent flycaster, using flies he himself had tied, though neither of us caught a thing. Paula sat in the middle of the canoe and shivered. On the way back to the cabin, I mentioned that I would like to bring out my tape recorder and spend the evening interviewing Ron. Very quickly, Paula interjected, "What questions are you going to ask Ron?" He was flustered and intimidated by the idea of a recorded interview without a script, and I gave it up.

This was a different kind of encounter than I had had with Morris, but then times were different. In the sixties the companies resisted the park proposal with a catchy line about their "working wilderness." Logging was conducted as Justice Douglas had described it, on a selective-cutting basis, with always a forest remaining. Ron and Paula, however, were obliged to defend clear-cutting, a system of shearing the earth, accompanied by extensive road building, which they justified on the basis of an infestation of spruce budworm, an insect that has long made its appearance in rising and falling cycles. Along with "salvage logging" of some forest stands, International Paper and the other companies were doing extensive aerial spraying of toxic chemical poisons to reduce the budworm threat to other stands.

Foresters provide technical explanations for these procedures, but theirs is a narrow profession, designed to produce a merchantable commodity. Their forest is composed of timber or pulpwood, "desirable species," which they prefer to cultivate like a crop of cabbage or corn. Their training leaves little room for romance or humanist values, or for insects or weeds.

My International Paper hosts flew me over the full length of the Allagash in the company float plane. It was a treat to count from the air no less than sixty canoe parties, demonstrating anew the desire of people to escape from supercivilization for a little while. Flying with a little elevation, the network of clear-cuts and roads was evident, though there were still extensive unbroken blocks. Just above the water, fifty feet or so, the Allagash looked more like I had seen it twenty years before. We landed at Lake Umsaskis for a close look. The state campground showed the sign of wear, but the same could be said of campgrounds in wilderness anywhere; there is too much public pressure on them to sustain a wild character.

I was dropped at Presque Isle, where the float plane set down on a small lake at the edge of my old military airbase. I had made arrangements to be met there by Ezra James Briggs, who had been highly recommended by a mutual friend as a vigorous, knowledgeable authority on the North Woods, ardently committed to their conservation. Consequently, I expected to face the figure of a tough, two-fisted outdoorsman ready to cross the woods in heavy hiking boots.

But that wasn't his appearance at all. Jim Briggs was a grayish sixty-five-year-old sporting the floppy hat of a confirmed fisherman. He was bent over, hobbled by some serious disease, and frequently out of breath even without doing anything. His spirit, however, proved to be anything but crippled. He spoke in a crisp New England voice, gentle but determined. Moreover, he didn't blink or show any change of pace when I brought out the tape recorder.

"Thoreau had a great deal about geology in his book, which adds to it. When I was a boy our woods were like his. The lumbermen were reaching out, but here they were too far from any market, so we had it all to ourselves. There was hardly any access. The only way in was by canoe, unless you wanted a devil of a walk.

"We put in near the mouth of the Allagash and went upriver powered by three horsepower motors. (Earlier everyone went by pole.) Then we came downriver, paddling, easy on the pole, fishing here and there. There was good trout fishing, and still is. I got interested in the wild places by hunting and fishing, by being in them and seeing them, what they were like and hearing the solitude and enjoying it.

"Now that I'm not able to walk like I could it's not too bad to take advantage of the truck roads and see some of the same things.

Of course, I see some things that aren't so pleasant, that aren't like they were before—like clear-cuts and streams running with mud.

"I was born and raised in Caribou, twelve miles north of Presque Isle, where my family has lived for three generations. In 1943 I was in the Tenth Mountain Infantry, training on the slopes of Mount Rainier in Washington State, but I was stricken by a form of rheumatoid arthritis. It was the finish of my military career and the start of a long series of medical problems. But I've never lost my love of the out-of-doors and of the sport of fishing.

"My goal from very early years was to devote a substantial portion of my life to promoting wise resource use in Maine. In the forties and fifties that was a unique sort of thing. I was a sort of lonesome voice in the wilderness. But I had financial independence. In 1952, at the age of thirty-six, I disposed of the family store (which sold sporting goods, hardware, and farm machinery) and retired. For a while I sold investments, but only casually, working at my own pace.

"I was involved in a sportsmen's club, but they only wanted to eat and belch and boast about their trophies, so I started an Audubon chapter, which has been a steady influence in its own small way. My interest, however, is not in birds, but in saving wilderness, the areas where I've had such wonderful experiences. We needed a good strong organization to embrace all the people who care, and I helped start the Maine Natural Resources Council to fill that role. I was elected as a Republican to the legislature for eight years—two terms in both houses—and served as chairman of the Senate natural resources committee. I was a lonely voice arguing against the use of DDT, against oil refineries that would foul the beautiful Maine coast, against factories dumping their waste in our clean streams. I fought the proposed Dickey-Lincoln Dam. It would flood one hundred thousand acres of flowering and animal wonderland for all time. It was awful.

"Of course, I wanted the Allagash to be designated a national river. If the paper companies told the National Park Service to roll over they wouldn't do it. Morris Wing knew me but wouldn't give me the time of day; he wouldn't say hello all the time I was in the legislature, let alone during the issue of the waterway. Others might smile and say hello. I just didn't have a happy experience with Morris, so I thought to hell with him. He could have a lot of good qualities for all I know. He might say I was all bad because I was such a thorn in their side. I'd get them before the Senate committee and do everything I could to give them a hard time. Part of it is showmanship, but it's the only way you can make progress. You're not going to get attention if you don't attract attention. We had wonderful editorials in the papers; we were making progress and they resisted. That's natural—we might do the same in their shoes.

"I'm not against the companies, just their dirty habits. They own the wood and want to turn it into money. They're anxious to get all the resources out of the earth and into the bank in one generation. Self-interest is the strongest motivation, but it's the degree of selfishness to which I object. They take advertisements in magazines telling about the good things they're doing, instead of trying to figure out what they really should do. People hate them. Many young people feel every big company is crooked, but I don't. I know that some foresters would rather manage the land properly than get more money out of it. Really good forestry, the kind advocated by Gifford Pinchot and Aldo Leopold, would have considered the total forest, all its creatures and values."

We drove to the woods. The Allagash Wilderness Waterway includes 200,000 acres, of which 30,000 acres are water surface. The state holds a narrow strip bordering the canoe corridor, while the companies control the remainder and the rest of the North Woods beyond it. Hundreds of miles of new, permanent gravel roads laced the woods. Logging trucks had the right-of-way, leaving clouds of dust, a sure sign of soil disturbance, of soil going up in smoke, imparting a sense of ugliness, of nature defiled instead of respected. Those roads only open the way to more visitors, degrading the backwoods experience they came to enjoy.

Loggers were extracting whole trees by machine, not leaving seed trees to provide another natural crop, or den trees or mast trees to provide for wildlife. The view from the river might be more or less as I had seen it years before, possibly even as Thoreau knew it, yet both clear-cutting and pesticide spraying must affect and alter the life-community. Insects like the spruce budworm rise and fall as part of natural rhythms. They regenerate a forest, then birds clean them out. But intensive aerial spraying year after year disrupts the natural system and perpetuates the problem; the poisons are likely to knock out natural enemies of the insects while the pests themselves develop resistant strains.

The study of wilderness and the study of Thoreau—not in any academic, organized sense, mind you—enables one to appreciate the wholeness of land. Ezra J. Briggs, perhaps because of his physical handicap, sees this with particular clarity.

"Some people are thankful they can use the logging roads on private property. Others feel they have the right to run over them and do as they damn please. If it weren't for the roads a person like myself couldn't go. That wouldn't matter. I would love to have certain blocks set aside. I don't care if it falls down or blows down or blows up, but there ought to be places where you can take students and interested people to see the succession of the forest the way nature functions. I can't hike in Baxter Park, can't climb anymore, but I revel in the greatness and wisdom of Percival Baxter. He tried to get the legislature to purchase Katahdin, but they had no foresight. So he bought it piece by piece—sometimes having to wait till Great Northern stripped it clean—and then deeded it piece by piece to the state. Now we have a gorgeous park."

Thoreau spelled it Ktaadn. He compared the view from the summit to a thousand fragments of a broken mirror that had been scattered far and wide; thus the lakes appeared to him. Though exercising scant influence on men and events while he lived, surely Thoreau's philosophy was in the mind and heart of Governor Percival Baxter, son of a wealthy Maine family, when he purchased and presented to the state Katahdin and 200,000 surrounding acres. He declared as follows: "Man is born to die. His works are short-lived. Buildings crumble. Monuments decay, wealth vanishes. But Katahdin in all its glory shall remain forever the mountain of the people of Maine." He gave the land to the people for recreational use, provided that it "shall forever be left in the natural wild state, shall forever be kept as a sanctuary for wild beasts and birds, that no roads or ways for motor vehicles shall hereafter ever be constructed thereon or therein."

Thousands in search of natural sanctuary now hike each year to the northern terminus of the Appalachian Trail, the summit of Katahdin, a massive uplift thirty miles in length. The final climb, on the famous Knife Edge, extends along a narrow ridge where the hiker can stand astride almost vertical walls and stare down on either side into great basins, gouged out of ancient glaciers—a choice vantage point to absorb the wonders of the Maine woods, as Thoreau did.

"Who shall describe the inexpressible tenderness and immortal life of the grim forest," he asked, "where Nature, though it be mid-winter, is ever in her spring, where the moss-grown and decaying trees are not old, but seem to enjoy a perpetual youth; and blissful innocent Nature, like a serene infant, is too happy to make a noise, except by a few tinkling, lisping birds and trickling rills?"

Who shall it be? Some future Thoreau will come along, of course, provided the North Woods remain for his or her inspiration.

Jim Briggs and I stopped at the bridge crossing the Allagash above Round Pond to snack on the lunch we had brought. Two canoes came down the river. It was a family group, a parent and child in each canoe. We talked with them and learned they were from downstate Maine.

"Are you getting the experience you came here for?" Jim asked.

"No," the man replied seriously, then adding with a laugh, "that's why I keep coming back."

You can say that again, friend—and make it for me, too.

CHAPTER VI

When the Mysterious Owl Called in the Great Smokies

It was raining in the Smokies.

Above us in the high places the mist formed, watery molecules arriving from distant spheres of ocean and atmosphere, converging briefly before continuing their long separate journeys. The rain was soft and warm, a summer spray to cloud one's glasses, or roll down the face like a child's teardrop, and mix with perspiration born of a hard climb. It was the kind of friendly rain to remind you the earth is good, splashing the air with smells of new life in the woods.

To me the image of the Smokies will always begin with rainfall, whether a faint fair drizzle or drenching downpour. The truth is the lines above are borrowed from the opening page of the opening chapter of my book about the Great Smoky Mountains, which first appeared in 1966. I might now think of some other words to describe the scene and mood, but none to better express my own feeling.

"Rain, rain, Smoky Mountains is thy name," I said.

But Harvey Broome, who had made his way in the mountains in every conceivable circumstance, answered with a laugh. "You don't complain about weather in the Smokies. You just learn to accept it."

My two companions and I were resting on a narrow, rocky

ledge, midway in our climb to the Chimney Tops. It was still early, a cool morning, alternately brightened with sunlight and darkened with the persistent showers. John Morrell and I were puffing. The climb was steep, almost vertical for several hundred feet, hand over hand from one rocky perch to the next, clutching tree roots and raw earth in between; not really a rugged ascent to anyone accustomed to western mountaineering, but the toughest the Smokies has to offer, and tough enough for me. As for Harvey, he was like a grayed eagle, light and wiry, attuned to wild nature; he had made his first trip of the year to the Chimneys in the quiet cold of January.

Why do people do these things? What is the attraction of harsh winter out-of-doors? Or the reward? Or the influence of wild nature on the spirit of the civilized human? When we reached the summit between the Chimney Tops, twin craggy pinnacles of rock, it was a world for dreaming on the manifest mysteries, myths, marvels, and meanings of the Great Smoky Mountains. The rains fell no longer. We sat and spread our lunch on a rocky island, surrounded by rolling haze and, at our fingertips, summer-blooming herbs, mosses, and dwarfed rosy-pink Carolina rhododendron, the "deer laurel" that grows high in the southern mountains and nowhere else. Quiet for a time were the three of us, the older eyes I fancied perceiving more than mine. Harvey Broome and John Morrell—scarcely lustrous names in the big scheme of things—yet they typify a certain breed who have given their energy to the Smokies and their love to the earth.

Harvey and John are gone, but there are others like them, many others, impelled by something inside that burns at times as love does. I've met these people in the Smokies (and elsewhere, of course), country people and city people, who want to rise above themselves and give their love for something money can't buy, hopeful it may make a difference in public policy.

My companions had been high school classmates in Knoxville during World War I. Both in time became lawyers. John went to work in the early twenties as a land buyer for the Great Smoky Mountains Conservation Association, acquiring parcels of private real estate that ultimately would comprise a national park of a half-million acres. Then he worked for the park itself, becoming more intimately associated with its development than any other person. Harvey entered private practice and made good, which was not quite good enough for him, for in due course he took a job as law clerk to a judge with the understanding that there would be ample free time to devote to affairs of the Wilderness Society, which he and a handful of others had founded while on a hiking trip in the Smokies and for which he served as president during the mid-sixties. And there we were, wordless for a while, finding ourselves in a breeze-swept aerie, watching and listening to the birds.

A towhee flicked her long, rounded tail while flitting upward toward the spruce and fir, where she builds her summer nest. An ensemble of tiny winter wrens, normally reserved, proclaimed their presence with melodious high-pitched trilling and favored us with their rare antiphonal song—as soon as one uttered the last bubbling *crrrip*, another began, for round after tuneful round. A flock of swifts, high, fast fliers on tireless wings, swirled in circles, feeding on insects while skimming the air, diving occasionally into deep, dark crevices in the rock which must have been their home. What could be more appropriate than swifts nesting in the natural chimney?

From our craggy perch we looked down on the valley known as the Sugarlands. It became the focus of our attention. It was filled with growing trees sweeping toward the mouth of the valley where the park visitor center and headquarters are clustered. My friends told how much all this had changed from their recollections of it. They began coming out from Knoxville as boys, in the teens of the century, when the high places were visited only by herdsmen tending livestock, bear hunters, and a few venturous hikers who would climb about through brush, briers, and downed timber, often losing their way in torrential rains and heavy fog, without maps, name places, or trails to guide them in many sections. The purple hazy range was visible from the hills of Knoxville, but barely anyone knew it by name.

In 1913, John Morrell, his father, and two friends came out to camp at the foot of the Chimney Tops. They first had to travel to Sevierville, the county seat, then follow a rough dirt road to Gatlinburg, an inconspicuous mountain village in those days. A guide met them there with a mule to haul their tent and other packs, and up they marched along Fighting Creek and the Sugarlands road, such as it was.

"One morning, while we were camped below," John recollected, "the Chimneys looked so close we started for the top to see if they really had soot in them. Instead, we found a yellowjacket nest that must have been upset by a bear the night before. We could see the cabins down in the Sugarlands, with their plumes of blue smoke rising over the cornfields and up between the bright, clear green mountainsides. That place could easily have been called Rocky-lands, for the people who settled there were compelled to stack the rocks before they could plant crops, and then had to dig holes between the rock piles to get dirt for covering the seeds."

As for Harvey, he told how he and his uncle would come from Knoxville through the sawmill town of Townsend to Elkmont, a logging camp with a small resort hotel on the other side of Sugarland Mountain. They rode the Little River Railroad, covering the fifty-two miles in two hours, fifteen minutes, the last portion filled with exciting hairpin turns where they could almost reach out and touch the gorge.

All this changed with the coming of the park. Unlike western national parks, which had all been part of the public domain, the land in the Smokies was privately held, some portions by timber companies, others by small holders. Backwoods communities were scattered in the hills. Nevertheless, the majesty was inescapable. In the 1920s the Southern Appalachian National Park Commission pointed to the Smokies as the prime site for a major new national park in the East. In 1930, when large delegations from North Carolina and Tennessee called on Secretary of the Interior Ray Lyman Wilbur in Washington to present the lands acquired by them as the nucleus of the national park-to-be, Governor O. Max Gardner of North Carolina declared:

"The Great Smoky Mountains National Park, when established, will create in the heart of the Appalachian Mountains a permanent sanctuary for animal and bird life and a botanical garden and arboretum which scientists say will be unequaled in the world."

Consequently, settlements were uprooted, and so were logging camps and logging railroads and herds of cattle grazing the grassy mountaintops. Hiking the trails along peaked and spurred ridges and across the plunging valleys, I can still find vestiges of settlement days in the crumbling rocky foundations of old houses, patches of daffodils and daisies, and ghostly fruit trees, but mostly the mountains have reverted to their own, upward through the natural cycle. The cornfield of four decades ago is a young forest of infinite variety, taking its place alongside older, primitive portions that were never cut or cultivated.

I marvel at how these forests, where natural creatures belong and are wanted, regenerate themselves, and at how myriad components, sturdy, graceful, exquisite, puny, and humble, fit together. Modest herbs flower in spring and by summer have withered and vanished. Woody giants survive for centuries. The genius of these mountains lies as much in the twenty-seven or twenty-eight indigenous types of gastropods, the lowly slugs, in the salamanders and millipedes, and the unique spider of Cades Coves that is native only to this place and to China—as much in these species as in the bear, the night-prowling bobcat, flying squirrel, turkey, and deer, and the two hundred kinds of birds that serenade the woods—for they are all part of the chain of life. Built upon the lowest of living things, they form a composition of endless themes and variations. Our species is part of it, too, for the Smoky Mountains comprise the national park that came into being as a testament of man's faith.

When it became time for us to start down from the Chimneys, Harvey suggested bushwhacking through a trailless jungle of heath thickets. The steep slopes of Sugarland Mountain were dense with masses of dog hobble, or leucothoe, intertwined with trunks and branches of dripping rhododendron and laurel, an almost impenetrable labyrinth with only an occasional patch of sunlight shining on red partridgeberries. We found ourselves following a bear path, over which Harvey loped gracefully and lightly. About all I could do, besides sliding, was to envy the old bear who could take it rolling downhill. It seemed more practical to step over the rocks of the mountain stream, and when rivulets filled my boots, my only thought was, *Let it rain!*

By his own testimony, Harvey had been a small, sickly boy

whose family felt that heading into the hills might do him good. I should say it did; he became a champion of high, wild places everywhere, serving as friend, hiking companion, and collaborator of such widely known scientific and environmental personalities as Olaus Murie, Aldo Leopold, Robert Marshall, Benton MacKaye, and William O. Douglas. Despite broad interests and influence, his heart was in the Smokies, his first hiking and camping country, his favorite wilderness.

He certainly influenced my life and attitude. I had come to research a book about the Smoky Mountains. Recently, I had written *Whose Woods These Are*, a successful book about the national forests, and the publisher thought there might be a market for one about the most heavily visited national park and that I might be the right author for it. I knew a little about the Smokies region, not much, but enough to feel I could do it justice. My thought originally was to write some kind of travel book, serving the practical need of park visitors, with chapters on natural history and mountain folk culture. That's not how it turned out, however. During the mid-sixties the National Park Service advanced a plan to construct a new and needless transmountain road across the Great Smokies that would desecrate the wilderness. I wanted my book to contribute to the efforts of Harvey and others to protect the park through public understanding and appreciation of its values. Every word in the book was designed toward that end, with this summary on the penultimate page:

"As I near the final paragraph, the public has been advised that hearings are imminent on the new Wilderness Act as it applies to the Great Smoky Mountains National Park. The immediate issue is whether to go ahead with construction of a proposed road from Bryson City across the park to Tennessee. In a broader sense, we shall write the record of our age in the pages of history; we shall demonstrate the degree of our respect for the ancientness of these mountains, and for the right of generations hence to see them in their natural state."

Harvey was an inspiring mentor. He recorded a scrupulous personal journal (which his wife, Anne, published privately following his death, a charming volume titled *Out Under the Sky of the Great Smokies*), written in gentle and cheerful language, though it revealed the author as a tough mountain hand, tough and yet contemplative. Harvey saw the Smokies in every season and in every mood. He was out there when the temperature dropped to fifteen below zero, and the trees cracked and popped throughout the night, and the ice froze on his eyebrows and eyelashes, and the water froze in his canteen. And yet without complaint because this was, after all, part of experiencing the natural world.

He met and marveled at bears, snakes, and spiders, along with the more acceptable plants and trees. "Trees," he observed, "are very satisfying. They stay put; they don't go out at night; they don't have dates. . . . Trees are in a sense more satisfying than pets because they are longer lived and more predictable. Living less complex lives, they are not as stimulating as people, although, on the other hand, they are less disappointing than many people."

Deploring the separation of urbanized Americans from their roots, Harvey related overhearing an Explorer Scout say that the water in the Smokies was better on the Tennessee side (than in North Carolina) because it came out of a pipe, thus leading him to challenge: "What sanctity is there to a pipe? Are the woods so forbidding that one is not at home unless there is a pipe?"

My friend was furious at policies of the National Park Service that make things easier for park visitors regardless of consequences to the resources. For him it was the "wind and sunset; the haunting dual notes of the varied thrush; the fugitive fragrance of the phacelia; the bite of the cold; the stir and challenge of muscle against mountain; the elixir of water cold from a stream; the flavor of rain-drenched blueberries"—the contact with raw environment—that bring living into focus.

Applying his influence as president of the Wilderness Society, Harvey led the fight to protect the Great Smoky Mountains from their assigned protectors of the National Park Service. His journal for 1966 recorded an account of the "Save Our Smokies" hike, when hundreds turned out to protest construction of the transmountain road. They came in family groups with little children. And there was Reverend Rufus Morgan, eighty-one and almost blind, the descendant of a proud old mountain family, moving spiritedly along the trail.

Nevertheless, one Park Service official, on learning that 576 hikers had signed the register at Clingmans Dome, retorted that only half had completed the full seventeen miles from there to Elkmont, Tennessee. Such is the mentality that later led to bulldozing a trail to Chimney Tops—a disfigurement defended by a high official on the ground that "parks are for people, aren't they?"

I attended the wilderness hearings in June 1966, conducted at Gatlinburg, Tennessee, and Bryson City, North Carolina. They were the historic first public hearings held by the National Park Service in fulfillment of requirements of the Wilderness Act passed two years before. The subject under immediate consideration was the fate of the Great Smoky Mountains, but the hearings also marked the beginning of a series of reviews of wilderness areas in other national parks, national monuments, and additional units of the National Park System.

"Conservationists the world over are looking to our National Park Service for exemplary leadership in the field of safeguarding the beauty and character of natural landscape and sites. It would be most unfortunate if the Park Service were unable to fulfill this role in the Smokies."

These words, spoken by Stewart M. Brandborg, executive director of the Wilderness Society, in his testimony, seemed to me to touch the heart of the issue with simplicity and directness. They made me conscious of the greatness of moment before a jam-packed audience in the hall and before the vaster unseen audience beyond it. For, as someone said during the flood tide of feeling and eloquence that followed: "A wrong decision will be severely judged by untold millions still unborn."

The government's opening presentation was devoid of such feeling—it was devoid of *any* feeling. This might be considered surprising, since the Secretary of the Interior of those days, Stewart L. Udall, was often depicted as wearing the mantle of Mr. Conservation and Protector of Wild Places, while the assistant secretary in charge of national parks, Stanley B. Cain, was a well-known educator and natural scientist, who in years past had personally conducted botanical studies in the Great Smokies. But something happens to people when they become elevated in importance and institutionalized; their values and loyalties become mixed. They rationalize compromise with a clean conscience and expect a public relations news release to bail them out.

Besides, top officials don't do the dirty work. They keep their skirts clean by sending others to do it for them. In the case of the Smokies hearings, it was a regional director of the National Park Service, who I knew as a decent fellow, behaving like a loyal lieutenant faithfully carrying out orders. I could accept this in a military circumstance, but to set one's principles aside for a paycheck and pension when one's whole career is focused on resource protection—that's not my idea of giving meaning to a life.

The regional director, Elbert Cox, read carefully and without digression from an uninspired and uninspiring statement. He offered nothing consequential in wilderness philosophy or park policy. He advanced a road plan for the Smokies intended to solve seasonal traffic jams, outlining the location of the transmountain highway plus corridors for additional inner loops. What was left over, less than half the park, was offered for inclusion in the National Wilderness Preservation System—not in one contiguous unit, nor even in two, but in six broken blocks.

More than two hundred witnesses spoke, mostly in brief, four-minute presentations in behalf of organizations or themselves. They expressed different views, but only one criticized the concept of preserving wilderness: a tourist promoter who said he would prefer to see the park paved with eight-lane highways. Public officials spoke first at both Gatlinburg and Bryson City, and, after hearing representatives of chambers of commerce and allied groups, departed. I hate that system. Representative Roy Taylor, the local congressman, chided outsiders for poking their noses into mountain business. "Many people attending this hearing have come a long way thinking it is their duty," he said, "to protect the Smoky Mountains National Park from Swain County and from the State of North Carolina and its citizens." Unfortunately, Mr. Taylor did not remain on the scene long enough to hear the elderly Reverend Rufus Morgan, properly dressed in gray suit and white collar. As founder of the pioneering Appalachian School at Penland, he had probably done as much for the advancement of Carolina mountaineers as any individual of his period, and far more than any roadbuilder or tourist boomer attending the hearing at the courthouse in Bryson City. White haired and erect, Reverend Morgan spoke proudly as a fifth-generation mountain man. He told of his adventures in studying wildflowers and ferns with young people, of enjoying the splendid solitudes, beauty, and grandeur of the Smokies, of hiking the entire sixty-eight-mile length of the Appalachian Trail in the park, and of his dreams that such opportunities be available for future generations. No outsider could have been more effective.

It was the "outsiders"—teachers and preachers, scholars and scientists, Scouts and Scout leaders, hikers, trout fishermen, botanists, and birders—who brought added power, poignancy, emotion, and intellect.

"I love the wilderness so much that I must oppose the transmountain road," said one. "As much as I like and admire the National Park Service, I just can't approve this plan," said another. They identified themselves with love of land and with idealism, speaking of the joys of wilderness, of spiritual exhilaration, and of the threats of a multimillion dollar political boondoggle. One man came from the Bronx, complete with Bronx accent, to describe the meaning of Central Park as the natural fragment New Yorkers must cherish and the meaning to him of the wild Smokies. In the morning at Gatlinburg the Tennessee Commissioner of Conservation testified for the transmountain road in behalf of the governor. That very afternoon a state park naturalist, Mack Prichard, testified as a private individual against the road. In time we became close friends and years later I asked Mack whether he considered his independent action fitting and proper. He responded: "No, I don't think it was fitting. It was pretty risky, in fact. I felt if it cost me my job it was worth it—being honest about the fact I thought it was a lousy idea. You do what you have to do sometimes. I thought it was a sorry idea to build another road. The park would be better off without the road it's got. Then you'd have twice as much wilderness."

Many scientists came to the hearings, not a single one to support the government position. They pleaded for large expanses of primeval land for biological, botanical, and ecological studies. "No road on earth," warned one, "is important enough to destroy the values inherent in these mountains."

When one woman spoke of the "emotional, religious experience," I realized that religion and veneration had been introduced repeatedly into the forum. A minister said he was shocked and disappointed at the Park Service plan: "I bring my young churchmen to master the challenge of the Appalachian Trail in the Smokies and to find an opportunity of self-reliance unmatched in the country." Judge Thad Bryson, of Bryson City, of the hometown business bloc, declared in his testimony, however, that wilderness people were like a religious group petitioning the Lord to keep all others out of heaven. Then somebody else said that nobody would tear down a beautiful church just because it was used by a minority faith. Harvey Broome, as president of the Wilderness Society, compared the Smokies to the *Mona Lisa*, which had been viewed only by thousands during its recent brief visit to the United States—but there had been no suggestion that it be sliced in parts to display before greater throngs. "As people came by the thousands for a fleeting glimpse of the *Mona Lisa*," he said, "they have come by the millions to the Great Smokies for a passing experience with wilderness. These matchless mountains deserve the same love and care that men have for centuries bestowed upon their finest works of art."

Those hearings for me were part of the learning process, perhaps a course combining history and political science above all. In 1912 John Muir attended the conference of national park superintendents in Yosemite. The major question was: Shall automobiles be allowed to enter Yosemite? "It overshadowed all others and a prodigious lot of gaseous commercial eloquence was spent upon it," he wrote. "But the Yosemite Park was lost sight of, as if its thousand square miles of wonderful mountains, canyons, glaciers and songful falling rivers had no existence." But in mid-June 1966, at the edges of the Great Smoky Mountains, the forum could not lose sight of the songful rivers, forests, wildlife, and the wonderful high places. These treasures and their survival were the inescapable questions.

Without the Wilderness Act, if you ask me, the bulldozers

would have been at work on the transmountain road. Because of the Act, concerned citizens had their place at the bargaining table, out in the open, where big issues deserve to be resolved, instead of in sequestered political corners. As a consequence, the transmountain road has never been built, at least not to this day.

Two years later I saw Harvey Broome for the last time. He had come to Washington on Wilderness Society business and we had dinner with a group of friends. Harvey had lately been ill with heart trouble. He looked pale and weak. Walking back to his hotel, the once tireless hiker felt he must stop to rest every few steps. He returned to Knoxville where, within a week or two, he died.

I was invited to the services and funeral, though these were hardly the kind that funeral directors conduct. Eight or ten of Harvey's intimates gathered in his study at his home on a Knoxville hillcrest facing the Smokies. Each took his turn in expressing some reminiscence. Words stuck in my throat as I looked at Harvey's hiking boots perched on a filing cabinet; I felt inadequate. Then we drove to the park to hike to Harvey's favorite area in the Greenbrier section. It was raining in the Smokies, a steady, drippy downpour that turned the forest misty, mellow, and mournful. Finally we stopped at what obviously was a chosen place. I hadn't realized what was coming and wasn't prepared for it. Anne Broome removed from her backpack a container about the size of a Mason jar. It held Harvey's cremated remains—all there is to any of us in the end, and no mausoleum, no matter how majestic, can make more of it. While we stood silent and thoughtful in the rain, Anne scattered the chalky ashes. It was time to leave, but no one seemed ready to take the lead. Ernest Griffith, an old scholar who had already lived a full life, broke the silence. He said it was fitting to express a few thoughts before we left this site. "This is a time of thanksgiving, not of mourning," he began a brief impromptu eulogy that brightened the mood. Harvey was gone, to be sure, but he left a marvelous memorial with his contribution to the Smokies wilderness.

Over the years I returned fairly often to the Great Smokies and surrounding mountain areas of Tennessee and North Carolina, often in company with my naturalist friend Mack Prichard. I would call him and say, "Can you meet me at the airport in Knoxville? I have to go to the park, and then to Chattanooga and Nashville." And he would be there, arriving just as I picked up my baggage, almost tardy but always timely because he had driven four hundred miles across Tennessee or had stopped to pick up a bottle of Scotch. We consumed a lot of whiskey of all kinds, including mountain moonshine, and would stop along the way to sample Tennessee's best barbecues roasted over hickory at the least likely places. Now and then he'd show up with his current lady friend or his ex-wife, each one of whom clung to him for dear life, but I preferred when he came alone because we had many things to do and to talk about.

We were involved in various issues. Either he would get me interested or I would get him interested. Or someone else would get us both into it. Some of these issues were pretty prominent in their time. There was the unsuccessful effort to save the Little Tennessee River (the home of the celebrated snail darter), at the edge of the Smokies, from the senseless and useless Tellico Dam. And then the successful effort to save Overton Park, a lovely urban forest in Mack's hometown of Memphis, from being bisected by an interstate highway. There was the proposed Cataloochee access road, which politicians and land speculators wanted to punch into a remote section of Great Smoky Mountains National Park. The park bureaucrats were ready to comply, but local Carolina mountain people, whose forebears had lived in old Catalouch', demanded that their heritage be safeguarded. It wasn't the "outsiders" who rose in righteous wrath, but it was a pleasure to help the cause.

Another time I was invited to speak at the dedication of the Gee Creek Wilderness, a rugged wooded mountain area in the Cherokee National Forest, named for a tributary of the Hiwassee River. The main activity at the dedication was serving and savoring burgoo, a huge stew concocted by Walter Williams, a trout fisherman friend of ours. Mack credited Walter for setting the area aside: "He noticed the beginning of logging and learned the whole place was scheduled to be cut and cut heavily. So Walter got sportsmen to write letters and start a wilderness movement. Tennesseans love a good fight. The Tennessee Conservation League, which supposedly speaks for hunters and fishermen, voted to support the status quo, but those fellows are too lazy to haul out their deer or wild pig and they don't want their Jeeps limited. They don't want to recognize that you're either part of the solution or part of the pollution."

Then there was Mack's effort to save Big Savage Gulf, which he first heard about from a fellow in Wisconsin:

"I went to a natural areas meeting there and met this fellow, Hugh Iltis [a feisty, impassioned Czech-born botanist whom I happen to know]. 'What are you doing to save Savage Gulf?' he demanded. Iltis had taken his Ph.D. at the University of Tennessee and knew our beautiful places. He set a fire under me with evangelism to go save these places. Huxley said, 'The use of knowledge is not wisdom but action.' If you don't act on what you know, then you just dropped the ball.

"I flew over Savage Gulf, then walked through it. The owner of the property was a Swiss descendant who had made a lot of money selling used Jeeps. He was sympathetic and interested. He said, 'I'd like to see those big trees reseed the whole plateau.' We started on the impossible dream. I contacted Governor Dunn, who had been a dentist in Memphis. 'Wouldn't you like to stretch those long legs and go hiking with us in Savage Gulf?' The governor said, 'Sure, call my secretary and make a date.' He came and helped us to acquire the area. He was a wonderful governor. When I went to Brazil I sent him a picture postcard showing a dentist who was a martyr. I wrote, 'Governor, be bold, be bold, but not too bold.'"

In early spring of 1983 I was coming east to Washington and arranged to detour en route for a couple of days in the Smokies. I wanted especially to climb Mount LeConte, a major peak in the park, just a shade under 6600 feet, and expected to see the first flowers of the new season.

Mack met me at the Knoxville airport. He was a state employee, yet insisted on living and working on his own timetable; he was often in trouble with his superiors and a step or two ahead of dismissal, but too many Tennesseans supported him. He had been chief naturalist in the state parks, and state archaeologist. At the time he was involved in conservation education, giving speeches and slide shows to more than a hundred audiences a year—

churches, schools, any and all groups that would listen to his message about conserving Tennessee's natural heritage.

My friend was like a Southern preacher with a banjo, a combination evangelist and minstrel, spouting conundrums and quotations, evoking laughter, tears, and wonderment. I've heard him before many audiences, mystifying, mesmerizing, and inspiring, though I imagine some of his superiors never heard him at all. He precluded questioning of an expense account by submitting none; he drove an official state car, which entitled him to gasoline at state pumps, and he would sleep under the stars or in his car.

I expected spring, but it was winter. Where wildflowers should have been bursting with color, the ground was mantled with snow, and with ice in places. Consequently, it took a while to get organized with the right gear for the weather, and it was after midday before we started up the trail. Mack carried the heavy pack. He was in his early forties, a good-looking fellow with dark hair and a round, full face, average size but size enough, carrying too much weight on his frame, which I insisted came from overeating the wrong foods and failing to care for the ecosystem of his own body. But he was selfless, impelled by purpose, enabling him to do things, whether crisscrossing the state or hauling a heavy pack, beyond the reach of others.

Mostly we were alone on the trail, rather strange considering its popularity and the fact the Smokies is considered a park for all seasons. We followed a stream thickly bordered by laurel and rhododendron. It struck me that mountain water in winter and early spring looks especially fresh and pure.

"That stream is a-flowing and a-going," said my friend. "The ancient Chinese asked, 'What of all things is most yielding and yet wears away the heart of stone? What is of all things most humble and yet is exalted under the heavens?' That's water. It just keeps flowing. And that's what we ought to do with our lives—let them flow, let them go."

On the way up the sky was generally clear, though scattered clouds, typical of the Smokies, hung low about the mountaintops and in the valleys. We could see forests dusted white with snow extending in rolling waves deep into North Carolina, the kind of picturebook scene you might associate with Bavaria or the Black Forest. The higher we climbed the colder it became. The major portion of LeConte had never been logged and its great trees were covered with snow. As we passed under the rocky outcrop of Alum Cave Bluff the tree limbs were weighted with glistening icicles, which now and then broke loose with thundering pops and whistled by like grenades. We passed a group of four men who had started early, been to the summit, and were on their way down. But they were traveling without backpacks. They were the only ones we saw above Alum Cave. The trail was coated with ice around steep, rocky ledges; only steel cable handrails riveted into the rock enabled us to keep our footing.

Finally we made it to the mountaintop. We had expected to see others, but were alone. It was late in the day but I was too cold to walk to Clifftop, the favored vantage for sunset watching. We huddled in the old stone shelter, built for summer use and downright breezy in winter. We hadn't brought a stove and couldn't gather enough decent wood to build a fire. There wasn't much point in setting up the tent. We crawled into sleeping bags on shelter bunks and made the best of it.

The moon was half-full, a pastel yellow. The frosted, snow-covered spruce and balsam stood like Christmas trees that needed no decoration, no carol or hymn to make them holy. Mack produced a bottle of rum. I was reluctant to drink, having given up the hard stuff, but my friend was disappointed considering we had had so many drinks together. Now, I decided, was the time to make an exception. That cheered him and warmed me. It is said that alcohol in cold weather induces hypothermia, but in this case it eased stress and reduced the shivers.

The snow fell all night and the breeze blew. I slept now and then, fitfully at most, stirred and shivered. In the middle of the night I heard an owl call. Mack had heard it too, for he sat up straight on the bunk and called back, but we didn't hear that fleeting song again. Around daybreak we did hear the peep of a junco, then saw the little bird creeping into the shelter, through one of its abundant cracks, to poke around for any pickings left by the last campers.

We decided to start down as quickly as we could. A sleeping

bag is comfortable and contains body heat. But once the hiker leaves it, he needs to move to stay warm. Heading down in the snow was about as tough as climbing up the day before. We were mostly in fog and mist. I was concerned about the chance of hypothermia, while Mack's mind was on the possibility of one of us slipping and breaking a leg or an arm.

But we made it back to the trailhead in fairly decent time, and celebrated by finishing the rum with beer on the side.

"I'll tell you what you've had," said Mack. "You've had an experience in endurance. There are not many places in eastern United States where you can go five and a half miles up a mountain while climbing twenty-eight hundred fifty-three feet and freeze your butt all night long."

"Yes, but you snored."

"We *both* snored, and were damn grateful for a chance to snore between shivers. Hiking up there helps build the body. It re-creates the human spirit, gives you the chance to lose yourself in ancient patterns of nature. That's what people need wilderness for."

Mack reminded me of how the year before he had accompanied his friend, Paul Adams, on Paul's 524th hike to LeConte—when he was well into his eighties. As early as 1925 Paul had established a simple camp at the summit, which the Great Smoky Mountains Conservation Association used to host potential supporters of the proposed park. His camp subsequently became LeConte Lodge, a rustic facility that makes it easy for hikers to enjoy the mountain (though shut tight till mid-spring).

What a difference between those days and ours. The mountain's untrodden recesses challenged Paul. He climbed LeConte in all kinds of weather and during every season, in daylight and in darkness. He'd climb at night because he couldn't sleep in the excessive heat of the valleys at the foot of the mountain, and found he could climb with greater ease at night, even when laden with camp provisions.

"I heard yesterday that some little lady of ninety-two has reservations at LeConte," Mack continued. "That's the way you get to be that age. Sure, it hurt a little going up and down, but that's what is good for us.

"Wilderness is something I like to know is out there. Wilderness means you still have someplace where you haven't made all the last decisions. Wilderness is the absence of people to me. Going up to LeConte and us being the only two people equals wilderness.

"Wilderness eats the unwary for breakfast. People are too durned lazy to put up the work to get there. I'm sorry about the fellow who got his leg shot off in the war, but wilderness is sort of the way God intended to manage the world before people came along and thought they could improve on it. We don't determine who gets to go; wilderness determines that.

"God had some of his best ideas here. 'Take care of the earth,' He said. 'Some of my best ideas are down here.' We've been using this planet as though we've got a spare in the trunk, as though we'd have another Smoky Mountains some day. We've been manipulating and changing and gnawing on this and that, a little piece at a time, a little clear-cut here and a little clear-cut there, till finally we haven't got very much.

"Wilderness gives you a perspective so you can measure the great changes in civilization, as we call it. Without such biological controls we don't have much chance to see the difference. During the night we heard a really beautiful owl call. I don't know what kind it was, but it was a different kind of owl than I've ever heard. I've been up there in the winter before and never heard that kind of owl. It could have been a saw-whet or a short-eared or something weird—it was not a great horned or barred owl.

"It was something mysterious that seemed to come out of the wilds of Mount LeConte as the voice of wilderness. Just waking in the middle of the night and listening to the little owl that you never heard before—and I've heard a lot of owls and talked to a lot of birds—that was beautiful last night. That was the highlight of the trip to me.

"I love an owl to call. Some people are superstitious about it calling their name. It's not calling your name. It's calling because it loves to be living, the life it wants and deserves to live. It's calling to say it needs a place to be wild in.

"Tennessee still has a lot of beauty in it: room for people to plant a garden, and not so many people that they feel hassled by one another. Their friendliness is a good indicator of that fact.

There is old-fashioned music in the mountain coves. They all come to Nashville to hear more of it. We try in our conservation efforts to hold on to some of these unique places where we can measure ourselves against the masterwork of the eternal.

"But Memphis is pushing eight hundred thousand, and the other cities are growing. We're being overurbanized. All big systems tend to self-destruct, with people passing each other in a hurry, unable to catch up with the beautiful things around them. That's why it's good for us to take a day of our lives to hike up LeConte to find the essential facts of life, to test our physical and spiritual capacity."

CHAPTER VII

A Wheelchair View
of the Rockies

In early 1971, W Mitchell was riding his motorcycle on the hilly streets of San Francisco, heading for work. At the moment he was not thinking of his job, but more likely of returning to the Colorado high country. Actually he had a job that most people would envy. It was glamorous, unique; he was the continuing center of attraction, with opportunities to meet girls, lots of tourists, people generally having a good time. Mitchell was a gripman on the San Francisco cable cars, one of a two-man crew (the conductor being the other member) on one of the only street rail cable car systems in the world. His particular function was to pull the cable lever, called "gripping the car," which made it stop or go. The job was fun, and it paid well.

Mitchell was an adventurous, healthy twenty-seven-year-old. He had just started flying lessons. He had spent the previous summer camping and part of the winter skiing in Colorado, and had returned to San Francisco to earn enough money on the cable cars to move to Aspen with his girlfriend. Fate, however, intervened. While heading for work on the fateful day, he never saw the laundry truck that collided with his motorcycle at an intersection. The gasoline cap on his vehicle, supposedly foolproof, popped open on impact. The fuel burst into flame. Mitchell, injured and helpless, was badly burned over 65 percent of his body. During the four months of hospitalization that followed, parts of all his fingers were amputated and plastic surgery was performed on his face. He credited his motorcycle helmet with saving his life.

This was for Mitchell the first of two installments in personal disaster. In November 1975, four years later, he broke his back in a freak airplane accident, which resulted in paralysis and loss of most functions from the waist down. The zestful motorcyclist, who had charmed the cable-car crowds, was now not only disfigured, but a wheelchair paraplegic.

I met Mitchell for the first time in the summer of 1981 on the floor of the Grand Canyon when we both went down the Colorado River with Martin Litton. He was an environmental celebrity who, as mayor of Crested Butte, Colorado, had led a campaign of opposition against AMAX, a powerful multinational corporation that wanted to develop a one-billion-dollar molybdenum mining project on the mountain just above his community. It was David defying Goliath from a wheelchair, carrying the battle to Washington and to the media wherever it would listen. The deposit lay on the slopes of Mount Emmons, 12,392 feet high, known locally as "Red Lady" because it takes on a red cast at sunrise, but Mitchell could have called it the "Madonna of the Rockies" and had people believing him. He was credible and convincing when interviewed on the morning network TV news programs and featured in assorted newspapers and magazines, with articles bearing such headlines as A TINY TOWN BATTLES A MINING GIANT (*The New York Times Magazine*), LIFE OR DEATH FOR A RED LADY (*Sports Illustrated*), and WILL MOLY MOVE A MOUNTAIN? (*The Wall Street Journal*).

One day we rode in the same dory through the biggest rapids. He appeared completely absorbed, at ease and unafraid. Another day I watched Mitchell swimming in a side channel with Sam West, the red-bearded Buddhist park ranger; I watched with admiration and envy. I would like to have approached this powerfully impressive paraplegic in some meaningful manner, but felt restrained by a barrier I myself had imposed, while Sam was free of artificial obstacles. As for Mitchell, he may have been disabled, but was hardly crippled. Any embarrassment was not on his part, but on the part of those who might see him as such. I hoped we would meet again. Luckily, roughly a year later, I saw him at a conference at Jackson, Wyoming. He was not really on the program, but I felt sure he would be heard. He spoke in a polished baritone, commanding attention not because he was in a wheelchair, but because of what he had to say and because of his poised, controlled delivery. He was clearly an articulate extrovert who would be heeded no matter what his handicap.

There was something important to learn from him—possibly a lesson in the value of wilderness without the physical exercise of hiking or climbing, or possibly some discernment of nature that comes only with impairment, or something about communication between humans that must be acquired rather than taught. At the Grand Canyon I had hurt my knee, which Sam West bandaged. One day later my friend Jill said, "You don't need that bandage any longer. He's only a ranger with first-aid training, while I'm a professional nurse and I know better." Though Jill massaged my knee, in a knowledgeable manner, I suppose, it was Sam's sense of caring while he administered the bandage that helped far more to ease the pain. Mitchell would say that he didn't do anything, that people did things for him, yet his presence and personality had a buoyancy that did a lot for the rest of us on that trip.

It was deep into winter, in the last days of 1982, when I saw him again. We had corresponded and he had invited me to spend New Year's with him in Crested Butte, though his young wife, Annie, would be away. I had spent Christmas with Sam at the Grand Canyon and the few days in between on the Navajo reservation and at Mesa Verde in southwest Colorado (all of which made me feel there is something to be said for being free to pursue one's own interests mobile and unentangled).

Crested Butte I found to be one of those romantic old mining towns cradled in the high valleys of the Colorado Rockies. Romantic to a point; the idea of a ghost town may conjure a picturesque image, but beyond it lies economic ruin, broken spirits, disturbed and degraded wilderness. Some towns, like Aspen and Vail, have found new life in recent times as ski resorts and mountain retreats, which makes the past easily forgotten.

Mitchell lived in a large, attractive Victorian house a block off the main street and catty-corner from the fire department. It was comfortably heated by a wood stove, contrasting with the biting cold outdoors.

"This house was built in the late 1880s, during the heyday of Crested Butte," he said while I thawed out with a glass of wine. "It started as a silver town. Lead and zinc came into the picture, but in 1896, when the U.S. went off the silver standard, lots of towns went broke. Crested Butte was lucky and survived on coal mining. But with abundant oil, there was no need to mine coal in such an out-of-the-way place, and in the early fifties the coal mines closed.

"The town looked about doomed, but wealthy outsiders came and bought the old houses and started refurbishing and refurnishing. The price of this house went up ten times. When I bought it in 1973, I paid thirty-five thousand dollars, cheap for me, but expensive for Crested Butte. The old-timers would put up wallboards, cover them with cloth, then with wallpaper; when they decided to fix the house they would add a few layers of paint and another layer of wallpaper. There was no insulation. In 1975 the house caught fire and completely gutted the upstairs. Friends rebuilt the house. The wooden doors are original and so is some of the old furniture, but the oak floors and the beautiful wainscoting on the ceilings were installed in the rebuilding. And now the house is insulated.

"That fire illustrates the sense of community here. The house burned in November, when the temperature was twenty-two below zero. That night the whole town showed up—it was the first house they ever saved. Having the fire department across the street is not such a bad idea. People kept bringing coffee and food to the firemen because it took from nine at night till two in the morning to get the fire out. Some of the women took my plants to their homes to keep them from freezing. Next day a group of men showed up and decided they were going to rebuild the house for me, considering I was in the hospital as a result of having broken my back."

At the time of my visit, Mitchell was nearly forty. He was born in a wealthy Philadelphia foxhunting suburb, quit high school when he wasn't doing well, and joined the Marine Corps. He was part of a restless generation: discharged in Hawaii, he worked as a radio announcer and bartender and became involved in Democratic politics; then he returned to Philadelphia to try out as an insurance

117

company management trainee, which he didn't care for at all, and left to join Robert F. Kennedy's 1968 presidential campaign in the West until the assassination. In San Francisco he attended college for a while and worked as a cab driver until he got his job on the cable cars. He started weekending in Yosemite, as many San Franciscans do, but as a motorcycle excursionist rather than a backpacker or naturalist. He and a friend cycled to the Grand Canyon, spent five minutes at the rim, and sped away.

Colorado was different for him, however:

"I was entering a world I had never experienced, as close to paradise as I could ever expect to be. Aspen was not really on our agenda; we had planned to motorcycle across the country, but we spent a week there, riding into remote places in the hills, road racing, meeting nice people. Each of us was riding his own bike. At Independence Pass I ran out of gas and my buddy went to bring some back. It seemed to take forever (because he ran out of gas, too), but there wasn't one moment that I minded being there, surrounded by the magnificent mountains and gorgeous foliage. When he returned, we headed back to Aspen for the summer."

Little wonder. Colorado's enduring appeal and value are in its high-mountain wilderness, though it has been well worked over for its minerals. In this state the rocky continental spine that extends from Alaska to the tip of South America reaches its climax, not in a single peak, but in massive ranges with more than fifty peaks above fourteen thousand feet. Rocky Mountain National Park is probably the best-known wilderness in the state, but it's not very wild, being extensively designed and developed for casual motoring use, and it covers only a fragment of the Front Range that rises above the eastern prairie. Wilder parts lie west in the national forests. Gunnison National Forest, in the Aspen-Crested Butte region of west-central Colorado, embraces magnificent wilderness areas, including West Elk, La Garita, Collegiate Peak, Oh Be Joyful, and portions of the Maroon Bells-Snowmass. In these sanctuaries, the natural composition of rolling clouds, snowy ridges, wooded slopes, high-meadowed basins, and lakes impart a sense of harmony derived from natural beauty. During the short spring season the saucerlike, star-shaped columbine, the state flower, leads the procession of wildflowers galore. Hummingbirds, mountain bluebirds, mountain sheep, golden eagle—they are all as native to the Rockies as the ancient rock; and so are the trembling aspen, growing in clusters, or clumps, from a single taproot, bending gracefully to the wind and brightening the autumn slopes with cloth of gold.

The Rockies are integral to the curious mixed history of this country. "Pikes Peak or Bust" was the lustful slogan of the 1858 gold rush. Yet, in 1893 the same Pikes Peak inspired an English professor, Katharine Lee Bates, to compose "America the Beautiful," the essence of idealism about this land, and rather a contrast to the "Star-Spangled Banner," whose inspiration was a military battle. The San Juans, in southwest Colorado, the largest mountain group in the state, are pocked with old shafts, mine roads, and ghost towns, but there are now more than a few current residents who eschew the notion of extracting or accumulating wealth and would rather live on dreams, folk songs, and poetry.

There are lots of places to drive to in Colorado, like the toll road to Pikes Peak, the Mount Evans Highway from Idaho Springs up through the walls of Chicago Creek Canyon to the highest point reachable by car in the country (14,259 feet), and the Million Dollar Highway between Ouray and Silverton. Those roads are well known. The Crystal Valley Highway, running from Carbondale south through the Elk Mountains, is lesser known, though readily accessible via Crested Butte, Aspen, and Glenwood Springs. It comes as a surprise, running alongside the aptly named Crystal River, within sight of Mount Sopris, almost 13,000 feet high, and Snowmass, over 14,000 feet. I recall, while driving this road, arriving at a fantasyland called Redstone. A forgotten, turn-of-the-century nabob named John C. Osgood planned and built what must be the most unusual coal camp in the world: a cluster of Victorian-style cottages, no two alike, a forty-two-room turreted Tudor manor house for himself, and a thirty-seven-room hotel, the whole complex still extant like something made for Disneyland. One nearby ghost town, Marble, yielded the largest block of marble ever quarried—for the Tomb of the Unknown Soldier. So much for incidental intelligence.

Mitchell had returned to San Francisco to work the cable cars one last time to get the money together to move to Aspen permanently. Then came the accident with the laundry truck.

119

"Some of the burns were third, fourth, and fifth degree, so the doctors said. The fingertips were so bad they had to amputate parts of all the fingers. The hands are fairly functional in spite of it. The greatest amputation was my left thumb, but the bone and muscle are still there and I'm thinking of an operation to put my big toe there.

"While lying in the hospital, my girlfriend and friends of the cable cars would come and ask what they could do for me. My eyes were bandaged so the skin wouldn't contract, as it often does in serious burns. I couldn't see, read, or watch TV. I had lately bought some Sierra Club books, including *In Wildness Is the Preservation of the World*, a combination of Thoreau's words illustrated by Eliot Porter's photographs. Finally I asked if someone would get that book and read it to me.

"Everything the hospital wasn't, the book was. The hospital was confining, the opposite of nature and the outdoors. I couldn't get up, move, or walk. I got to thinking about John Muir, travels, self-sufficiency, skiing at Badger Pass in Yosemite without poles and falling down.

"Once out of the hospital I went to Yosemite as soon as I could, this time with completely different awareness. I hadn't seen nature or wilderness or the outdoors as I saw it now. I went to every campfire talk they ever gave. I absorbed all the information I could. My girlfriend and I got a little camper for the pickup truck. We took more day hikes as I got stronger."

It was very cold in Crested Butte, but we walked two or three blocks to dinner, Mitchell moving in his wheelchair faster than I did on foot. "Go inside and ask the bartender if he would help you bring in Mitchell," he directed when we reached the steps of the Chinese restaurant. "You bet!" the tall man behind the bar (who turned out to be the town's chief marshal) responded without hesitancy. That's how the evening went. A stream of people came to our table to visit. After dinner we stopped in two or three pubs and ran into more friends. Mitchell said his face was stinging from the cold, but it didn't deter him. At the Wooden Nickel he was mobbed by good-looking women. Later, when I asked him to explain the fascination, he laughed. "I know all their secrets and won't tell."

At his house again the hours passed. We talked with music as a background. He had an elaborate turntable and a large collection of records and tapes spanning a wide range in taste. He kept the fire going in the wood stove, dispatching me to the front porch now and then for more wood.

"After the accident my girlfriend and I came to Colorado. I was in love with the mountains and the outdoors. I got a larger camper, with a place for my Great Dane's dogfood. Meantime, I brought suit against the laundry company and against Honda, the manufacturer of the motorcycle, for the defective gas cap. In the spring of 1973, almost two years after the accident, the trial began. One week into it, we settled with them for a large amount of money—almost a million. After the lawyers got theirs, and after medical expenses, I wound up with almost half a million. I was able to invest it, principally in a wood stove company in Vermont and real estate, office buildings, and apartments here in Crested Butte. I wanted to settle in Colorado. Though I couldn't be called an environmentalist, I appreciated the natural environment and wanted access to it, to be part of it. I was living in Aspen, which is only thirty miles north by air, but two hundred miles by road, with the great mountain barrier in between. I looked at Telluride, but when I found this house in this little town in the heart of the Rockies, I knew it was for me."

Mitchell settled in Crested Butte and went back to flying. He had soloed the day of his accident in San Francisco. Even in the hospital he was studying flying again. Once released, he and one of his lawyers bought an airplane, a six-seat Cessna. Despite problems with his hands, he received a pilot's license. He did considerable flying in Colorado and earned an instrument rating, commercial pilot's license, and multiengine license.

"I got pretty proficient in the airplane, but I guess not proficient enough. In November 1975, I was planning a trip from Gunnison to Denver to San Diego. I had three others with me. Gunnison Airport was cold; it was a beautiful day, but extremely cold. The plane had been sitting outside and there was some ice on the wing. It clearly wasn't ready to fly. You don't fly with ice on the wing—that's a cardinal rule. I turned the plane around into the sun so the sun was beating down on the wing and went to have breakfast with these guys. I came back an hour later. It was still extremely cold, but it seemed like a lot of the ice and snow were gone. I was satisfied that virtually all of it was gone. That was poor judgment on my part. One careful look would have revealed there was still some ice. There was another commercial pilot in the front seat with me who was going to fly the first leg. He started the takeoff roll and the plane just didn't seem the way it should have been. We stopped and checked the engine. Everything seemed to work right. I decided to do the takeoff myself, started down the runway, got in the air, probably about a hundred feet. It didn't feel right at all. I was concerned and thought the best thing to do would be to abort the takeoff. So I chopped the power. The plane stalled—without power the plane came down very rapidly, settled hard on the runway, on the wheels, but very hard.

"The other guys were pretty shaken up. Two of them I think actually hurt their backs, but they were able to get out of the plane, which I told them to do immediately. I realized immediately, however, that I couldn't move my legs, that I couldn't get out.

"In retrospect, you could look back and wonder what you might have done instead. Who is to say? Five of us got out alive. Had we crashed in the mountains and rocks directly in front of us, who knows what would have happened? On the other hand, maybe the plane would have flown. It was flying then. With more speed it probably would have kept flying, not as well as I would have liked, but I could have come back and made a landing. I had about seven hundred and fifty flying hours—a pretty fair amount, with a lot of training. But I broke the cardinal rule. When they investigated the accident they found about a quarter inch of ice on the wings. You don't take off with ice on your wings.

"You make mistakes and sometimes you walk away and say, 'Wow, that was a close one.' In this case, four other guys walked away from the accident. One was dancing that night. I was in the hospital. Sure, I was upset, but I didn't have great fits of depression. Nor did I when I was burned. I adopted the attitude, 'That's what's happened. Now what do you do from here?'"

Because the plane had come straight down, all of Mitchell's weight bore down on one vertebra, the twelfth thoracic, and crunched it. The severity was not at first apparent. The night of the accident, while in a Denver hospital, he called physicians he knew in different parts of the country asking their counsel, feeling sure that paralysis was only temporary and that he would overcome it. Late that night Denver neurosurgeons performed a laminectomy, peeling away bone to examine the spinal cord. Mitchell's hope was that some broken bone might be pressing against the cord or digging into it, and that by relieving the pressure he would be okay and able to walk. Following the operation the doctors gave him reason for hope. "Your spinal cord appears completely normal. There is no indication of any damage."

Later it was explained to him that one could be so badly injured that his spinal cord resembled a hamburger, and yet lose almost no function. On the other hand, as in his case, one might be struck only lightly and suffer permanent paralysis. He learned a lot about anatomy, the spinal column, cell structure and cell regeneration, the difference between the recuperative kind of broken back and the permanently disabling. He went to an acupuncturist in Santa Fe, a faith healer in Mexico; he did exercises, drank herbs, ate carrots, and visualized himself walking.

"Some people are paralyzed, totally paralyzed, and two weeks later are walking around. But if you're totally paralyzed two weeks after the accident, chances are slim that you're going to be up with completely normal functions six months later, or ever. In my case, I am seven years post-injury. There is no record of anyone recovering his function after seven years. That doesn't mean it's not possible, or that I have a negative attitude, but I found that after two years of thinking positively, a certain frustration set in. I was frustrated in seeking a cure and not finding it. I had never denied the injury, never said, 'I don't have to learn to live as a paralyzed person.' I accepted the fact that this was going to be a long-term condition.

"A lot of things happen to you after you've been paralyzed a long time. You have problems of atrophy: muscles not getting used on a regular basis, bones getting brittle. Some people have done these things to themselves, but I don't look at this as a suicidal impulse. I feel one of the reasons I've been able to deal with the injuries and not let them drag me down is the attitude that I'm responsible for my own life.

"The accident was totally my responsibility. In the motorcycle accident, people said it was the other driver's fault. Technically, legally, that is true, but I tell people who ride motorcycles that anything that happens to them is their fault—because they're the ones it happens to. That means they have to watch their own asses. If they're not paying attention to what happens around them, to someone running a stop sign, or driving drunkenly, or anything, if they're not paying attention, then they're the ones who are going to get hurt. They can blame someone else for their being injured, but that gives very little satisfaction when you're in a wheelchair. Plus, it's a complete waste of time. So I take complete responsibility for my own life, the good and bad. When you weigh it all out there's been so much more good than bad."

This is what I had come to hear. It may for some have nothing to do with wilderness in America and its values, but for me it has everything to do with wilderness—for Mitchell, through his experience and narrative, evokes the value of wilderness equated to the human species. His physical misfortunes and adventures in an almost perpetual boyhood are structured into fulfillment in coping with the world, the better and worst of it.

"After the accident I became a bit of a bum. I bought a motor home and cruised around with two girlfriends (or I should say two friends who are women). We traveled in the Southwest and Mexico; we had a nice time. I fell in love briefly in Bisbee, Arizona, with just a wonderful woman I'm still very fond of. Qualities don't evaporate—they weren't false qualities that made our relationship so worthwhile. Sure, sometimes I'm an asshole and difficult to live with, temperamental and obnoxious, but there were things about me she found loving. The same with me. And those didn't go away. We found we no longer could live together, but that doesn't mean she lost all those wonderful qualities that made her such a rich and beautiful person.

"I owned a building in Crested Butte and had a bar, the Tailings, and by default of the tenant wound up running the bar. It was not of my own doing. I used to be a bartender and had managed a bar in Hawaii when I was going to school, and that was a great experience. I loved it. I finally decided, however, that running a bar is a terrible business. Bartending is not bad at nine or ten at night; people are pretty friendly, having a nice time in a nice social atmosphere, a little more relaxed with a drink or two, but by two A.M., when it's time to close the bar, people can become quite obnoxious, and they are not your casual social drinkers having a drink or two before dinner, or coming down to dance to a band and maybe having a beer. These people are usually pretty hard core. They don't have much to do in the daytime, otherwise they wouldn't be up drinking till two A.M. I decided running the Tailings was not the most fun in the world. It was great earlier in the evening, and I had some great parties over here at the house with some of the bands playing after the place closed, some really good musical groups. But alcohol is one of the worst drugs and those who abuse it tend to be the most victimized people I can imagine.

"In 1977 the marshal, mayor, and county judge approached me at different times. There were two vacancies on the town council and they wanted me to be a candidate. Council itself would make the selections for these seats, which would be filled for only three or four months until the election. I didn't like the idea of giving up two Mondays a month for council meetings; besides, I thought I might lose. They made me feel guilty that I wasn't contributing to the town. But they might have been trying to do me a favor, getting me pointed in the right direction. I was also aware that the AMAX Corporation was starting to do some exploration on Mount Emmons, the Red Lady, and that big things might be coming our way. I agreed to put my name in. I was unanimously elected.

"Soon after, the mayor announced he was not going to run for reelection. Then, one evening, Ken Hall, the leading candidate to become mayor, and I were walking to the council and talking about AMAX. They had a big mine at Leadville and it was pretty awful. I was concerned. This town had two good newspapers in those days, both weeklies, so we had gained more knowledge than most towns about AMAX and their track record, so I had some foreboding. That night, while we were walking, Ken Hall expressed his idea that AMAX was inevitable and we might as well get together with them and see what we could get out of the deal.

"I was not at all sure. There are cases where things are inevitable, and maybe that attitude makes sense. In this case, we had a town of people above average intelligence, above average educational background. We had something really worth saving; we weren't in need. AMAX was going to offer us nothing, as far as I could tell, except problems that I later really became aware of—boomtown problems, the cyclical boom-and-bust problems of mining. Anyone who looks at boomtown glamour knows the only glamour is for the bank president, real estate developer, and the guy who sells mobile homes. Again, that's until the bust."

That night Mitchell decided to run for mayor. He felt the town needed someone articulate who sensed the potential danger of the Mount Emmons mining project and was prepared to take on AMAX. His opponent, Ken Hall, was well liked and had been campaigning for months. Hall went door-to-door and talked to a lot of people to get their support. Mitchell talked to people, too, mostly by positioning himself in front of the post office. The issue was the mine and who would speak for Crested Butte. At that point Mitchell was not totally opposed to AMAX. He told the voters: "I have really negative feelings, but why don't we do some intensive investigation before we put up the welcome sign? It's not inevitable if we don't want it." Mitchell won by 20 votes, 176 to 156, though he had expected his margin to be larger.

The morning after the election he began his first two-year term as mayor (at an annual salary of three hundred dollars) by attending a meeting at the county courthouse in Gunnison with representatives of AMAX. These included Gordon Allott, a former United States senator, and Wayne Aspinall, a former congressman, both of whom I had observed during the years I lived and worked in Washington, D.C. Allott was an ultraconservative Republican who responded almost instinctively with hostility to virtually every progressive wilderness and environmental idea that came before the Senate. Aspinall was much more interesting: a powerful Democratic wheelhorse in the House, a crafty wizard who understood environmental arguments better than most environmentalists and who kept foes frightened and humbled. Through seniority he became chairman of the House Interior Committee, which he dominated by controlling the flow of legislation. The first Wilderness Act was introduced in 1958, but Aspinall bottled it in committee year after year. When he finally allowed it to pass in 1964, he insisted on a proviso to allow mining in wilderness. December 31,

1983, was set as the cutoff date for locating new mineral claims, creating problems likely to last years beyond that deadline.

Mining on federal lands through the influence of elected officials such as Allott and Aspinall has long been sustained as a democratic right. The Mining Law of 1872 is still considered valid and sacred, though enacted at a time in history when the country had more land than people and could afford to provide portions of it as encouragement to "the hardy miner opening new frontiers." That law gives any citizen or candidate for citizenship unqualified right to enter federal lands—except for national parks and other areas specifically closed by law or administrative action—and therein to stake a claim, explore, and extract. Should the miner work his claim as prescribed and strike a valuable mineral source, he becomes entitled to "go to patent" and purchase the land at a cut-rate bargain price. The Mineral Leasing Act of 1920 changed things to some extent and for some resources, such as oil and gas, but the 1872 law still sanctions and stimulates exploration of "hard rock" type minerals, such as gold, uranium, lead, zinc, and molybdenum.

Aspinall, as the kingpin of western resource policy, defused critics by establishing the Public Land Law Review Commission in 1964, with himself as chairman. He had the power in Congress to do that. After six years of study, the Commission recommended some minor reform, principally in payment of patent fees and administration of mining claims. It conceded weaknesses, but viewed them from the needs of the industry:

"Mineral exploration and development should have a preference over some or all other uses on much of our public lands. . . . We also urge the establishment of a program to determine the extent of mineralization of public land areas where mineral activities are presently excluded but mineralization appears to be likely." These areas are specifically the national parks and classified wilderness of the national forests, which remain under protection from these surveys, as they should be.

Mining constitutes a powerful threat to wilderness all over the world. Multinational conglomerates are accustomed to having their way. Governments mostly welcome them. Corporations have dealt with and brushed off, or bought off, tougher opponents than the paraplegic mayor of little Crested Butte. In 1979, for instance,

President Carter established by proclamation Misty Fjords National Monument in Alaska, an area with superlative qualities on a par with those of Denali and Glacier Bay. But the U.S. Borax and Chemical Corporation wanted a piece of Misty Fjords, called Quartz Hill, to pursue a molybdenum claim. That firm, despite its name, actually is a subsidiary of a British conglomerate, Rie Tinto Zinc, which in the 1960s was poised to mine one of Britain's loveliest places, Snowdonia National Park in north Wales. Caring English and Welsh mounted a campaign of opposition and succeeded in saving Snowdonia, an unparalleled victory for nature. R-T-Z, however, wins more often than it loses. Defeat at home was succeeded by conquest abroad, in Alaska.

The U.S. Borax molybdenum claim was a focal point in the bitter Alaska lands fight, with environmental groups striving to save the integrity of Misty Fjords. The minerals claim covered 2500 acres, but when Congress passed the Alaska Lands Act of 1980 (formally, the Alaska National Interest Lands Conservation Act), it excluded from wilderness nearly 150,000 acres—ten times the size required for the mining operation. The act guaranteed a permit to U.S. Borax to construct a road, regardless of need or environmental impact studies or impact on salmon-spawning rivers. U.S. Borax was expected to produce less than three pounds of molybdenite for each ton of rock; the remainder would have to be discarded as waste either on land or in one of those hitherto unscarred fjords. Don McKinney, manager of the Quartz Hill project, in a statement in the *Anchorage Times* of September 6, 1981, brushed aside environmental values and environmentalists: "The law mandated it, I really don't think the judge is going to give them a stay. With the climate in the Reagan Administration, I don't think we'll have any trouble with administrative rulings from the Forest Service."

AMAX, in contrast, would rather be known as a corporation with a conscience than with a strong arm. "We're not going to mine if you don't want us," a company spokesman declared in May 1977. Officials were willing to meet and listen to critics, with assurance that the Mount Emmons mine would be different from its unappealing Climax Mine at Leadville. It would, in fact, be "first of a new generation of mines serving as a model for the nation as to

128

how people can work together in a timely, coordinated manner to meet their natural resource needs without undue delay or unnecessary impacts on life style."

Nevertheless, the company proceeded on a determined course. It had acquired the site of an old lead and zinc mine, a tract of private land above eight thousand feet, surrounded by Gunnison National Forest, where it proposed to develop what it claimed to be the world's largest deposit of molybdenum, a metal with industrial and military uses. It would hollow a portion of the mountain above Crested Butte, removing twenty thousand tons per day in order to extract a molybdenum concentration of less than 1 percent. This would necessitate construction of a mill to refine and extract the mineral, utilizing large quantities of water, then disposing of immense residues into tailing ponds or, in earthy vernacular, slime pits. The construction project would require a force of around two thousand, the mine and mill in operation, around sixteen hundred. The year-round population of Crested Butte, in contrast, was about twelve hundred.

As the town's first full-time mayor, Mitchell went after AMAX. Two years later he was reelected overwhelmingly, indicating a clear mandate. He succeeded in putting his town on the map and AMAX on the defensive. At first he thought he was not photogenic, that he was too disfigured to appear on television or in the newspapers. Yet, he was pictured with the governor of Colorado in the Denver newspapers, and other media showed interest, which spurred him to capitalize on every opportunity.

"Vice-President Mondale was scheduled to speak in Grand Junction. I received an invitation, as did every public official in western Colorado, to come down. There would be eight hundred people in this huge hall and I was going to be in row one ninety-two, with no chance whatsoever to meet the Vice-President. Cecil Andrus, the Secretary of the Interior, Senator Floyd Haskell, and Governor Dick Lamm were also going to be there. This was a measure of my sense of media, or my sense of how you have to be more aggressive than just accepting a seat in row one ninety-two, which is where the Secret Service wanted to put me. I said, 'I can't. I'm sitting in this damn wheelchair and can't see a thing.' They moved me right along the roped barrier in the front. I was much better off. I still didn't think I'd have a chance to talk to the Vice-President, but at least maybe I'd have a chance to ask a question.

"I watched the aisleways and figured they would be coming up the aisles. In twenty minutes, in came Floyd Haskell. He came over to me and said, 'You're Mayor Mitchell. I've heard a lot about you. You're doing great stuff.' I was excited; that was a big deal. A few minutes later Governor Lamm came in. We had met several times. Then came Fritz Mondale. The governor said, 'Mr. Vice-President, I want you to meet a very special public official in Colorado, a great Democrat.' Mondale and I chatted for several minutes.

"Sitting in the front row, I was with some staff, some White House or Vice-Presidential staff. I got their names. They said, 'When you're in Washington, look us up.' That kind of thing. The Vice-President said the same. After the session was over, Cecil Andrus was talking to a number of people. I went over and waited. Finally he turned to me and I said, 'Mr. Secretary, you don't have time to discuss my problem here, but if I'm in Washington at some point can I come by and visit you?' I followed all this with letters. Outside I positioned myself where Mondale was leaving. The Secret Service didn't hassle me. When he came out they took pictures of us and that made the press. The press, of course, means a helluva lot to the politicians. Somebody who is getting ink is someone they will see."

In spring of 1978 Mitchell and Myles Rademan, the town planner, headed east to Greenwich, Connecticut, the headquarters of AMAX. "They were going to put on a dog and pony show, take us to Windows on the World in New York, razzle-dazzle for the little guys from Colorado, and persuade us that they were going to do the best job." Mitchell and Rademan left a week early to make the rounds in Washington. They found considerable interest and support, which heightened after *The Washington Post* appeared with a full-page, illustrated article on page two about Mitchell and Crested Butte.

"It was a big deal. Floyd Haskell's office called me at the hotel. 'Could we have you up here? Reporters are lined at the door. We have requests from three television stations. I feel like your press secretary this morning.' I had interviews with TV guys and Haskell in the office. He loved it, naturally. They followed us to the train to New York. When I got back to Crested Butte, NBC News wanted a story. They came and did a big piece. Then *The New York Times Magazine*. Environmental groups wrote a lot about the little mining town taking on this big company. We had a cover story in *Historic Preservation*, a beautiful story, in the publication of an organization run by a lot of wealthy Republicans. The spotlight was so bright that AMAX and the Forest Service had to walk the line. Good people in the Forest Service wanted to protect the resources, but others claimed the 1872 act was inviolate, that mining was an inalienable right. One of these was Tom Nelson, one of the highest Forest Service officials in Washington, who retired soon after and went to work for the American Mining Congress. But the company and agency were forced to look closely at their responsibilities. It didn't stop them, but it raised the price of the mine."

Colorado environmental and wilderness activists, often derided as crazies and liberal hippies opposed to everything, had some new sense of legitimacy. It had been coming a long time, particularly since the defeat of Allott and Aspinall in the 1972 election, and the election as governor of Richard Lamm, who had kept the winter Olympics out of Denver. The state of Colorado and Crested Butte succeeded in obtaining a court order requiring AMAX to stabilize old dumps and treat water seeping out of the mine site it had acquired, which proved an expensive undertaking. "AMAX wants to do very well what shouldn't be done at all," Mitchell insisted, an argument that giant company, for all its power, had a tough time refuting.

On August 7, 1981, AMAX announced deferral of the project for at least two or three years because of a slump in the molybdenum market. Mayor Mitchell celebrated by helicoptering to the summit of Mount Emmons and asserting public sentiment as a factor in the company decision. "We demanded they do the job right, and that means higher costs," he said. "There are other deposits they will explore first."

It was New Year's Eve and friends were coming for wine and cheese. Mitchell had all the right paraphernalia and plenty of champagne. He ended the discussion of the AMAX mine on this note: "They never got the mine started, so their commitment in investment was not appreciable. Hopefully that means they won't have the incentive to come back. When and if the economy turns around and there's a great boom in the steel industry, they may return, but I doubt they'll ever be as strong as they were. There is a legal right to mine and to patent, under the 1872 law, if you can show you have a viable economic deposit. The argument we've made for a long time, and which the Forest Service has had to accept, is that mining companies must meet certain standards to contain their wastes, protect air and water quality, and the physical environment surrounding the site of their activities."

Mitchell was no longer mayor. He had been defeated after the second term, but he conducted his New Year's party like the hero who had just been treated to an overwhelming vote of confidence, thanks to all those present. Politics was his mission, part of his life. He was like old Boss Curley with his Boston flock. Most people there that evening, as generally in America, willingly concede political leadership and responsibility to someone else. The crowd was bubbly bright and lively, mostly young, articulate individualists, though tied together by common threads: the jeans, beards, sensitivity, intellectuality, and rootlessness. All part of the crowd flowing from unfulfilling education and marriages through seemingly safe harbors like Crested Butte. Largely harmless and undirected, they get carried away with social injustice and then complain about the stress involved in trying to do something about it. One young man I had met earlier at the ski shop talked to me about cross-country skiing, then switched to the subject of drugs and the pleasantness of "trips" derived from their use. But a young woman in the circle countered that she preferred to get her trips naturally, though it might require more effort. I felt a little stuffy for agreeing with her, yet it seems senseless to corrupt a natural environment and one's body when the object is to find relief from social corruption.

Next morning, New Year's Day, Mitchell was on the telephone, calling people all over Colorado and all over the country, like the politician going through his book to build his connections. Between times friends stopped by. I got acquainted with one or two who voluntarily confided how people loved to be spun into Mitchell's web, but how they, themselves, when they got too close, resented being manipulated and used. The charmer, however, caught up in his own cause, never sees it that way.

In the afternoon we went for a drive in his car to view the mine site and the mountains around Crested Butte. The vehicle was engineered so that he could manage behind the wheel without the use of his feet. I mentioned that this reminded me of the Colorado River trip, where people wondered how he would get by, and yet he had proven more self-reliant than me. He plainly preferred doing things for himself. There were times when he needed help, or was helpless, yet he resisted dependency.

"The great thing about rivers is that, as a paralyzed person, you are confronted with the least limitation. Everybody is much closer to being equal in the water. Your legs aren't nearly as important to row the boat or paddle the kayak; conditions are not nearly as difficult when you have the benefit of the water.

"Going down the Colorado through the Grand Canyon, actually, was my fourth or fifth river trip. The first was on the Gunnison River not far from here, just below Black Canyon of the Gunnison National Monument. Because of its steep granite walls, access is almost impossible. Parts of the canyon are totally inaccessible to man except by the river. It's such an incredible trek that very few people have made the trip. Jerry Mallett, a great river runner, and other friends carried me down and it took us almost all day. It was a wild and beautiful place. No backpackers, no beer cans, no campsites. No cows had gotten down there, so the native grass grew tall and untouched.

"Next I went down the Dolores River, a three-day trip in a rubber raft, again with Jerry. We put in at Bedrock, Colorado, but almost got caught in a flash flood. We pulled out at Slickrock to camp in a torrential rainstorm. I was shivering like crazy. They took me up to a lean-to and two of the more beautiful women I've ever known changed my clothes for me. That warmed me immediately.

"Another time Jerry and I went down the upper Colorado, above Moab, Utah. I rowed some on that trip. We were running Skull Rapids, one of the great rapids on the Colorado River, when we went into a big hole and I got tossed out of the raft. I was drinking a beer, while they were filming and photographing me for a story. I wasn't paying enough attention, lost my sunglasses, hat, beer, and almost lost my ass.

"It was wonderfully exciting and I'd love to do it again and again. The excitement of coming out of that boat and wondering where you were and where the rocks were and how you were going to do—I don't think I was scared even for a second. I'm a pretty good swimmer. At first I flailed around a little, then swam to the boat and they pulled me back in. I just loved it. Oh, the boatman got tossed, too. And the next rapid we did with one oar.

"Once I went to testify at a wilderness hearing in western Colorado, either at Montrose or Delta. Representative Aspinall was presiding. To his pleasure, one witness after another said that wilderness keeps out the old, infirm, handicapped, and poor. Then I got to speak. They must have thought that here comes the ultimate argument for their position. But I said that wilderness keeps out fancy machines the poor can't afford. I spoke on how vital it is for all of us, me included, just to know it exists. I use wilderness in a lot of ways. I go into it occasionally, though I can't get very far under my own power unless I'm in a boat. The ultimate value is not for you or me to go walking, though it's nice to have that luxury. The ultimate value is preservation of a variety of species, to save a little of what's left to show where we came from.

"My first trip to the Grand Canyon was when I was ten, at a Cinerama movie in Philadelphia. I enjoyed and felt it. Of course, it's not the same as going down the Colorado, but still, had the Grand Canyon not been there, or if it was blocked by dams, I wouldn't be able to experience it at all. Nor would it be available to people who follow me.

"Yes, it's harder for a person in a wheelchair to hike into the deepest part of Oh Be Joyful than for a twenty-year-old Olympic athlete, but it's also hard for a person of seventy-five with a heart condition. All that says is maybe Oh Be Joyful isn't there so everybody can hike into it.

"There are few people who see it, and I say the fewer the better. If there was a stream of hikers, as on the John Muir Trail in the California High Sierra, where they say, 'Don't drop anything because if you bend to pick it up you'll get trampled by the people behind you,' where they have to issue permits, and where you have to make a reservation to go hiking—that makes it wonderful to have places where people can get closer to nature without a crowd.

"Deer, grasshopper, and gopher all have rights, too. Aspinall may not understand that, but they have as many rights as he does. They are as important as he is in the final sense, and in some senses more important. Life on this planet would be pretty unpleasant without field mice, elk, mosquitoes, and all kinds of animals and plants. Because I can't go into Oh Be Joyful without a four-lane highway makes me love Oh Be Joyful all the more. I'm more fortunate than most people because I've been able to see it. If a four-lane road was built, nobody would be able to see it, not even through photos and films, because it would no longer be what it is now."

We were parked near the gateway to Oh Be Joyful. The sky was a clear, deep blue, the mountains and fields covered solidly with snow. Mitchell had wanted me to bring my skis and take off into the wilderness, but I figured that while that would be a treat, I could ski anytime. He was gregarious, self-assured, yet everything he said held special value for me. He hadn't finished high school (as he had confessed earlier) and had gotten some, but not many, college credits, yet his perceptions and sense of purpose went far beyond classrooms at their best.

"Through investments I'm blessed with material comfort. I have freedom to spend my time doing something useful. People are taught to have television, nice cars, lots of stuff. I spend time visiting the local school, supplying materials about the future, about what it takes to make the planet livable. I want to have fun, too, go to parks, listen to park rangers describe geology and species, see and learn about a lot of different things.

"When I was defeated I didn't feel too good about it, but it was mostly my own fault and responsibility. If I had worked harder on the local front and been more sensitive to community needs, and tried to work on some of the chamber-of-commerce-type issues, and gotten people a little more involved and been in touch with people, I might not have lost. Some of that I didn't choose to do. If I had it to do all over I still wouldn't, but some of it I could have done and not sacrificed any values.

135

"People were convinced that, while I was out there doing great things nationally and internationally, I wasn't paying enough attention to the problems of Crested Butte. My antigrowth environmental stands discouraged some builders. But the article about us in *Time* magazine described this place as Shangri-la. People really had something to fight for. That Crested Butte hadn't been destroyed, that it was worth coming to see, as described in that article, was worth millions to this town, which it could not have gotten without me. I didn't do it to be the chamber of commerce; I did it because it was the only way to fight the battle, and for my own self-growth—not so more people would come and ski in Crested Butte.

"Another factor was that people said, 'Mitchell is going to go on and do other things anyway, run for secretary of state, governor, or United States senator. He doesn't really need this, and how long is he going to be around anyway?' Four years hence they could be right.

"Explaining to people what happened to me is not one of the most exciting parts of my life. People stare and whisper, 'Look how ugly he is.' Children point and say, 'Monster, monster.' It's reasonable to question and wonder. I like children and spend a lot of time at the school. I explain how I'm a part of life that they, too, that they could easily be.

"Once we get over those descriptions we can talk about the very important things. I did a *Today* show live in New York with Jane Pauley. She concentrated on the physical parts of my life and I wasn't able to discuss the exciting thing of being mayor of a small town and trying to save our beautiful valley. I do recognize my physical handicap. In fact, one of the services I can do for the handicapped is in being able to go out and let people know, 'Yes, you can be in a wheelchair and have short fingers and a burned face and still be a thinking, intelligent, active, important person.' It does a lot for people in my situation who don't have the benefit of the exposure that I get.

"My fingers are short, so I don't have the dexterity that most people have, but I'm a licensed pilot, drive a car, use chopsticks, play a fairly good game of blackjack, and open a bottle of wine. I no longer have control of my legs or some functions below the waist, such as bowels and bladder, so I have some moments that are awkward or embarrassing. There hasn't been a total unmitigated disaster, but at times it gets very difficult. On the other hand, a person who experienced my kind of injury in 1930 had almost zero chance of survival. There were very few paralyzed people running around in 1930. Usually nobody could catheterize them and the kidneys would suffer. Or they would get bladder infection from improper catheterization. Or skin problems from sitting too long or from not sitting on the right kind of cushions, developing serious sores and ulcers which can lead to infections. Today my life expectancy is that of a normal person because of all the knowledge gained about paraplegia.

"The wheelchair is a pain in the ass; it's no fun at all to be stuck at a curb and not be able to get over it, to be at a building and not be able to get into it, not to be able to go hiking in the wilderness. I'm not sad that I can't downhill ski anymore. I only did that about six times the winter before I broke my back, but I am sad that I never cross-country skied. That was one opportunity that I never availed myself—to be able to go into wilderness in winter—just the idea of being able to do it yourself.

"Before I was paralyzed there were ten thousand things I could do, now there are only nine thousand. I can either dwell on the thousand I lost, or concentrate on the nine thousand that are left. Most of us do only a few hundred of those ten thousand things. If I get to eighty-nine hundred ninety-nine and have done all of them, maybe I'll have the right to be frustrated."

I experienced a brief lesson in frustration the morning I left. Frustration I would define as a sense of helplessness in a circumstance where one feels the need for control. Such was exactly the case that morning. I was anxious for an early start, but it was very cold, below zero, and my car wouldn't start, though it had never failed me before. The one or two service stations of Crested Butte were nearby, but neither would open for at least two hours. Mitchell phoned a friend, whose wife reported he was out, and then called another. Within a few minutes both arrived. I was frustrated by the delay. It was something I couldn't do a damn thing about, and I was dependent on others. Suddenly I had a flashing image of myself paralyzed in a wheelchair. I realized the trivial quality of my grievance and the genius of my friend Mitchell in coping with bona fide frustration. I turned attention to the two men who had come to my aid. We shared some interests. One was an ex-engineer who wanted to write. The other was a mountaineering guide who wanted to teach at a university. The time I had lost was regained by being with them, and by being with Mitchell a little while longer.

CHAPTER VIII

Of Two Classy Guides in the Minnesota North Woods

I met Sigurd Olson for the first time in 1960 at his home in Ely, Minnesota, an earthy resort town that serves as principal gateway to the Boundary Waters Canoe Area. I was fresh from a canoe exploration of that singular composition of lakes, marshes, bogs, ponds, and cool forests shared by the Canadian province of Ontario and Minnesota. Now I felt that I was paying homage to the keeper of the kingdom. The Boundary Waters was more than Sig Olson's backyard, it was his empire, though I'm sure he wouldn't have thought of it quite that way. He was warm, friendly, and relaxed, displaying a neatly wrapped package ready to mail: the manuscript of his latest book. Sig hadn't started as a professional writer and didn't complete his first book until he was fifty-five. Yet, it became the first of nine, the last appearing following his death early in 1982 at the age of eighty-two. Those books are filled with his perceptions of North Country water wilderness in the center of the continent. The titles tell the man: *The Singing Wilderness, Listening Point, The Lonely Land, Runes of the North, Open Horizons, Wilderness Days, The Hidden Forest, Of Time and Place.* As I scan his writing now, I regret that I didn't ask at that first meeting, "When can we canoe?"

Over the years I saw him a number of times. One of the most

memorable was at the 1967 Sierra Club Biennial Wilderness Conference in San Francisco. He suffered from palsy, which made his hands shake, and later, it seemed, his whole body, which perhaps accounted for his sitting alone near the front of the large hall. When he was called to speak before the Wilderness Conference, however, the quivering stopped. He was in total command, of his delivery and his audience. He had been a teacher before becoming a writer, and I can picture him holding the class in the palm of his hand.

"The stakes are so high, the threat so desperate," he said, "we can no longer think of wilderness as being a minority need, a need of two percent of the population. I feel that the wilderness is the concern of all Americans and all humanity, that if we do not save some wilderness, mankind and his spirit will suffer, and life will not be so happy for future generations.

"My only suggestion to this conference is to consider, as wilderness battlers, ways and means not for reaching each other—we are converted—but for reaching the other ninety-eight percent of the people. Make the wilderness so important, so understandable, so clearly seen as vital to human happiness that it cannot be relegated to an insubstantial minority. If it affects everyone—and I believe it does—then we must find out how to tell the world why it affects everyone. Only when we put wilderness on that broad base will we have a good chance of saving it."

His books are fulfillment of that self-assigned mission. He wrote that everyone was tuned in, consciously or otherwise, to the song of the wild. He found a place of his own in the North Woods and called it Listening Point—"because only when one comes to listen, only when one is aware and still, can things be seen and heard. . . . Anyone can have a Listening Point. It does not have to be in the North or in the wilderness, simply some place of quiet where the natural world still lives and one can look into the cosmic distances of space and time and hear the eternal music to which man has always listened."

Derived from his extensive canoeing, which took him far north to the Canadian Arctic, he wrote chapters abundant in universality, about the seasons, the sound of rain, the trapper's cabin, campfires, the way of a canoe, and about the witching hours:

"When the rapids glint and their shouting is glad and free, the treachery of hidden rocks and ledges is forgotten, and the canoe moves in and out with a sureness of the bright spirit that comes from them. Running before a gale, when spume is white and blowing in the wind and the water is in a sparkling champagne mood, is no time for somber thoughts. On such days you can shout and sing to the wind, for witching hours are there for the taking."

The wilderness writing, philosophy, and advocacy in Sig's work, and in the work of others as well, is lofty and uplifting, looking beyond any mere moment or place. At that San Francisco conference, the Sierra Club honored Sig with the John Muir Award, with a fitting lofty expression of its own: "in recognition of the excellence of his writing and leadership in conservation that we believe will truly make a difference a hundred years from now in the face of this land and in the mind of man."

The award was given to Sig not only for his writing, but for his activism in defining and defending the wilderness qualities of the Boundary Waters. In a sense, "Boundary Waters" is an artificial designation, like the boundary itself. Nature created only forms of land and water; it took humankind to classify and title forms and masses entirely for its own purposes. There would be no need to call anything "wilderness" in a less populous, less lustful age; but except by doing so there would be no wilderness. When Sig arrived at Ely in 1922, this was simply a country that had endured heavy logging and now was attracting attention among canoers. Over the years to follow, Sig would stand in meeting halls urging that the natural values be protected from assorted mining, logging, motorboating, and snowmobiling. He was treated for his troubles to hoots of scorn and derision from fellow Ely citizens; little if anything would be left of it today if it were not for the framework of the Boundary Waters Canoe Area.

Arthur Carhart was an early contemporary of Sig Olson's on the scene. He worked for the Forest Service from 1919 to 1923 as a landscape architect. When he was dispatched to the Superior National Forest to prepare a plan for recreation development, he recognized the area could be "as priceless as Yellowstone, Yosemite, or the Grand Canyon—if it remained a water-trail wilderness." His bosses thought that was wild talk; they were considering a master plan to build roads to reach every lake and to line the shores with thousands of summer homes. Carhart persisted, won support, and laid the basis for a policy statement that "no roads will be built as far as the Forest Service can control the situation, and no recreational developments will be permitted on public lands except waterways and portage improvements and such simple campground improvements as may be needed to prevent the escape of fire or to protect sanitary conditions."

Carhart went elsewhere, but years later he would pay tribute to Olson for leading a small group, which held, as he said, "a thin line of defense protecting this exquisite wilderness until help could rally to save it."

What was it they found worth defending? Based on my own experience, I would call it the feel of freedom above all else. Freedom from crowds, cars, and mechanical noises. Freedom that comes from doing for one's self, without dependence on technological support. Freedom in nature, derived from being among critters that get up and fly when they want to, or run, swim, wiggle, dive, and crawl, all admirable modes of self-propulsion. I felt free to pick and savor wild blueberries. I felt free to swim in cool waters, cool and dark, but as pure—well, almost as pure—as in the days of the nomadic Chippewa.

There are so many lakes in the land of lakes that explorers ran short of names for them. On the Canadian side, one chain is composed of That Man, This Man, Other Man, and No Man's Lake. Dozens of wives, sweethearts, and just plain girls are memorialized in other lake names. On the United States side, the Insula Lake Route, on which I traveled, begins with Lakes 1, 2, 3, and 4—but numbers understate their beauty. The largest lakes are more than twenty miles long, while others are broken by peninsulas and islands, giving the impression there is no end to the sheltered water wilderness.

The Boundary Waters Canoe Area lies in the southern portion of the geological province called the Canadian Shield. We could set it all aside as a national park or designated wilderness and some future generation would be grateful. Or at least a large, solid, and unbroken portion of the Shield. Lake Superior, the largest and cleanest of the Great Lakes, would be the centerpiece, if I had my way, while everything around it on the Upper Peninsula of Michigan, northern Wisconsin, the North Woods of Minnesota, and Ontario, on the top side of the lake, would be included. What we have now are fragments, bits and pieces of national parks, national forests, state parks, and Canadian provincial parks. We have only that much to show for our generation.

For what we do have, Sig Olson is responsible to a significant degree. When he came to Ely he was a student looking for a summer job. Though born in Chicago, his family lived mostly in northern Wisconsin, so the ways of the woods came easily and he was hired as a canoe guide. He studied geology and biology, which he later taught at Ely Junior College while continuing to guide in the wilderness.

Here he explored, as all canoers do, a surface carved by continental glaciation into some of the world's most tranquil scenery. In at least four distinct periods, each lasting hundreds of thousands of years, ice masses advanced over mountains, grinding and scraping soils and subsoils, planing the center of the continent, then retreating and leaving in their wake a landscape of lakes, bays, lagoons, cliffs, and kettle holes ready to receive the arboreal forest of fir, spruce, pine, aspen, and birch.

The Sioux lived in the country until evicted by the Chippewa (called Ojibwa on the Canadian side). The Indians lived on game, fish, wild rice, and maple sugar. Nature was implicit in religion, as evidenced by names of clans and totemic emblems: bear, loon, heron, moose, eagle, and catfish. In summer the Indian traveled in a birchbark canoe, light and maneuverable, which he paddled while kneeling, without benefit of centerboard or seats. In winter he switched to snowshoes or to sleds pulled by dogs. He managed without a snowmobile.

The Indians were preempted by Europeans. For a century and a half, French-Canadian voyageurs plied the lakes and streams in large canoes, transporting explorers, missionaries, and soldiers to the West, returning to Montreal with furs. They were somewhat like the cowboys on the Plains, rugged stock, now romanticized, doing hard work in exploiting natural resources usually for the benefit of eastern or European syndicates. The route of the voyageurs became so well established that the 1783 treaty with Great Britain ending the American Revolution specified the international boundary should follow their customary waterway between Lake Superior and Lake of the Woods.

Sig Olson wanted to preserve the country as the Indian and voyageur had known it. He joined with Carhart in blocking the development of roads. He and others fought a plan to construct a chain of power dams across the vast Rainy Lake watershed; it would have reduced all the lakes east of Rainy into four great reservoirs, submerging streams, forests, and islands. That fight continued until 1934, when the International Joint Commission, the United States-Canadian agency that adjudicates boundary disputes, set it to rest with the declaration, "It is impossible to overstate the recreational and tourist value of this matchless playground. Its natural forests, lakes, rivers and waterfalls have a beauty and appeal beyond description and nothing should be done to destroy their charm."

That battle led to establishment of the Boundary Waters Canoe Area, but it hardly brought all issues to an end. Local entrepreneurs felt wilderness was theirs to exploit, not to exalt. Following World War II, Ely boasted of being the "largest inland seaplane base in America." The noise of engines shattered the age-old spell for the bear, beaver, and eagle. The poor canoer would round a rocky headland and see the lights of a new fishing lodge glowing from a campsite where for years canoers had built their cookfires. Sig once paddled a number of days to a specially beautiful waterfall. There he encountered a group of plane arrivals. "Grand spot," said one. "Sure," agreed another, "but think of all this power going to waste." Then, turning to Olson, he said proudly, "We made it from Ely in just twenty-seven minutes. It will take you a good three days to get out." On my trip in 1960, a large speedboat, bearing the name of a resort blazoned on its side, carried guests past my little canoe for a sample of instant wilderness.

These things don't happen any longer. Some businesses suffered, but the wilderness, and the world, are better for it. Sig Olson, for all his recognition, awards, and honorary degrees, was not the most popular man in his hometown of Ely. Though revered by some, he was rejected and reviled by others. It depends on one's viewpoint, the long or the short of it.

"If the country is destroyed by progress, then what do you have left?" Sig would ask.

"Take this country here. What brings people up is the wilderness. If they log it, mine it, and rape it, then there would be nothing left. Don't look at it today, tomorrow, or next week. Ask, 'How is it going to look a thousand years from now?'"

A couple of years before he died, Sig underwent a cancer operation. He was pretty weak for a while and walked with a cane. His handsome face was deeply furrowed. His days of rough woodsmanship were gone, though he recovered some of his strength. In January 1982, while snowshoeing near his home, Sig suffered a heart attack and died. It was a wonderful way to go.

I returned to northern Minnesota the summer following Sig's death, but to International Falls rather than Ely. Since the 1960 canoe trip, I had been in the North Country several times, visiting Isle Royale National Park, the largest island on Lake Superior; Ontario provincial parks, on the north shore of the lake; the Apostle Islands, part of Wisconsin, at the south end of the lake; and Voyageurs National Park, which lies a little west of the Boundary Waters. I had been to Voyageurs soon after its establishment in 1975 and wanted to see it again and to observe how this new park was progressing.

There had been some of the same conflicts, but centered at International Falls instead of Ely. Resort owners resisted the idea of a new park that might impose restrictions upon them. Unlike the Boundary Waters, which was largely federally owned as part of Superior National Forest, Voyageurs was composed of lands held by the state of Minnesota and large timber companies. Those firms talked much like their confreres in Maine in confronting the proposed protection of the Allagash Waterway. They were opposed to parks in principle, asserting that parks and wilderness are unproductive and interfere with economic progress. They would cite what they like to call the differences between preservation and conservation, their way being the appropriate conservation way. This has been a fundamental premise of forestry since the days of

Gifford Pinchot, pioneer and patron saint of this profession. Timbermen don't have to make the point, since foresters willingly do it for them. Nevertheless, the park was established and the companies were obliged to cede their properties to the government at fair market value. Sig Olson was one of the key personalities in pursuing the cause of Voyageurs to its climax.

Another instrumental figure was George Esslinger, a man I had known during World War II as a dogsled driver working on search-and-rescue missions in the Army Air Corps. Someone had mentioned his name on my earlier visit to International Falls. He was, I remembered, a resort owner in the region. It turned out that he was virtually the only one willing to speak during the controversy in support of the park proposal. I had tried to locate him. Though he still lived in town, he had sold his resort and was traveling. Now, in 1983, after almost forty years, I saw him again.

George was still a wilderness man by instinct and inclination, but his wilderness days were done. He weighed about two hundred pounds, at least twenty more than during his days in the military service. He was hard of hearing and suffered from bad knees. But then, he was nearly seventy-one years of age.

He wasn't certain that he remembered me, but was hospitable and insisted on being my guide. George had been a fishing and hunting guide for half a century. During the campaign for the national park he had guided prominent and influential personages, including the governor of Minnesota, Sigurd Olson, and Charles A. Lindbergh. I contrasted George and Sig, both North Country wilderness guides. One was well schooled in formal science and letters, polished and worldly, while the other was purely a product of his environment. Though he had traveled, his world was local. The disparity was inconsequential. In the woods, woodsmanship counts and that comes from doing and observing, not from classroom exercises.

We talked about this for almost three full days while covering portions of the national park. Mostly we traveled by powerboat over the big lakes, Kabetogama east through the Narrows into Namakan, then south into Crane Lake, almost to the western edge of the Boundary Waters Canoe Area. George stayed in the boat but waited patiently while I got out to walk on shore.

I followed trails on the Kabetogama Peninsula, which separates these lakes from Rainy Lake on the north, and which we cruised the following day. Except for these large, broad lakes, Voyageurs and the Boundary Waters are composed of similar landscapes. Once away from powerboat lanes on the large lakes, the park was filled with fresh and sparkling vistas. A chain of internal lakes on the peninsula was well suited for canoeing, which I hoped I could do another time. The arboreal forests reached the water's edge, broken here and there by bogs, surprising palisades, and sand beaches. Wild rice grew in shallow bays and streams. On the trail into Agnes Lake, I heard a rustling in the brush, which sounded at first like the wind, but the air was calm. It was a bear cub scampering up a tree. The beaver ponds I saw created habitat for aquatic plants, which in turn fed insects, which fed fish and birds. I saw nests of eagles and great blue herons. We stopped at a rocky islet, where I took a swim. That unusual bird of wilderness, the loon, emerged on the surface, displaying its long, slender neck and ducklike head; it scanned the scene, then dove for lower depths as suddenly as it had appeared.

At the extreme east end of Rainy Lake, more than twenty miles from International Falls, we stopped for a beer and lunch at the Kettle Falls Hotel, an odd little backwoods inn, built in 1913 and run by the Williams family continually since 1918. It began as a hostel for lumberjacks, trappers, and traders, then for fishermen, and now survived as a curio and conversation piece for tourists. Because the boom logs in the foundation had rotted, the floor was warped and tilted, especially in the bar, adding to its character, if not stability. At Kettle Falls, nature played a queer trick on mapmakers, or vice versa; for this was one place—probably the only place outside of Alaska—where I could stand on United States soil and look south into Canada.

The little hotel seemed fitting to its setting. On the way back, however, I grumbled about a table of people near us in the dining room. "There wasn't anything wrong with them, but they could have been riding in a high-powered motorboat anywhere," I said. "They were pretty well oiled with booze and will probably drink their way back. They didn't do any work to get in or out of the national park and I doubt they appreciate it very much. I can't see that's what the wilderness was saved for."

George saw it differently. "It's not all canoe country," he countered. "There's too much open water—most people can't handle it. There is ideal canoe country on the inland lakes and the kind of terrain a good sturdy hiker and backpacker likes. But on the big lakes motorcraft have to be large to give the visitor plenty of safety.

"I don't want to contradict you. I hope it doesn't hurt your way of thinking, but it's just not that type of park. It wouldn't be utilized, it would be like putting a chain across and calling it quits."

He wasn't arguing. George was too polite to be argumentative. Besides, if anyone had earned a right to a viewpoint, it was he.

"I wouldn't want wilderness set aside where nobody could go to it. I have met some people too much to the left—they didn't want anybody to be in it. I want others to have the same privilege that I had. When I was in the resort business, a lot of people came up to go back into the brush. They paid for the chance to see and enjoy where God made nature.

"I had a friend who was a doctor in a town in Minnesota. One of his patients, an attorney and former state senator, was prosecuting a handyman at a farm accused of killing some people in an axe murder. He lost the case because he didn't have enough evidence and went to the bottle to down his defeat. The doctor thought too much of this man. He called me and made a reservation for a week for his friend. 'Don't let him near a bar. Keep him out in the wilds. Get his mind off what he left behind.'

"We went on the trail to where he could see a deer. I took him fishing and we had a fish fry. After five or six days he went back and told the doctor it was wonderful medicine. To me wilderness is like a medicine. People who live in Chicago or San Francisco need to get away from that daily turmoil of go-go-go, they need to get to the lakes and mountains—not to commercialize them, but to be able to touch and feel them."

George himself came north from St. Paul to work at a resort on Lake Kabetogama in 1931, during the Depression, soon after graduating from high school. He never really went back. His family bought a resort, which George and his wife, Livona, operated until they retired in 1969.

"I became conservative about using natural resources. Instead of seeing rocks and trees and ferns and grass, I started seeing footprints and signs and manmade cement. Wilderness deteriorating and exploited. I wanted fishing and hunting for the future, but you can't burn your natural resources and expect them to continue forever.

"When word first came that the Shoepack area on the Kabetogama Peninsula, where I worked with my dog team, was being considered for a national park, I became quite interested. To my way of thinking this might be the way to do it. I met Governor Elmer Anderson, a leader in the park movement, and through him, Sig Olson. They came to my resort with Chuck Stoddard [a well-known environmental personality, at that time regional representative of the Secretary of the Interior in the upper Midwest, and later president of the Wilderness Society] about three or four times during 1966 and 1967. Whenever that group came to survey the area they worked out of my resort. They depended on my service to get around.

"Sig Olson was down to earth, the kind of person who enjoyed the kind of work I was engaged in. I idolized the man. He was a guide himself, who taught the ways of the woods. I wish I had known Sig when he was a lot younger because he had a way of telling such adventures out in the wilderness in book form. He didn't have to shout to demand attention. He got attention the minute he spoke. He was sensible, intelligent, and experienced on what he talked about. Nobody contradicted him.

"I decided that if their way of thinking was to preserve the woods through a park, I'd go along with it. When we first brought up the idea of a national park, the timber companies objected. One of them owned property in the heart of the Kabetogama Peninsula, where it planned a condominium development. It was amazing that the wilderness would be used for modern ideas. They had done it at Rockford, Illinois. They owned the property and said that would happen here, with bowling alleys and beauty parlors. I just couldn't believe it. It would be for the filthy rich, people who could afford to own an airplane and fly out from Chicago or Florida to enjoy the wilderness with ease. We didn't want it that way and had to stop it. The country would have gone down the drain."

Once the park was established, the resort owners who had sided with the opponents discovered it was a good thing. It assured the

resource upon which they depended. George, who had been a minority voice in International Falls, was proven correct in insisting
that wild nature has a value in its own. Now, he told me, the
wolves have come back. At one time they were down to only three
or four families, persecuted and secretive. As a consequence of protection, the park literature attests, nothing so symbolizes Voyageurs' enduring primitive character as the presence of its wolves.
The park is in the heart of the only region of the country south of
Alaska where they survive in any numbers. Once wolves were
thought to be only on Isle Royale, though now they are known to
be in Superior National Forest, Voyageurs, and possibly other areas
as well.

I mentioned to George the contrast I had noted between his
country and the Allagash in northern Maine. Big timber had fought
the establishment of national parks at both places. At one location,
where timber lost, people see and feel unspoiled nature, while at
the other, in Thoreau's Maine woods, they hear the song of chainsaws instead of warblers and grosbeaks; they see clear-cuts and logging roads all over the place.

"Yes," George agreed, "big companies are fighting for their
right to make a profit, not for the public interest. They may win
now, but what good does it do the country in the long run?

"Here they gave us arguments about multiple use. Multiple
use, sure, as long as it didn't hurt the companies. Water came out
of their mills looking like ink, with a horrible stench. That's their
bread and butter, while the rest of the people suffer."

My last evening we spent in reminiscing at his little house at
the edge of International Falls. George wore hearing aids for both
ears and managed pretty well. Someone telephoned to discuss the
town's arrangements for Christmas. He wore a headset to amplify
the caller's voice. For years he would transport Santa Claus on his
way from the North Pole, not all the way, but picking him up by
dogsled at the Canadian border. For the past ten years George himself had been Santa, calling at hospitals, schools, and the homes of
needy families. His build and personality were ideal for the role.
Everywhere I had been with him he was held in high esteem, a
small-town elder statesman, if not quite a guru. International Falls,
as I saw it, was not an attractive place; it had lost the opportunity

:o conserve and cultivate the frontier flavor, but instead was blighted by the same planless commercialization afflicting towns and cities across the continent. All of which make Voyageurs National Park more precious, and which perhaps accounts for the respect given to George.

He showed me his scrapbooks about his dogsledding exploits and military service. One photograph taken at our old air base in Maine showed Harriett, my Red Cross friend of those days, riding on George's sled with another officer. That was forty years ago.

"I thought that was you," George said politely.

I gulped, then laughed. "Well, that picture probably was taken after I was transferred. He looks like a good fellow."

I asked him about guiding and dogsledding.

"I would take fishermen out in summer, deer hunters in winter. We liked to hunt like Indians, stalking the deer, the hard way. The area had burned over in 1936, and the new growth of willow and aspen made wonderful hunting for whitetail, particularly in the Shoepack area, where I had a cabin. At first I got three dogs from a fellow at St. Francis, on the Canadian side of the border, then started breeding my own. We would dress deer in the woods, then haul the carcasses out on the sled. A couple of winters I worked for the Department of Natural Resources, hauling hay to feed deer near Wolf Island and helping the game warden, who was snaring wolves as part of a habitat study.

"There were quite a few dog drivers. We put on endurance races across the lake, of seventeen to twenty miles, that were more fun than anything else. I traveled on snowshoes, not skis. Skis are too slow. In going through deep snow I would put a rough lock— that's like a chain—on my dogsled. I'd get ahead of the dogs and open a trail on snowshoes. If it's too easy they'd gang up on me. Then I'd come back and take off the lock.

"I'll run for a while till I get sweaty (which I do even if it's forty below), then ride for a while. If going up a steep hill, I'll get off and push to help those dogs along. If you just ride, you're going to get colder than hell. In an hour you'd freeze to death. You have to control your body temperature.

"When I came back from World War II, I was a kind of celebrity. I worked in parades. At the St. Paul Ice Carnival I would be hired to show my dog team. One year I was hired to work on a float, with a team of four dogs running on a treadmill. At the end of the parade we rode into an auditorium packed with thousands of people. The announcer said, 'Ladies and gentlemen, the dog team you just saw won the war for the United States and its allies. Now the dog team and driver have just won first prize on this float!'

"After that appearance a booking agent asked me to go on a speaking tour. 'Hell,' I said, 'I'm a dog driver, not a lecturer.' At first I was shivering in my timbers, but I did it for three or four seasons, through Minnesota, Wisconsin, Illinois, North Dakota, Iowa, and one season around Texas, mostly before students, everything from kindergarten to college. I'd give a demonstration of about forty-five minutes, then take kindergarten or first grade children for a ride around the gym floor. (The sled was on wheels.) I'd show the commands, 'Gee' to the right, 'haw' to the left. 'The dogs are anxious, so the minute you release the sled, give a whistle or handclap and down the trail you go.'

"I worked for a number of sport shows, demonstrating on the stage or riding out on the streets, again on a sled on wheels. One time I'm on Michigan Boulevard in Chicago, following my lane. A cop sees me coming down the street. He's busy out in the middle of the street directing four-way traffic. The light changes from green to red. I stop, put the brake on. The light changes from red to green. I give a whistle and we start. As we go by, he shouts, 'Hell, you're a better driver than them taxicab drivers!'

"He thought I would cause a big traffic jam, but I had the dogs well trained. Around animals, if you train them properly, they react to your actions. If you're mean to them, they'll resent that. With gentleness your dogs will come around.

"Snowmobiling is popular in International Falls, but it's decreasing. For a while everybody in the family had a personal snowmobile. Not now. In the wilderness, stuck out there, I'd rather have a dog team. Anything manmade can't cope with the cold and climate. Give me a dog team anytime. It sounds brutal, but if I'm down to my last bullet I've got one more shell to kill the dog. If I had to, I'd eat it. Some dog drivers and explorers, when desperate, have done that. If I'm out on the trail or don't think I'm going to make it, being with dogs and having somebody to talk to would keep me from getting ice happy.

"In the Boundary Waters the Forest Service is going to use dog teams from now on, for transportation, getting equipment back into places where they can't use snowmobiles. They're discussing doing that here in Voyageurs and giving demonstrations for visitors. I always felt I was part of the wilderness riding the dogsled.

"My running days are over. I've got a lot of memories, met a lot of nice people, made a lot of rich friends. One night Governor Elmer Anderson phoned me. It was during the time we were trying to get the national park. He was staying at the lodge on Rainy Lake. 'I have a gentleman here and would like you to guide us. But he doesn't want any publicity.' I went over the next morning and here was this tall, gray-haired gentleman. It was General Charles Lindbergh. He was a native of Minnesota and quite influential. I just about fell through the floor because it was such an honor.

"I took them across Rainy Lake to Kettle Falls. On the way back I stopped the boat so we could watch a couple of eagles flying around. General Lindbergh didn't seem enthused because he wasn't commenting at all. About two or three weeks later I got a letter from him mailed from Singapore, telling me what a wonderful trip it was, how those blueberry muffins at Kettle Falls pleased his palate, and how he enjoyed those eagles flying around."

Sigurd Olson and George Esslinger, a couple of classy guides to the North Woods, leave important works. They lived well-defined lives, with their ambitions fulfilled. When I went to the 1967 Sierra Club Wilderness Conference, the main issues were still new to me. Sig opened the heart of the matter with challenge and inspiration. Politicians and bureaucrats on the program missed the mark. They were like self-sentenced prisoners who couldn't let themselves go to exult in their personal encounters in the wild, but felt, instead, constrained to follow narrow concepts that come from laboring in offices for too long.

Because I was on the program, too, I was invited one evening to appear on a panel on the San Francisco public television station in company with Estella Leopold, a paleobotanist and the daughter of Aldo Leopold, and Roderick Nash, just finishing his Ph.D. They were also speakers at the conference. Our panel moderator was a local attorney, a personable, up-and-coming Republican politician with an excellent grasp of the wilderness issue, Caspar Weinberger by name. Later he would become the militaristic Secretary of Defense in the administration of Ronald Reagan. He might have done better by sticking to the wilderness and becoming a guide, too. If he could have handled it.

CHAPTER IX

❧

Yellowstone: Where Have All the Grizzlies Gone?

It was the grizzly bear that did it. No, not really, it's simply an idea I like to explore in odd moments, those odd moments we all experience while going through a mental exercise starting with "If this had happened," or "If that hadn't happened," and assigning responsibility to somebody else for whatever did happen. That grizzly, I admit, was an innocent bystander, trying to get by on its home ground, but its very presence sparked a considerable change in the scenario. Not on a very large scale, except when measured in the lives of people, including my own.

The bear made its appearance the very first night on the trail. Ralph K. Miller, the lean, grizzled outfitter and guide, spotted it about one hundred yards outside of camp. It was curious but kept its distance, doubtless sniffing the aroma of the dinner we had just finished.

It was mid-August of 1980. That day we had ridden from Soda Butte, a natural curiosity shaped a little like a thirty-foot obelisk, in the Lamar Valley, the northeast corner of Yellowstone. The night before, our little party had met and stayed at a modest, neat motel at Cooke City, which is no city at all but a gateway to the national park. In its earlier days Cooke City was a mining town and rendezvous of game poachers, and still has about it the flavor of unfinished defiance. It is doubtless quiet in winter, when snows pile deep and tourists have long vanished, except for hardy, or foolhardy, snowmobilers.

The horses had been trailered from Cooke City to Soda Butte for the start of a week on the Mirror Plateau, a wilderness portion of the park, which few visitors explore. From grassland and sagebrush at 6600 feet, we had ridden through fields of wildflowers and pine forests to almost 9000 feet. Rocky ranges reached to the horizons in Wyoming and Montana. We were in Yellowstone as it was meant to be, the sanctuary in which we could easily consider ourselves the intruders.

Miller proposed that we saddle up and ride for a closer look at the grizzly, larger than a cub but not yet full-grown. The older couple, Roswell, or "Ros," and his wife, Louisa, declined. Ros's routine proved to be that once his day's riding was done he closed it with a couple of pre-dinner Scotches, and maybe one or two post-dinner. Barbara, who had come alone on the trip, the wife of an eastern businessman, also declined. That left Jane, her name was, and me. She sat at the end of the log in front of the campfire, putting down her dinner plate. Jane was somewhere in her forties, not unattractive, but cool, reserved, self-assured or possibly defensive, a loner. She had brought her own herbal tea and said she didn't eat meat. She hadn't taken to me especially, nor I to her, but she was up for the ride. It was complicated, however, by the fact that the horses were unsaddled and out to pasture. Miller suggested that we take only two horses, he riding one and the both of us on the other. We never got close to the bear, but Jane got close to me, her arms holding tightly around my waist while we galloped over the meadow. She wasn't very large or heavy, no more than five feet four and possibly 105 to 110 pounds. I could tell she was sliding around the back end of the horse and doing her best to stay onboard. I wasn't overly confident myself, this being the first time I'd ever ridden double; still, the feel of her was stimulating, a flashing reminder of how I have always envied motorcyclists riding with their girlfriends.

The bear took to the brush and we returned to camp. Daylight seems to linger longer at high elevations, particularly in the northern latitudes, but once twilight shadows cross the meadows, time passes quickly around the campfire. Our four tents were scattered in the grove of trees: Louisa and Ros in one; Jane and Barbara in another; Ralph and Candace, or Candy, his attractive, red-haired girlfriend, camp cook, and wrangler, in the third; and me, with a tent to myself. Normally that would be a luxury, but at the time I felt uneasy about sleeping alone. My tent was pitched on the outer edge of the trees and I pictured that grizzly bear finding me a handy midnight morsel. When Ralph and Candy secured the loose food by hanging it from tree limbs, I suggested to Jane and Barbara that the bear might be back and there was safety in numbers; I could crawl in with them and we'd each be in our separate sleeping bags anyway. They readily agreed, evidently having apprehensions of their own.

I lay quietly for a long time between the two women, dozing lightly at most. Barbara turned on her side away from me and seemed asleep, though Jane remained close. Nights tended to be mild (though early mornings would be frosty and cold). I had my arms out of the sleeping bag and touched Jane, sensing that she was conscious of it but not repelled. Without aggressiveness, I let a hand lay against her side. In a few minutes I moved it across her sleeping bag over a breast. She placed a hand over mine, a response that was like an electric signal. I put both arms around her and drew her close. She wanted to be held; it was as though she *needed* to be held. Thus we spent the entire night, the sleeping bags still largely between us, but the arms and upper torsos and cheeks and lips never out of contact, all this while the third tent-mate lay asleep.

What next? Next morning I wondered. I had a firm idea of what I wanted, but how would I bring it up? Now, while the night's embrace was fresh, or wait until we pitched the next camp? Jane solved the problem. "I've been thinking and I've talked to Barbara. I would like to be in your tent with you tonight. But I might not stay, we'll have to see. Is that all right?" I saw a touch of uncertainty in her brown eyes, as though she knew what she wanted but was asking whether it met with my agreement. But, of course!

After the first night she announced, "I'm moving in with you. We'll find a spot where we can pitch the tent and be alone." Thus began a marvelous wilderness romance, sharing and enjoying days as well as nights. We observed herds of elk and buffalo in their summer range of high, lush meadows, an occasional moose, grouse, and coyote. We'd see different kinds of birds, the species varying with elevation and terrain: bald eagle and rare black rosy finch, birds of striking form and elegant beauty such as the sandhill crane, trumpeter swan, and western tanager. From the top of the Mirror Plateau, views unfolded of the great ranges surrounding Yellowstone: the Beartooth and Snowy ranges, the Gallatin Mountains, the Absarokas, and the snowy Tetons far to the south, dramatic because they rise so sharply and starkly from the valley floor. Yellowstone itself, for all its marvels, is essentially a high, rolling plateau, or series of plateaus, without jagged peaks. Even mountains more than eleven thousand feet above sea level do not appear high because they rise from elevations of almost eight thousand feet. But Yellowstone embraces space, a frontier as it must have been a hundred years ago, when adventurers rode through glacier-carved valleys and alpine meadows abloom with Indian paintbrush and lupine; space and solitude, free of complication and encumbrance. Yellowstone is almost as large as Massachusetts, but, for the present at least, they could have been planets apart. The romance and Yellowstone itself were indivisible, one as fresh and vital as the other. For almost a week our little party didn't see another human or hear a motorized sound. Jane was a good rider and camper. She had read about Miller's trips in the Sunday travel section of *The New York Times* and saved and budgeted for it. She was a professional nurse who specialized in education, teaching advanced nursing to nurses at a medical college in Philadelphia. She had divorced three years earlier after twenty years of marriage and three children, and had programmed this trip for herself.

We shared the days with the others, though they could tell that each day brought the two of us closer together. Candy cooked cheese blintzes for breakfast one morning, crepes and strawberries the next. For lunch on the trail we had quiche, or cold chicken, with fresh fruit, raw vegetables, cheese, nuts and raisins, and wine. We stopped at scenic settings, the edge of a waterfall or at a cliffside, looking into distances that went on forever. At dinner we ate steak or trout with fresh-baked bread. Miller liked to say he ran trips first-class, start to finish. Doing so, he added, enabled his guests time and energy to better observe the natural environment. I'm not sure that view is correct. The outlay of effort is an important factor in appreciation of wilderness. Yet, we did our share. In trail riding, the horses bear the heavy burden, but riding requires a degree of stamina, if not skill. We followed steep trails, climbing spiny mountain ridges, then zigzagging down switchbacks into meadows and river valleys. Only a few were officially designated trails; Miller chose well-trod wildlife routes, or made his own. He would stop the party now and then to allow his horses to rest. They weren't any prize winners to look at—one of them, Lingo, was one-eyed—but they were surefooted and responsive. The end of the day's ride meant it was time to unsaddle and hobble the horses with cuffs around their ankles, allowing freedom to graze and find water while keeping them from straying, and time to brush their blankets. Somewhere between each day's ride the horses themselves had to be brushed down. These chores took a lot of time, but they're part of the routine. Then there was the kitchen to set up, with the canvas fly over it, and the nylon-domed tents, so easy for those who know how (preferably on level ground, for those who could find any).

For Jane, this was her first visit to Yellowstone and her first western horse trip. I had made my first ride, the first of several, twenty years earlier, in the Bridger Wilderness, in the Wind River Range, which lies on the west slope of the Continental Divide about one hundred miles southeast of Yellowstone. That is classic country in its own right, though scarcely known as compared with Yellowstone. Being in the Wind Rivers was a moving experience that impelled me to learn about history, art, and wilderness.

On that trip I traveled in the environment painted in 1837 by Alfred Jacob Miller, places he found "as fresh and beautiful as if just from the hands of the Creator." It was the same setting into which John C. Frémont ventured in 1842, with Kit Carson as his guide, and a full military expedition, in search of headwaters of the Green River. Frémont was drawn to the high peaks by their shiny ice caps, and determined to scale the highest. From our camp at Fremont Crossing, I could see the peak he climbed and named for himself: a jagged, truncated mesa of stone, by all odds the most spectacular. Frémont and five companions rode beneath a perpen-

159

dicular wall of granite, working their way to the summit, then dismounted and climbed on foot in thin moccasins made from buffalo skin. Ever dramatic, he drove a ramrod into the rock and "unfurled the flag to wave where never the flag waved before." He mistakenly assumed himself at the highest point in the Rockies and was overcome by the "concourse of lakes and rushing waters, mountains of rock, dells and ravines of the most exquisite beauty, all kept green and fresh by the great moisture in the air and sown with brilliant flowers." In the decade following, Albert Bierstadt was likewise inspired and used this setting for at least a portion of his massive painting, *Rocky Mountains*, a showpiece of the Metropolitan Museum of Art in New York.

My own trip into the Bridger was of a different kind. There were more than twenty riders, plus a crew of almost ten. I would never go on such a trip now; nor would I recommend it. With eighty-plus horses and mules for riding and pack stock, wildlife was driven away. The wranglers used chainsaws to cut firewood, without much objection from members of the party, some of whom did a lot of drinking.

Jane disapproved of drinking, though not violently, and she had personal reasoning behind her. Her husband had been an alcoholic and had ruined his career as an industrial psychologist. As a nursing educator she had taken up holistic health, or holism. Those were only words to me, so I was curious. She explained and I questioned, at meals, on the trail, in the tent, sometimes in the middle of the night between passion and soft embrace. The more she told of holism the more meaningful it became. It was something for which I had been reaching, and searching, in my own way; it was thoroughly complementary to environmentalism, or the "ecosystems approach" to natural resources.

In articles and speeches I had developed a line that each individual must lessen his demand on the earth's raw materials. "We must alter the life-style that makes us enemies of ourselves," I would say, urging people to stop confusing standard of living with quality of life. But I wasn't sure that I was doing much of it myself, beyond turning down the temperature or switching off the lights. Two years before, as I told Jane, I had been in northwest Montana, speaking in behalf of a group called the Flathead Coalition against commercial developments threatening the integrity of Glacier National Park. These included a proposed mining project a few miles from the park in Canada and logging in the adjacent Flathead National Forest. At Kalispell, a heckler piped up and demanded, "How did you get out here? You flew—that's how. Quit telling us to use less resources while you use more." Though I defended myself, I was abashed that he was challenging my own overconsumption. Sometime after that I had gone to Malaysia. Kuala Lumpur, the capital, was smitten with the machine-made worst of the West. But in a village on the coast of the China Sea, I found people using bicycles, not for play and pleasure, but for normal transportation, eating fish they caught themselves, and purchasing fresh fruits and vegetables daily, without need of refrigeration. They were backward by some standards, but progressive by others.

Holistic health, as I interpreted it from Jane, meant taking care of one's own ecosystem, of assuming responsibility through healthy living rather than relying on prescriptions and pills. It was the unity of body, mind, and spirit, as some primitive peoples scattered across the world have long understood it. She tried teaching me diaphragmatic breathing, the simplest, most immediate natural answer to stress, but I was too much of what she called a "chest breather," and had never discovered my own diaphragm. We talked of visualization, yoga, Tai Chi, and autogenesis, a lot of approaches to personal living of which I had not been aware.

We talked about each other. Our romance in the wilderness started for me as a game, a brief fling. "A honeymoon without benefit of ceremony," I referred to it jokingly. But something was going on here, changing and deepening the relationship. During the day Jane was one person, making the most of Yellowstone, hiking, riding, pitching in with chores, enthusiastic yet still a little reserved. Throughout the night she was another person, making the most of being with me, warm, responsive, scarcely out of my arms, her lithe, light body fitting snugly and weightlessly against mine. I found out something about myself: that I was able to give love and receive it as I had never been able before. Our domed tent was colored blue and gold; it became our blue and gold spaceship as we traveled into orbit. The ground was hard, of course, but it couldn't have mattered less to two persons transported. She was deeply moved; one night, as the trip neared its end, while I stroked her graying blondish hair she cried in my arms, lamenting what we both thought would be a final parting.

We could have remained in Yellowstone forever. At one campsite we stayed two nights, settling for day rides and avoiding the complications of breaking and setting up camp. Mornings were cold and crisp, but when we opened the tent flap we saw buffalo in the meadows, a dozen or more, huge animals grazing gently, undisturbed and undisturbing. I would tell Jane now and then that she ought to see the high spots of Yellowstone as well—Old Faithful, the mud pots, Yellowstone Lake, Grand Canyon of the Yellowstone River—along with the crowds that come from all over the world to admire these natural marvels. No, thank you, this would be Yellowstone for her, the way she had always planned to picture it.

I myself had been to Yellowstone a number of times, but it was refreshing to see it with her and through her eyes. It was the Yellowstone of limitless distances, of sagebrush desert, open meadow, and high forest; the forest of trees rather than timber, allowed to die and decompose, to the forester's despair; of rocky places, where minerals lie undisturbed, to the geologist's despair; of grasses reserved for wild animals rather than for domestic livestock; of fumaroles, bubbling hot springs, and mud pots of scalding water and superheated steam, yielding the earth's energy free and unfettered; every part of Yellowstone vibrant, alive, and changing. It was the Yellowstone that mystified the early explorers and held them spellbound.

Going to Yellowstone in the 1860s, I imagined, was like going to the moon a century later, an incredulous adventure into the unknown. The official expedition of 1870 verified and legitimized the wildest tales. The story of how this group of men, while sitting around a campfire along the Firehole River, agreed to work for designation of the area as a national reserve, has sometimes been challenged by historians. While the skeptics could be right, the eloquence and conviction in the reports speak for themselves. As for example, the official account to the army of Lieutenant Gustavus C. Doane, whose cavalry detachment guarded the civilian explorers from the unpredictable Crow and Blackfeet: "As a country for sightseers, it is without parallel; as a field for scientific research, it promises great results; in the branches of geology, mineralogy, botany, zoology, and ornithology, it is probably the greatest laboratory that nature furnishes on the surface of the globe."

Yellowstone the laboratory has fulfilled its promise in some respects and failed in others. The wonderland we saw provides sanctuary to bear, bison, moose, elk, deer, bighorn sheep, antelope, mountain lion, coyote, badger, beaver, almost every kind of mammal present before the park was established, with exception of the wolf. We didn't see all these species, but enough to believe all must be present. The sight of abundant bison stirred me to think of the mystique of this massive, stocky, noble animal, the mystique derived from Indian and frontier history, and from the unrestrained slaughter of millions across the Plains. When the American bison was at the brink of extinction throughout its habitat, a small band somehow survived in the drainage of Pelican Creek, which lay across our route. That band provided the source stock that makes Yellowstone today the only place in the United States where bison are able to range free, without cropping or hunting, subject entirely to natural regulation. The park perhaps was established primarily to protect scenic spectaculars in public ownership, but presently it would be recognized as a wildlife sanctuary. It provided refuge for the last significant herd of bison, and the largest elk herds in the country, and beaver still common in streams and brooks, though outside its boundaries these species were at the brink of extermination or sharply reduced in numbers.

Nevertheless, it's not the bison that make Yellowstone Yellowstone, nor the bears, beaver, elk, scenery, or panoramas. It's the naturalness, the natural functions that humans let be. University wildlife courses, particularly at land-grant schools, focus on what is called management, manipulation, really, of vegetation and wildlife in order to produce favored species or to control numbers of given species. Where hunting is sanctioned, the favored species are game animals. National parks are presumed to preserve natural ecosystems, but their wildlife is subject to manipulation as well, not only in the United States, but virtually everywhere in the world. Kruger National Park, in South Africa, is twice the size of

Yellowstone. It gives the impression of naturalness, but the impression is misleading. The park is completely fenced, in order to contain lions and elephants from getting out in the neighborhood, and systematically compartmentalized to provide so many of each species in each compartment. Whenever any large species grows too numerous, the excess is systematically removed by culling, otherwise known as killing. A wilderness park, however, should have its boundaries defined and limited for man, not for wildlife, so that its wolves, wolverines, bears, and lions can truly be wild. Restrictions have been imposed on the wildlife species in Yellowstone because wilderness has been sacrificed to build access roads, campgrounds, hotels, and souvenir shops. Wildlife management, for its part, may meet specific objectives, but a specific element of wilderness can hardly be separated from the rest of it.

Ralph Miller thoroughly understood certain aspects of wilderness. He was a rough-cut frontier throwback, seemingly unlearned and self-taught, dressed for his role in a sheepskin jacket and a well-worn western hat no larger than a fedora. His work was hard, but chosen; he was a flagellant, punishing himself, and sometimes punishing, or challenging, his riders as well, though he would insist he never conducts an endurance contest, or a race. He was paying for something in his past, or proving something to himself.

Our party lived closely and learned about each other, even down to what each looked like without a stitch of clothing. That happened the day we went to Hot Springs Basin, one of those wonders of Yellowstone, reflecting heat and pressure inside the earth. After hiking around bubbling paint pots, pools of boiling water, and spouting geysers that few park visitors get to see, Miller brought us to the pool of hot water he had promised. We all welcomed the opportunity to bathe.

Louisa and Ros had no reluctance. They were older, but contemporary. He was retired from an office job with an oil company, while she was a schoolteacher. They were humanists who had worked as volunteers for three years on an Indian reservation in North Dakota. Barbara, a buxom lady, likely in her early fifties, was contemporary, too, approving the romance between Jane and me, and enjoying her role as Jane's counselor and confessor. I saw my tentmate without clothing for the first time. She was slender but not small boned, well proportioned with slender hips and small breasts, soaping herself easily and gracefully, enjoying the luxury of warm water.

Ralph in the buff proved scrawny and raw-boned, an unglamorous figure. In settings such as the communal bath, we learned his story. He was born in Boston, his father a physician, his mother a successful interior decorator. As a born rebel, he went through reform school, drugs, military school, and a year of college. He learned about horses by working around race tracks, then bought, sold, and trained them. Between summers he was in school again, at Montana State University, planning to become a veterinarian. Candy, the cook and wrangler, was not his first live-in companion. Nor was he hers. She had all the elements of physical beauty: cascading reddish hair, clear eyes, well-defined nose, lips, and chin, and a slender, erect figure, but she was bony and burned from a hard summer on the trail. She told me her parents were from South Dakota, but they divorced early in her life. Her mother remarried a man whose work took him from Vermont to California, so she saw a lot of the country. Candy had a worldly glamour about her, an inherent sophistication, but her interests, at least as I saw her, were neither worldly nor urbane, but fundamentally earthy. Her career was hers by choice: She loved the outdoors and Ralph provided the means to be in them. While Ralph studied veterinary medicine at Montana State, she was there, too, studying architecture.

One evening around the campfire we talked about grizzly bears. I thought I knew something about them, having read a lot of the literature and having interviewed various experts. Ralph alleged that bears—not only the grizzlies, but the smaller black bears—were being killed by park rangers without official accounting or reporting. This struck me as unverifiable gossip, the kind circulated around a national park by individuals with personal grievance against the park administration. Still, he cited the noticeable absence along the roadsides of the blacks, the chronic "beggar bears." Black bears by the dozens used to line park roads during daylight hours, chewing on candy wrappers and kosher dill pickles. But not any longer. They just aren't there. I could only respond that the National Park Service had pursued a successful policy of retraining the bears to make their own way in the wild. But all that successful? With *all* the bears?

The facts, likely, will never fully be known. Books will be written asking, "Where have all the grizzlies gone?," or in defense of the policies of the National Park Service, or trying to set the record straight. For the grizzly bear is the conscience of the country. When the white man crossed the Mississippi, grizzly bears were everywhere, estimated to number fifty thousand. For some Indians, the great bear, sometimes weighing more than half a ton, was a figure of reverence, or a kin; to others, killing a grizzly was a mark of bravery. Still, they took only a few, as contrasted with the whites who followed. Few Americans of our time ever see a grizzly in its native setting. There are none in California, although the bear is the symbol of the Golden State. Outside of western Canada and Alaska, only a few hundred remain, most of them in Yellowstone and Glacier National Parks and adjacent national forests. Funding goes into research and meetings and so-called recovery plans, but it is conscience money that yields little to protection and perpetuation of the bear.

Red and black leaflets warn visitors about "hazards," the principal one being the possible grizzly encounter. The public notion is of a mean, ferocious beast, unpredictable at best. Bears attracted to campgrounds by food are classed as "rogues"; they are removed and, when considered sufficiently roguish, dispatched to bear heaven.

"He is a harmless, peaceful giant, perfectly satisfied to let you alone, if you let him alone," wrote the pioneer naturalist Ernest Thompson Seton, painting quite a different picture.

"When he was the unquestioned monarch of the range, trapper and cowboy knew right well that they need only exercise a little self-restraint, show some decent courtesy to this big dignified giant in the fur cloak, and they need not fear but what he would respond."

The trappers were deadly foes of the grizzly. They overcame its size and strength with the repeating rifle. Each year the grizzly was the victim of more deadly traps and guns. It was at the mercy of those who knew no mercy.

"Man, aggressive, brutal and destructive, has forced him to

change many of his ancient habits," wrote Seton. "The heedless bear that roamed the open and fed by day is gone. His place is taken by bears that feed secretly, silently, by night, in cover— always secretly. . . . He has retreated to secluded fastnesses, to wild and inaccessible regions of thicket and mountainside. He is changed in temper as in life, and the faintest whiff of man scent is now enough to drive him miles away. Repeating rifles have instilled the idea that man is master—omnipotent, merciless."

I don't mean to advance an overromantic view, especially one that spurs encroachment and disturbance. Grizzly bears are as different and unpredictable as people. I have no idea of what bears were like before men saw them, except from what I've read. However, I have had personal contact and communication with the late Adolph Murie, who for years conducted wildlife ecological studies in the national parks. His approach was aimed at true research. This means living with the animals, or at least out among them, trying to think as they do, and establishing an intimate relationship with the creatures that reveals their motivations in all they do. Such intimate, on-the-ground contact with animals, as his brother, Olaus Murie, commented, leads to an understanding of nature that is desperately lacking in this age of exploitation.

In his classic book, *A Naturalist in Alaska*, Adolph Murie discussed recreation and grizzlies. As he related, a friend was about to embark into bear country and sought his counsel. Adolph replied that a traveler had nothing to worry about: He could enter the wilderness with a light spirit; all he needed was faith. The chief difficulty would be to preserve one's faith, but if his friend did so, respecting the bear's potential for causing injury and keeping a respectful distance, all would go well.

National parks ought to be spacious sanctuaries for bears in whatever number they can sustain. There should be room for humans, too, but the needs of bears should come first. Enos A. Mills, a Seton contemporary, in his book, *The Grizzly*, told how different things were in his time. When Mills arrived in the Colorado Rockies in 1884, grizzlies were still common. During the autumn of one year in the early nineties, Mills made an eight-day trip in what is now Rocky Mountain National Park. He saw the tracks of between forty and forty-five grizzlies, eleven in one half-day alone. But grizzlies soon decreased sharply in numbers, under the pressure of stockmen, settlers, and professional hunters. Mills lamented the slaughter:

"The grizzly bear is really the greatest animal on the continent. The grizzly walks: there is a dignity, a lordliness of carriage, and an indifference to all the world that impress themselves on the attention. Someone speaks quietly to him: he halts, stands on hind legs, and shows a childlike eagerness of interest in his expressive face. His attitude and responsiveness are most companionable and never fail to awake the best in everyone who sees him in these moments. He even seems to have a sense of humor."

That might even have been the case with the young grizzly we encountered on the Mirror Plateau. To Miller, it was a curiosity to display to guests. In my own mind, however, I hadn't given the bear the chance to express his sense of humor. Enos Mills recounted these two episodes that I wish I had read first:

Once, in the southwest corner of Yellowstone, a number of boys were bathing in a stream when a young grizzly came along. For a moment it stood watching their pranks, then slipped quietly behind some trees on the stream bank. When the boys approached the spot, the bear gave a wild "Woof, woof," and leaped into the water among them. This caused great excitement and merriment, evidently what the bear desired. As it swam hurriedly away, it looked back with satisfaction.

In another case, as the stage arrived at a Yellowstone hotel, one of the passengers, who had been having much to say concerning bears, put on his raincoat and got down on all fours, proceeding to impersonate a bear. Presently a grizzly arrived, made a rush at the man, and chased him up a tree, amid laughter and excitement. The bear made no attempt to harm anyone and plainly enjoyed its prank.

That was in the days before park visitors became imbued with a sense of fear and fright, as though programmed to panic. "The grizzly," wrote Mills, "is an animal of high type and to develop his best he needs fine, high consideration." Such consideration has been denied, less and less of it being granted as visitor numbers rise. For years they were fed at garbage dumps, near the hotels inside the park, and at the gateway communities, mostly for the amusement of tourists. One sign, in fact, proclaimed Lunch Counter—For Bears Only. Bits and pieces of the bear's range were transformed into tourist facilities. The point has often been made by officials, in responding to complaints of zealous nature lovers, that developed areas cover only 5 percent of Yellowstone, leaving the remainder for native wildlife. But wild animals don't understand or follow this human reasoning. The grizzly covers a lot of distance in its flatfooted way to follow its nose to fill its stomach. It is drawn to plants at the pre-flowering stage of growth, when succulence is greatest. In June and July it feeds on spawning trout in the arms of Yellowstone Lake, and in August on small, sweet raspberries ripening under the cover of lodgepole pine. It tears dead timber to shreds in search of ants and termites. It is drawn into campgrounds for what it considers to be a cheap and easy meal.

Between 1959 and 1971, John and Frank Craighead studied the movement of bears in Yellowstone through the use of radio tracking collars, a system they pioneered. These identical twins have been highly respected as popular wildlife biologists, which accounts for part of their problem—they became *too* popular for their peers, writing articles and books, and producing and appearing in television specials, the kind of thing that bread-and-butter technicians don't do and which they resent in others. Moreover, the Craigheads demonstrated independence and principle, concern for the cause of the grizzly, rather than for any bureaucracy.

The Craigheads stirred a fuss in Yellowstone—or I should say they were at the eye of the controversy—yet they are not aggressive people. I remember meeting John Craighead at West Yellowstone in the early seventies. He was only five feet six and soft-spoken to the point of shyness. I can't recall the exact year, but the next day I was in park headquarters noting an item on the bulletin board that Superintendent Jack Anderson had just received the first annual award of the International Snowmobile Association for opening the gates of Yellowstone to snowmachines and encouraging their use. It was that year. The award struck me as ludicrous. Anderson had barred the Craigheads from continuing their research in the park because he didn't think it was natural for bears to be running around with collars on their ears, yet sanctioned the intrusion of snowmachines during the one season when Yellowstone is quiet enough to be natural.

In the late sixties the National Park Service wanted to close the open-pit garbage dumps in order to restore the park as closely as possible to pristine condition. The policy was instituted rather hastily following a 1967 incident in Glacier National Park, when two young women were killed by grizzlies that had been intentionally attracted to a certain area by the use of garbage. The Craigheads did not oppose closing the dumps, but warned that abruptly doing so could seriously disrupt grizzly feeding habits and movements, forcing bears into areas where they could come into conflict with humans. That became the issue of heavy debate, but behind it lay the future of the grizzly. In 1973 the Craigheads announced they had data to prove that during 1970–71 a total of ninety-one Yellowstone grizzlies were killed or placed in zoos—a loss rate exceeding cub reproduction by 50 percent. "The general conclusion," they said, "drawn from analysis by computer, is that a high mortality rate for the period 1968–71 has caused a rapid decrease in population size that if continued could cause extermination in a relatively short period of time."

In due course the Craigheads would be vindicated. Because they wouldn't quit, despite abundant insult and abuse, the country at last has a better grasp on the condition of the grizzly bear. But if they were right, somebody had to be wrong. A lot of people were wrong. One of them was Anderson, the park superintendent of those days. I knew him and had traveled with him in the park a time or two. He was a great big fellow who reminded me of a game warden, or some kind of law enforcement officer, intimidating by sheer bulk. He had done some good work, including trying to educate fishermen to be respectful of the resource, but his antagonism to the Craigheads declined from issues of principle into personality conflict. He was strongly supported in Washington by the Assistant Secretary of the Interior, Nathaniel P. Reed, a young man in his thirties, tall, highly motivated, and well intended, who looked down a long, aristocratic nose on those who disagreed with him. On September 12, 1973, he addressed a letter to *The Washington Post* responding to a commentary on Yellowstone bears (by Lewis Regenstein) it had published only the day before. He cited the report of a science advisory committee (composed of Dr. A. Starker Leopold, University of California; Dr. Stanley A. Cain, University of Michigan; Dr. Charles E. Olmsted, University of Chicago, and Sigurd Olson, of Ely, Minnesota) recommending the policy of closing the Yellowstone dumps. "When I took office in May 1971," Reed wrote, "I was warned by some of America's best-known biologists that I would be criticized by well-meaning bear lovers and the perpetual Park Service critics if I reaffirmed the policy. I was also advised that if I had the courage to follow through with the policy that after an initial loss of bears which could not adjust to living in a non-garbage dump ecosystem a healthy natural population would evolve that were free-roaming, fully self-sustainable and indeed wild."

My files show that he sent this to me with a little typed memo. I wrote to him soon after with a few questions. His response of November 16, 1973, includes the following: "I am pleased to report that the appraisal of the park's bear management program shows it has been successful and is proceeding as anticipated. The grizzly bear population appears to be healthy and viable and maintaining itself in a wild, free-ranging state independent of garbage as a food source. Also, reproductive success was reported to be very good this year as compared with previous years. Control actions in developed areas were at a minimum this past summer, e.g., no grizzly bears have been destroyed and it was necessary to capture and move only two bears (sow and cub) as of late September."

Maybe so, but in 1980, Dr. Richard Knight, leader of the Interagency Grizzly Bear Study Team (a group of biologists assigned to replace the Craigheads after their research contract was dropped), began issuing pessimistic statements about the bears' status. Asked by the *Denver Post* about the grizzly's future, he replied, "Bleak—eventual extinction in twenty to thirty years."

All kinds of measures presumably have been taken in behalf of the grizzly, but in August 1982, Roland Wauer, chairman of the Interagency Grizzly Bear Committee, which supervised the study team, issued an urgent memorandum saying the Yellowstone grizzly population had declined seriously and that quick action was imperative: "Unless some change occurs to reduce the grizzly bear's mortality rate soon, the probability of retaining this wildland species in Yellowstone National Park is minimal."

In 1983 a colleague at the University of Idaho, Dr. Maurice Hornocker, provided me with a little additional reading. Maurice was a member of the Craigheads' grizzly research team for five years before branching into his own studies of mountain lions and other wild cats, a field in which he is recognized as the foremost expert in the country, if not the world. He showed me a letter he had written to a professional journal, *The Wildlifer*, referring to Wauer's report: "This statement and the essence of the memorandum fully support what the Craigheads have been saying for fifteen years. Some will say that conditions have changed, that mortality is higher now, that 'development' outside the park has taken its toll. That may be, but the park still has the fundamental management responsibility. And the hard facts remain that had the Craigheads' views been heeded, had a more conservative approach been taken in the bears' management, had those measures now called for been implemented in the 1960s, then there is a strong possibility this obvious crisis would not exist."

His view was endorsed in a subsequent letter by Robert B. Finley, Jr., Research Associate of the University of Colorado Museum, who had been involved in grizzly bear research as an official of the Denver Wildlife Research Center of the Department of the Interior. But he was not hopeful: "I agree that the Craigheads have been vindicated, but I am not so sanguine as Hornocker when he says, 'Now, presumably, the Craigheads' recommendations will be followed.' My experience indicates that research is likely to be mismanaged until the last bear has been counted. . . . My efforts to promote a sound research effort convinced me that the Department of the Interior was more interested in suppressing disagreement than in finding the truth or saving grizzlies."

Will the record ever be clarified? Will the grizzly be gone first? On our pack trip I had taken along a recently published book, *The Bears of Yellowstone* by Paul D. Schullery, published by the Yellowstone Library and Museum Association. It was essentially an apology for the bureaucracy, an attack upon the Craigheads, and a preachment to the public and media to be more respectful of authority, as illustrated by these excerpts:

172

"The public asked whoever was handy why there were no bears to feed. Most often they were told, by store clerks, gas station attendants, and other highly qualified observers that 'the rangers shot 'em all.' . . .

"Most popular writing about the grizzly controversy in Yellowstone has been strong on the rhetoric of wildlife preservation and weak on fact. A lot of the outcry was patent nonsense, such as the local rumors that big pits had been dug in secret places in the park and filled with the bodies of *hundreds* of bears, but many respectable writers jumped on what amounted to a bandwagon. Virtually none of them did enough homework to fully understand either viewpoint. . . . The Park Service scientists (professionals whose careers depend on their ability to accurately gather and interpret data) were identified with the Big Government, and throughout the controversy it was only their judgment, and even honor, that was challenged. . . . The roles into which the Craigheads and the Park Service were cast for the convenience of public consumption did not do service to them. It did not do service to the public. And, most of all, it did not do service to the bears. This was a major failure for the press. . . .

"*The Track of the Grizzly* (by Frank Craighead) will certainly bring the Doctors Craighead much public sympathy, and it will probably also add fuel to the now simmering controversy. It is required reading for serious students of bears, not only for its wealth of information but as a model of controversy journalism at its worst."

We rode through the heart of grizzly country, but far removed from the issues. The weather had been fair and favorable, on the whole, now cloudy and breezy (with clouds dramatic in color and form, fitting companions in the wilderness), then clear and warm. On the last day the heavens unloaded in a steady downpour. Despite rain gear, we were drenched. It was miserably cold, yet none complained—and not because we were riding out. It seemed a reasonable part of the experience and much was still going on. Passing the shores of Tern Lake, Fern Lake, and White Lake, while heading down the trail into Pelican Valley, we observed flocks of Canada geese, nesting eagles, and a pair of trumpeter swans. Jane pointed excitedly to one of the swans stretching its snow-white wings, about seven feet from tip to tip. The bird squawked its distinctive, low-pitched resonant beep, and glided gracefully across the lake. That little vignette of nature enriched our day. The trumpeter swan, Yellowstone's largest bird, is no common sight. Once it bred over a vast area of the continent, but its range was preempted for settlement and development, and its great size made the swan an easy target for shooters. The trumpeter was pressed to the brink of extinction; in the early 1930s, barely more than thirty remained. Under protection, it has made a comeback and no longer is considered endangered. The trumpeter swan is one of more than two hundred species of Yellowstone birds. On the lakes, streams, sloughs, and backwaters one can find one species or another: bald eagles, ospreys, sandhill cranes, great blue herons, and kingfishers. Unfortunately, it is easy *not* to see them, particularly for the casual visitor intent on driving from Point A to Point B, taking a few snapshots, and moving on to something else.

We had only begun to sense Yellowstone's limitless recesses, its magnitude and grandeur, but at least we had slowed down to let impressions penetrate outer defenses. Perhaps that's how it was with Jane and me. We had only begun to know each other, although the relationship was deeper and stronger than a casual holiday romance. It was not to be the end, as fate developed, but it was not to be endless either. For the present, as we returned to our little Cooke City motel, the main idea was to be together, to luxuriate in the same bed, on a mattress instead of a thin pad above hard earth, with a soft, warm comforter instead of tussling with sleeping bags, and to embrace each other's freshly bathed body. That was the idea; however, I was assigned the same single room I'd had on arrival, adjacent to Louisa and Ros with only a thin wall in between. How inhibiting that would be! Happily, love finds friends. Our faithful duenna, Barbara, who was to have shared a double room with Jane, graciously offered to change with me. No strain, and nobody the worse for not knowing. For Jane and me it was starting anew, our first night in bed. We had made love for five consecutive nights, yet were both incredibly filled with desire. She wore an attractive little white gown, but only for a few moments. We left on a small light and looked into each other's eyes, deeply and endearingly, through embrace and passion.

In the morning the group ate at breakfast together for the last time. Miller was a good host, though now he had his mind on preparation for the next riders arriving that afternoon. John Townsley, the national park superintendent (who had succeeded Jack Anderson on his retirement), joined us. By prearrangement, he came to meet me at Cooke City and to take me for a couple of days with him in the park. Officials have done these kinds of things for me. Though I have no status, title, or delegated authority, I think they assume that I have a certain influence, or conscience they need to turn to, or some instrumentality of principle by which to measure their performance. On the other hand, some are frightened, intimidated, or repelled at my inquisitiveness into their management of public property and at my published criticism of their agency or the leadership of the Interior Department. They would rather not have me around or provide me with legitimacy by association. What they want least in their lives and careers in controversy. Townsley could handle it. He was a huge fellow, at least six feet four and 250 pounds. His father had been a ranger before him, a point of pride, but his belt lay around his frame well below the equator and he clearly lacked the carriage one might expect of a park superintendent. Running Yellowstone is considered the second most important job in the National Park Service, second to the director in Washington. That park is a principality in its own right, with wild animals, millions of visitors, crime, politics, and a thousand pressures, and the park superintendent is the prince in power. Many of the park personnel held Townsley in scorn, considering him more politician than preservationist, but it is difficult to be otherwise.

Jane was going back to Billings and to a convention in Colorado. Her expression at breakfast reflected an afterglow of the last night together, and of the entire week. Her eyes filled with love and longing. We sat next to each other and touched hands beneath the table even while Townsley was answering questions about one thing and another relating to Yellowstone. We rose and walked outside while the others sat and talked—for a final kiss and embrace, scarcely daring to think we would ever be together again. As the future unfolded, we did meet. I would phone her and we would rendezvous once a month. She was always ready while love was still fresh, even when it was difficult for her. One night in New

York we had dinner at the Carnegie Tavern, the glassed-in side-walk-café section, from which we watched the snowflakes outside. Though she was pale and seemingly cool as always, her face was aglow from the candles at the table. Jane leaned forward, took both my hands in hers, and shaped the words to her lips, "I love you," without uttering a sound. "I love you more than loving," she said another time. Perhaps she felt this way, loving, longing, and yearning, because I lay beyond reach, except for these stolen little interludes, and would always be going home; I cared not what her inner reason might be, and responded in kind.

Ralph Miller invited me as his guest the following summer. I couldn't make it, but the second summer I was able to and accepted. He wanted me to bring Jane, but she was busy studying for her doctorate, busy with her professional career and holistic health interests, busy with other pursuits, and she didn't want to return to Yellowstone, having been there once, which, she said, was enough for her. Our relationship had endured more or less through temperamental lows as well as romantic highs. She wasn't sure that she wanted me, but didn't want to lose me either. Despite the uncertainties in my life, I was also now possessed of a new freedom. I accepted the opportunity to be at the University of Idaho for a year, at least, with Yellowstone conveniently en route. Jane and I would have a respite, time to determine our respective and mutual futures.

I returned to dear little Cooke City, with its one street through town, and the same motel, with its memories, and the single room in which I had stayed before. It was Rendezvous Week, the liveliest time of year, with entertainment in the bars, cancan dancers in the street, and all kinds of vehicles, from massive motor homes to motorcycles and bicycles, and all kinds of people, old straights and young shaggies, backpackers, Boy Scouts, and artsy-craftsy groupies. Summer is the time when Cooke City, West Yellowstone, and a hundred other communities like them must make it for the year. Wilderness in their backyards is their bread and butter, yet they are dissonant, like flimsy stage sets thrown up for the moment, in contrast with the backdrop of wild nature, designed to last forever.

Ralph and Candy were still Ralph and Candy, lean and pressured by logistics of one trip after another throughout the summer and by bills to pay during their brief interludes in Cooke City. Ralph was a bit of a masochist, pushing and punishing himself, alternately kind and brusque to others, as though the trip itself were part of some larger mission. He had succeeded in getting into veterinary school at Tufts in Boston. (Apparently the route to becoming a DVM is even tougher than to becoming an MD.) His speech was still rough and unrefined, but now he could spice his horse talk with academic jargon and explain with ease the anatomy and behavior of the animal. Candy had studied sculpture in Minneapolis, pottery in Vermont, and had managed a restaurant in the Berkshires. Now she was studying architecture and had transferred from Montana State to the Rhode Island School of Design in order to be with Ralph.

The two cash customers on the trip, Jeff and Cindy, were a married New England couple in their mid-thirties, both lawyers. I mentioned them in Chapter I as having been out with Ralph a couple of years before. Oddly, even with two clients he could still make a profit—predicated on his own and Candy's long hours and hard work. I also mentioned Mary Ellen, age twenty-seven, a friend of Candy who joined the party after driving her microbus solo across country without evident pain or strain.

From the familiar Soda Butte trailhead we rode across the meadows and into the mountains. Candy led a foal, age two and a half months, named High Roller, sleek and frisky, a luscious golden tan in color, that wanted to be with its mother, Dakota, one of the string. Candy, graceful, unprepossessing, slugging it out and taking the hard knocks on the trail, and the foal could have been clipped from a western movie. And so could the scenery. We passed a lone bull moose, then a herd of elk. Rolling clouds and light rain gave way to a clear blue sky. In every setting different combinations of wildflowers grew. Masses of bluebells, buttercups, and tall sunflowers swept across the open meadows. Small wintergreen with white flowers claimed the shady dells. We saw lots of lupine, penstemon, and paintbrush, reminders of how colorful and rich the Yellowstone can be; or any wilderness for that matter, ever endowed with natural forms and colors, though less gaudy, or showy, on one day than another. The challenge is to observe and perceive, without demanding all the answers, as scientists and re-source technicians in forestry, range, and wildlife insist upon doing. The ultimate answer is wrapped in mystery anyway, and you don't have to understand nature in order to respect it and to want it left whole.

We camped the first night in the high meadows at the head of Opal Creek, the very site from which we had seen the grizzly on the trip with Jane. The horses stood quietly at pasture, most of them resting on one hind leg, locking moving parts in place so they could sleep standing up. Candy had loaned me a bizarre paperback novel, *Pinball*, by Jerzy Kosinski, which I read until dark. The promotion blurb on the back cover called it "a forceful new novel of genius and evil," then adding: "Ricocheting with humor, burst-ing with sensuality and exploding with violence—it is a game as intricate, unpredictable and complex as life." The book was all of that, yet its unlikely scenario could not compare with the wilder-ness life around me. Wilderness is intricate, unpredictable, com-plex; it evokes emotion and sensuality, and stirs genius and evil. It explodes with violence and conflict—the violence of weather in its many moods, the conflict among species in the mosaic of life and death, the broader conflict of man against nature, the resistance of wild places to the genius of technology, with the end foretold in natural law, the movements and forces of earth beyond understand-ing and control.

Wilderness as I see it demands humility. It places princes and peasants on the same footing in a magic, hypnotic time frame. Nor-mal relationships lose meaning or relevance, at least for the while. Jeff and Cindy, alas, remained consciously upscale. He spoke repeatedly about his and his wife's accomplishments and worldly acquisitions as though they really mattered. He would trot his horse when told not to, and ride too close to the pack animals. He and Cindy were bright and physically strong enough to manage on their own, and it would have done them a lot of good if they had to.

Mary Ellen was more appealing. She was raised at Stamford, Connecticut, from which her father commuted daily to some corpo-rate headquarters in New York. She was never interested in his work—sad, I'd say, for them both. She had studied environmental horticulture at the University of Connecticut, disappointed that it had nothing to do with the organic approach, but then universities by their nature tend to be conservative and cautious, close to established ways of business. Instead of following a professional route after graduation, she worked at little jobs—the restaurant, a farm, a ski resort, gardening—in Vermont, the Berkshires, Santa Fe. She was a willing worker, with no assignment around the camp too small for her. It wasn't simply repayment for a free trip, but rather that she wanted to experience each and every aspect of camp life, to learn to care for horses, and to be useful.

One evening Mary Ellen, Ralph, and I rode our horses to observe sunset from a high ridge above our camp on Pelican Creek. We had been through a long day on the trail, but Mary Ellen, like Jane, was determined to capitalize on every opportunity. We rode through magic moments, time that is timeless. Far from city lights, I followed with my eye the course of changing natural colors, soft white and gradient blues and bronzes, light and shadow of fading day merging with oncoming night under a waxing moon, nearly full.

In virtually every meadow a herd of elk fed undisturbed. Once elk thrived on the grassy plains. As settlers claimed valleys and meadows, the handsome wapiti retreated to high, timbered country. They adapted to Yellowstone, benefiting from annihilation of wolves and mountain lions, and multiplied. During brief spring and fleeting summer, elk make the most of the lush meadows (as do bear and bison) before snows force them to retreat to the lowlands. During a harsh winter, elk are subject to die-off, their carcasses feeding scavengers, including the grizzly.

We rode past a massive solitary bison feeding on rich clover and grasses, and then three coyotes scouting the edges of an elk herd, ready to pick off one that might be weak or stray. I listened intently to the songs of twilight in wild country, variously shrill, soft, groaning, cooing, and melodic and harmonic in their own way. They were mostly, but not altogether, eventide voices of elk. We looked across Yellowstone's unscarred forests, here and there vapors rising like clouds from the thermals, and Yellowstone Lake reflecting the rosy alpenglow, and beyond, far to the south, the jagged snowtopped Tetons scraping the clear Wyoming sky, and, to the east and north, the granite Absarokas and Beartooths.

It was a momentous experience, of course, but I have wondered about rights and privileges, including my own, in wild country. I wonder about the effects of people washing in a stream in which native fish are dependent on clean, clear water, about the impact of horses on vegetation and terrain, about the impact of horses and people on elk in their feeding and resting areas, and about the principle of wilderness invaded for the pleasure of cash customers. One day we rode past an eagle's nest, which Ralph had particularly wanted to show. We were very close to it and Jeff was taking pictures, while the male eagle was dive-bombing and shrieking and trying to divert us. That concerned me and I asked myself, "Do I belong here? If so, by what right?" Near the end of the trip we went to Hoodoo Basin and climbed Hoodoo Peak, a soft formation crumbling under our feet. How many pairs of boots could Hoodoo absorb and still be a peak?

Whatever the answer, I don't have the right to moralize either. But I will try to make it through the question by recounting the time I was engaged to write a guide to the national parks for Kodak. About midway through the project, an official of that company telephoned. "Listen," he said, "you're making it too difficult for people to take pictures." "Maybe so," I responded, "but I'm not writing this book to sell your film. I'm writing it to show people how to appreciate the parks through the medium of a camera." There ought to be a way and we may get to it yet, hopefully before the last grizzly is gone.

CHAPTER X

─────── ❧ ───────

William O. Douglas: Child of the Cascades, Following His Own Star

In the kitchen of their little wilderness resort, which was semi-retired like themselves, Kay Kershaw and Isabelle Lynn of the Double K Ranch reminisced about their next-door neighbor at Goose Prairie, the late William Orville Douglas, their hero and mine.

"We took him on many, many pack trips," said Isabelle. "He was an absolutely great person to have on a pack trip. The worse things got the better Bill liked it. I have a mental picture of Bill standing at the campfire with his poncho blowing straight out and a big grin on his face while the rain came down. He loved it. He wasn't a glutton for punishment, but he liked the idea of being an outdoor man and he was good at it."

I never made a wilderness trip with Justice Douglas, as did some of the friends we shared, but I had known him in Washington—not well, but well enough to grasp Isabelle's description and flesh it out in my own mind. Douglas epitomized hardiness, the vigor of the outdoors. We had lunch together a time or two and I would see him at parties here and there. Once he generously counseled my daughter when she was considering studying law. His

181

mind was quick and his body kept up with it. He was built sturdy, ruddy-complected from his life outdoors, and twinkle-eyed. I knew Joanie and Cathy, the last two of his four wives, younger than the children of his first wife, but then vitality is ageless. I admired his writing, not that it was literary quality, but he knew whereof he spoke. I doubt that any judge, or any lawyer, has had a better comprehension of conservation issues, wilderness in particular, and been more influential with bold ideas. From Justice Douglas I received a supreme compliment when in a Supreme Court opinion (the Mineral King dissent) he quoted from some things I had written, not once but four times.

"We had one disaster with him," Isabelle continued. "Not a disaster. We had a pack trip planned that he was part of and we had eight or nine other people signed up. Just as we were about to start the rangers closed the national forest because of fire danger. This was the first time they had done so.

"Once the danger was over, Bill came by and said, 'I want to go on this pack trip.' We told him that all the guests had left. 'That doesn't make any difference. I'll pay for it. I want to go.' The packer who was going to do this job for us had left to drive a truck somewhere. Kay and I spent the night till eleven o'clock trying to find somebody to pack this trip. It was for Bill and Cathy and Jack Larson, Bill's friend, a botanist, who had been with the Forest Service. He came into the Forest Service with ideals, but didn't stay.

"We got a packer who turned out to be no packer at all. Things were strewn all over the hillside before we got anywhere. Luckily, we had our own wrangler with us; he had no experience in the packing line, but he learned fast. We were going to Carnalita Basin, a marvelous place right under Bismarck Peak in the Cougar Lakes, with rock walls all around it. It was September, but it wasn't marvelous that night because there was a blizzard. The packer had all the tents and stoves and sleeping bags, but he got lost and never got there. We had nothing.

"I had a pint of brandy in my saddlebag and passed that around. Most of it leaked in the night. Everybody said, 'You drank it.' I didn't. That was some kind of night. Anything can happen when you go out in these mountains. It was cold and the wind was blowing—it was like a mixing bowl."

"When you say you're not going to do it," interjected Kay, "don't do it." I've heard that idea variously expressed, the general idea being that a wilderness trip starting poorly will be jinxed all the way. Kay and Isabelle were good talkers, self-reliant women, each with opinions of her own, interrupting, correcting, and complementing the other. Kay was a little older, I thought, in her early seventies, but in this little dialogue Isabelle was principal narrator.

"Kay and I were lucky. We both had rain suits. That's all we had, just the clothes we were wearing as we stood out there. We built a fire, but you couldn't get close to it because the wind was terrific. Nobody really suffered. Bill entertained us all night telling about similar horrible situations he had been in. Where guides went off and left him. Things like that. He was terrific. You might say he got us through the night."

"It let up the next day," Kay added, "but you can't go into the mountains and not find yourself in some kind of snowstorm or rain. But don't go out and look for trouble!"

I came to Goose Prairie in the summer of 1983, combining it with a visit to Mount Rainier, which rises high above it a few miles to the west, with the crest of the Cascade Range between them (or sixteen miles from Goose Prairie). Goose Prairie is not a town, but a settlement of homes, cottages, and cabins spread across 160 acres, the standard size of a homestead claimed under the historic Homestead Act. Tom Fife, the original homesteader, owned all this fragment of mountain paradise perched at 3,400 feet elevation between two mountain ranges about a mile and a half apart. There is mail delivery, but no telephone, which makes communication with Kay and Isabelle a little old-fashioned, but plenty adequate from their viewpoint. The community is encircled by national forestland, which the two ladies, aided by Justice Douglas until his death, and by many others, have long campaigned to be classified as the Cougar Lakes Wilderness, though not yet with success.

This is the country that Bill Douglas called home. And what a home it was: in the heart of the evergreen Cascade forests and the mighty snowcapped volcanic cones, Mount Rainier, Mount Adams, and Mount St. Helens. Bill knew this country as well as he knew the law books. "I am part of the rhythm of the place," he would say. He had experienced the country since his boyhood in Yakima, forty miles east. He hiked, rode horseback, camped, and fished all over the Cougar Lakes and Little Cougar Lakes, and doubtless was deeply influenced by the setting and spirit of the deep-blue lakes cradled by green conifers and sunlit patches of snow on the surrounding ridges.

Douglas sat on the Supreme Court in Washington when it was in session, and traveled to many places all across the globe when it was not, but Goose Prairie and the Cascades were his home turf. He purchased twelve acres on high ground adjoining the Double K Ranch (for Kay Kershaw), and built the house for himself and Cathy, planting around it Canadian dogwood, mountain azalea, Oregon grape, and other Cascade plants. He could follow trails in any direction into the high country. He observed a few golden eagles frequenting the peaks, the ferruginous hawk sweeping the valley in search of its favorite prey, the golden-mantled ground squirrel. He noted abundant life in wilderness and its edges, from toads and weasels and deer feeding in clover every summer evening to snowy owl and horned owl, the great Bubo, master of the night air.

My friend Harvey Broome came out from Tennessee while he was president of the Wilderness Society to ride the Cougar Lakes country with Bill (and Kay), just as Douglas would go back to the Great Smokies to hike and camp with Harvey and his wife, Anne. Bill was anything but provincial, relentlessly exploring a lot of places with different kinds of wilderness people, like Willard Jalbert, the canoe guide in Maine; Caroll Noble, the Wyoming rancher; Olaus Murie, the field biologist; Wade Hall, the forest ranger of eastern Oregon, and Richard L. Neuberger, Oregon journalist, author, and United States senator (whom Douglas considered pretty much of a drugstore cowboy—that is, inexpert in outdoor ways—but a solid citizen nonetheless). Every place was important to him. "If we are to survive," he wrote, based on a Maine experience, "we must make Katahdin the symbol of our struggle for independence from the machine that promises to enslave us. We must multiply the Baxter Parks a thousand-fold in order to accommodate our burgeoning population. We must provide enough wilderness areas so that, no matter how dense our population, man—though apartment-born—may attend the great school of the outdoors, and come to know the joy of walking the woods, alone and unafraid."

Everything about Douglas marks him as a democrat. From a childhood of poverty he rose to prominence and security. The same was true of Richard M. Nixon and Ronald Reagan. They, however, allied themselves with wealth, conceiving wealth to be indivisible with power, while Douglas saw nobility and grandeur in all things humble. I think of him as the epitome of the old Northwest populism—in his carriage and conduct, and in his attitude toward the land and the law.

He and friends would recount experiences in mistaken identity of the Supreme Court Justice on the trail. Once Douglas was headed for a rendezvous with a companion with whom he planned to climb Mount Adams. But his car broke down on the way and he had to hike several hours under a hot sun to find a mechanic. He had on climbing shoes, without extra socks, and developed a painful blister. He decided to seek medical attention and located a doctor's office, where the nurse seemed horrified at this nondescript person coming off the street in tattered shirt and Levi's. The doctor thought him an indigent and directed him to a clinic a "half dozen blocks down the street that takes care of all the bums." When Douglas waved green bills, the doctor apologized and treated the blister. Still not revealing his identity, Douglas said the law was ahead of medicine: that if the physician lost his license and was indigent, the highest court in the land would hear his case, while waiving all filing fees and assigning him a competent lawyer. "How do you know all that?" the physician demanded. "Because I seem to spend a lot of time there." (Which recalls a Mark Twain story. Arriving in town early for an evening lecture, the celebrated humorist was dismayed at the lack of posters in evidence. Slipping into a chair at the barber shop, he inquired slyly, "Anything to do around here of an evening?" "Yep, Mark Twain's at the lyceum. Every seat is taken. You'll have to stand to hear him." "Hmm," groused the author, "that happens to me whenever that fellow makes a speech.")

Despite my admiration for Justice Douglas, I had not originally thought of him as one of the personalities to be treated in this work. I had not considered the Cascades either, though they consitute the major stronghold of wilderness in the lower forty-eight states and they were only four or five hours by car from my new home in north Idaho. Luckily, I was invited to Wenatchee, in central Washington, in the spring of 1983, to speak at a workshop of Forest Service rangers. The day following the meeting Dick Buscher, a Forest Service veteran, took me for a look at some of the country, including a short hike in the Alpine Lakes Wilderness. In years past I had seen other portions of the Cascades, but this was my first visit into this domain in which more than seven hundred lakes, formed by glaciers, lay in the wooded valleys and among the high, rocky peaks between Wenatchee and Seattle. Dick mentioned the Cougar Lakes, then Justice Douglas and Goose Prairie, the Double K and Kay Kershaw and Isabelle Lynn, and I knew that I must go there. A few years earlier I had had some correspondence with Isabelle while she was on the board of the National Parks and Conservation Association, so we were not exactly strangers. Dick mentioned that they had no phone and I would have to make arrangements by mail. But to which of them should I write? "Be smart. Address your letter to them both," he cautioned.

To me the Cascades have always been a high wave of western green glory, untamed and unbroken except for the distinctive volcanic summits that whiten the horizon with perpetual cover of snow. In our time significant portions have been civilized and scarred, but I prefer this primitive image. Each part of the range has its distinct personality, clinging to its natural origins. Mount Rainier, the loftiest volcanic peak, is a gleaming landmark visible for hundreds of miles when the weather is clear. The summit reaches 14,410 feet into the atmosphere, intercepting tides of moist air flowing eastward from the Pacific. The consequences are spectacular cloud halos—they appear at times like rounded icebergs floating on a sea of clouds—and world record snowfalls. About forty square miles of icy glacial rivers cap the mountain in its perpetual winter. But Rainier is only one of the fraternity of giants in the range, extending nearly seven hundred miles from Mount Baker and Mount Shuksan, at the Canadian border, south to Mount Shasta and Lassen Peak, in northern California, including between them in Washington State and Oregon: Mount Adams, Mount St. Helens, Mount Jefferson, the Three Sisters, Mount Hood, and Mount Mazama, the collapsed volcano of Crater Lake. The violent eruption of St. Helens in 1980 came as a reminder that this region has been the scene of earthly cataclysms over millions of years. St. Helens, most symmetrical of Cascade volcanoes, the "American Fujiyama," has been the most active volcano in the country outside Alaska, scarcely going more than 100 to 150 years without an eruption. They all form part of the Pacific "Ring of Fire" that arcs from South America to Alaska, Japan, and Indonesia and includes three fourths of the world's active volcanoes.

There is more to the Cascades than the volcanic giants. The most dramatic section, the North Cascade Range, mostly between eight thousand and nine thousand feet, comprises an untouched landscape of what the Swiss would describe as pinnacles, massifs, ridges, and cols, flanked by glaciers and snowfields feeding cirque lakes and streams. The Alpine Lakes Wilderness is one of the few large masses of land in the Cascades not dominated by a volcanic peak; it embraces the handiwork of glaciers in those seven hundred lakes.

Cascades—the word has a liquid, magic ring to it. The name evidently was bestowed by another Douglas, David Douglas, the roving Scottish botanist, during his travels in the 1820s. John C. Frémont twenty years later added his approval, noting the flow of rivers, especially of the Columbia, from the heart of the range. On the western slope, where the mountains meet the Pacific winds, moisture and rain are abundant. Plant life rises to giant ferns, flowering plants, and shrubs, and trees to the dominant species, the Douglas fir, a massive, mighty tree of Northwest wilderness, named for David Douglas after he had brought a specimen back to England for the Royal Horticultural Society. But after crossing the Cascade crest, moisture diminishes sharply. Douglas fir yields to ponderosa pine, which grows on drier sites. Then moisture all but disappears; the landscape becomes an arid, treeless plateau better suited to farming and ranching than to timber.

I began to learn the vegetation of the Northwest and the different ways of viewing it when I came out in 1960 researching my first book on the national forests. On the Olympic Peninsula I walked with a ranger along Willaby Gorge, in the heart of a glorious rain forest. I asked him to identify one species of tree or shrub, and then another and another—there were so many of them, each somehow distinctive, whether in size, form, or coloration—but the ranger knew only a few and they were principally the "merchantable" species, those with commercial market value as timber. He seemed oblivious to the crooked vine maple sprawling over the water in the bottom of the gorge, where it mingled with red alder, denigrated as a "weed tree," yet covered with lovely grayish bark (in reality a mass of lichens feeding on the bark), and to the pointed sword ferns growing on the bank as tall as young trees, furnishing a green background to blooming shrubs, berries, and wildflowers. A few days later, on the west slope of the Cascades, I walked with another ranger in the Suiattle drainage. He loved the tall trees, the big Douglas fir, and felt they were of more value standing in place than as logged timber, but his professional forestry colleagues mocked him as a "dickey-bird watcher."

The big trees of the Northwest, growing in the country's last significant virgin forests, have beauty and personality. They appeal to those who love living things. The western red cedar, growing largely in moist valley bottoms, reaches heights of 175 feet; it has a cinnamon-red fibrous bark and flat, lacy sprays of almost fernlike leaves. The western hemlock, a little smaller, grows at elevations up to 3000 feet, a tree of dignity, with dark russet-brown bark, showing abundant and long cones at the ends of its branches, the top shoot, with glossy green leaves, bending in a graceful arc. Of all the trees on this continent, the Douglas fir, thriving in deep valley soils above the undergrowth of fir, hemlock, and cedar, is second in size only to the giant sequoia. Stately, wonderfully proportioned, the Douglas fir grows to 250 feet, sometimes 300, with a clean shaft, clear of limbs for 100 feet; the larger trees may be from 400 to 1000 years old. It bears resemblance to spruce and fir, as well as hemlock and yew; its scientific name, *Pseudotsuga taxifolia*, means "false hemlock with yewlike leaf," though it is now known as *Pseudotsuga menziesii*. As a timber source, it is the most important tree in Northwest, prized for its strength and immense size, free of knots and other defects.

Douglas-fir forests are sheer green-gold. In the national parks of the Northwest—Mount Rainier, North Cascades, and Olympic in Washington, and Mount Hood in Oregon—trees are beyond the reach of loggers, much to their chagrin. The national forests, far more extensive in size, are open territory, except for those portions specifically set aside and classified as wilderness. From an airplane window, or from the summit of any mountain peak, telltale signs of modern logging in huge, brown, open blocks checkerboard the green. Because the remotest portions of the Cascades are accessible and conquerable, the sense of beauty and naturalness is degraded.

Trees have value, whether as scenery or timber, that has been determined, but do trees have rights? If so, who speaks for the trees? In 1974 a California law professor, Christopher D. Stone, published a challenging slender book titled *Should Trees Have Standing?*, with the subtitle, *Toward Legal Rights for Natural Objects*. To some degree it was derived from a work already done by William O. Douglas; Part II of the book consists of the Supreme Court decision in the Mineral King case. The Sierra Club had brought suit to block the Forest Service from opening Mineral King Valley in the Sierra Nevada Mountains of California to commercial development by Walt Disney Enterprises, Inc. The majority of the high court ruled the Club lacked standing, that it was seeking to vindicate its own value preferences through the judicial process. In his dissent, Justice Douglas declared as follows:

"Contemporary public concern for protecting nature's ecological equilibrium should lead to the conferral of standing upon environmental objects to sue for their own preservation. . . .

"The ordinary corporation is a 'person' for the purposes of the adjudicatory processes, whether it represents proprietary, spiritual, aesthetic, or charitable causes.

"So should it be as respects valleys, alpine meadows, rivers, lakes, estuaries, beaches, ridges, groves of trees, swampland, or even air that feels the destructive pressures of modern technology and modern life. The river, for example, is the living symbol of all the life it sustains or nourishes, fish, aquatic insects, water ouzels, otter, fisher, deer, elk, bear, and all other animals, including man, who are dependent on it or who enjoy it for its sight, its sound, or its life. The river as plaintiff speaks for the ecological unit of life that is part of it. Those people who have a meaningful relationship

189

to that body of water—whether it be a fisherman, a canoeist, a zoologist, or a logger—must be able to speak for the values which the river represents and which are threatened with destruction. . . .

"Those who hike the Appalachian Trial into Sunfish Pond, New Jersey, and camp or sleep there, or run the Allagash in Maine, or climb the Guadalupes in West Texas, or who canoe and portage the Quetico Superior in Minnesota, certainly should have standing to defend those natural wonders before courts or agencies, though they live 3000 miles away. . . . Those inarticulate members of the ecological group cannot speak. But those people who have so frequented the place as to know its values and wonders will be able to speak for the entire ecological community."

Though his fellow Justices remained unmoved by his plea, they plainly respected his singular wisdom in wilderness and nature issues based on intimate, first-hand field experience to complement his legal acumen. In another important case, involving Hells Canyon on the Snake River, the deepest gorge on the North American continent, the court ruled, with Justice Douglas writing the decision, in behalf of river values without a dollar sign.

That was an exciting event, wholly unexpected, reopening a case that already seemed signed and sealed, in a cause that seemed lost. In 1964 a syndicate of four private utilities had been granted a license by the Federal Power Commission to construct the 670-foot High Mountain Sheep Dam, south of Lewiston, Idaho. But it was opposed in a legal dispute by a combine of eighteen public power utilities, the Washington Public Power System. These promoters, public and private, called Hells Canyon, which lies between Idaho and Oregon, "the last major hydroelectric site in the United States," as though it's indecent and sinful to leave alone the works that God hath wrought.

The Snake is the second longest river in the Northwest, flowing from headwaters in the mountains of western Wyoming across Idaho, picking up the waters of its tributaries (including the Salmon, a major stream in its own right) before joining the Columbia. When the case came before the Supreme Court, the Snake had already largely been bottled by dams. Only a little more than one hundred miles remained untamed, unspoiled, in the very middle, flowing through the deepest canyons and embracing the wildest stretches of white water. This section holds a magic fascination for scientists, boatmen, fishermen, hikers, hunters, botanists, and archaeologists.

The Supreme Court afforded Hells Canyon a second chance when in June 1967 it directed the Federal Power Commission to reconsider its license—not simply as to which utility should receive it, but whether *any* dam should be built. Aren't there other criteria than economics, the high court asked, for determining the fate of wild land not specifically protected? To put it another way, though Hells Canyon may not be as renowned as the Grand Canyon of the Colorado, this doesn't mean it is any less of a national treasure, or less worth saving in its natural state. As Justice Douglas declared in behalf of the court: "The test is whether the project will be in the public interest and that determination can be made only after an exploration of all issues relevant to the public interest. These include future power demand and supply in the area, alternate sources of power, and the public interest in preserving reaches of wild river in wilderness areas and the preservation of anadromous fish for commercial and recreational purposes, and the protection of wildlife."

The decision gave heart to conservationists, who renewed their fight to save Hells Canyon from any dams. Dr. William L. Blackadar, of Salmon, Idaho, turned up at a Lewiston hearing after riding thirty-five miles in his kayak through huge waves and rapids. "We do not realize the potential of this area," he said in his testimony. "Eight years ago the first fiberglass slalom kayak was designed. At that time less than five hundred people were rafting the Middle Fork of the Salmon River annually. Now over ten times that number run the river and for the first time sizable numbers of kayaks have appeared. This area will soon be alive with these 'banana' boats. Isn't it great these challenges await us? Wouldn't it be sad to think these bigger waves might be hidden under hundreds of feet of water? There are few areas left and these will become priceless."

I went up Hells Canyon from Lewiston in 1969. With three companions from the Forest Service (which administers most of the land on both the Oregon and Idaho sides) and a photographer, we rode aboard the stubby, forty-eight-foot *Idaho Queen II*, which held the contract to deliver mail to isolated upstream ranches; then we switched to horses to camp and ride out on the Oregon side. The river flowed swift and deep, winding through bend after bend of great gorges, with rapids as wild as boiling water. I was amazed at the number and variety of birds: eagles and falcons using the high canyons for isolation in breeding; herons soaring overhead and gathering food along the riverbanks; Canada geese nesting in the cliffs; partridge, quail, and grouse, and, most numerous, chukar coveys popping up everywhere, though this species of game fowl had been introduced from Europe only fifteen years before.

The dam has never been built, despite efforts of the Department of the Interior, under one of our conservation heroes, Stewart L. Udall, to see it through. I won't say that Hells Canyon remains unchanged, but it remains undammed. Likely it would have been otherwise had Bill Douglas been a country lawyer or a country teacher or the dean of a law school.

Wilderness and conservation were not the only personal interests that Douglas infused into his Supreme Court opinions. He was a strong-willed civil libertarian, bucking the public tide when need be. In 1953 he issued a stay of execution in the espionage case of Julius and Ethel Rosenberg. He alone voted to grant a new trial to Alger Hiss. As he recorded later: "Apart from the legal issues never conclusively resolved, the result of the Hiss case was to exalt the informer, who in Anglo-American history has had an odious history. It gave agencies of the federal government unparalleled power over the private lives of citizens. It initiated the regime of sheeplike conformity by intimidating the curiosity and idealism of our youth. It fashioned a powerful political weapon out of vigilantism."

The Rosenberg and Hiss cases were hallmarks of the 1950s, the season for blacklists and witch hunts, for Congressional scaremongers such as Martin Dies, J. Parnell Thomas, the young Richard Nixon, and Joe McCarthy, reaching out to stultify expression and communication. "The bureaucracies, both inside and outside government," Douglas wrote, "became more staid, more like-minded, less imaginative, and much, much less courageous." My own experience in environmental writing tells me this assessment

192

is correct. Editors scarcely stimulate or welcome or tolerate ideas that depart from a safe norm. And society is the loser.

Douglas epitomized bold intellectuality. He suffered enemies, who insisted he must be a secret Communist, a Communist sympathizer, or, in the least, a dangerous screwball. They clouded the issues of principle; they obscured the essence of his critique of institutional bureaucracy. Referring to the Tennessee Valley Authority, a New Deal agency which in time became strongly aligned with antienvironmentalism, he wrote as follows: "I was for TVA when it was launched, but what I saw of it in the next decade appalled me. TVA was viable in purpose but run by men over whom the people had a very remote, attenuated control. These administrators fulfilled the legal standard of the 'public interest' by applying their own personal conceptions of the public good. They were inspired to perpetuate their regime and make it bigger and more powerful by building dams endlessly and branching out in numerous similar fields. Later when I got to communist lands, I saw monolithic bureaucracy in all its crushing power; it exploited the common man and was beyond effective control even by the Politburo."

His detractors detested his far-ranging activism. Why, they demanded, couldn't he exercise judicial restraint and propriety? He brushed them off, unbending: "A man or woman who becomes a Justice should try to stay alive; a lifetime diet of the law turns most judges into dull, dry husks."

He and his court colleague, Hugo Black, were close in their concept of civil liberty. Douglas especially favored this statement of creed by the Alabaman:

"Our own free society should never forget that laws which stigmatize and penalize thought and speech of the unorthodox have a way of reaching, ensnaring, and silencing many more people than at first intended. We must have freedom of speech for all or we will in the long run have it for none but the cringing and the craven. And I cannot too often repeat my belief that the right to speak on matters of public concern must be wholly free or eventually be wholly lost."

President Nixon, Vice-President Spiro Agnew, and House Minority Leader Gerald Ford in 1970 sought to impeach Douglas. They tried to prove that no individual can buck the system and make it, that the establishment is bigger than any or all of its parts. Douglas, however, was too much of a scrapper, a frontier populist, to be silenced or intimidated. He was one of the movers and shakers of modern times, based on a simple principle of freedom in an industrial age, which he expressed as follows:

"In this century big business has been anti-free enterprise. Acquisition of wealth and power took priority over the development of the moral capacities of the individual. Big business behaved like bandits raiding a frontier. The gospel of wealth was equated with man's dignity before God; exploiting the community became a way of life. Material values were bedecked with moral or ethical values. The 'liberty' of industrial giants to become heads of powerful principalities with great political clout was honored by the courts though these giants had no technical competency to do anything except to make money. It is indeed ironical that in this technological age industry cannot make a pollution-free car or mine sulfur in smokestacks rather than in the ground."

Bill Douglas followed his own star, though the course was not always easy. He was born in rural Minnesota in 1898, the second of three children. His father, a Presbyterian minister, took the family west, settling in rural Washington. Bill was a weakling with puny legs, a victim of polio at the age of two or three; an attending physician, in fact, predicted he would not live past forty. When he was six his father died, leaving the family impoverished so that, even as children, he and his brother and sister were forced to work as fruit pickers in the fields. It was the beginning of tough youthful labors that showed him the humble side of life, and the seamy side. At one time or another he was a pinboy in a bowling alley, a ticket taker in side shows at the county fair, a stool pigeon for a sanctimonious preacher spying on prostitutes (for whom he developed more empathy than for the preacher); he drove a one-horse ice wagon, worked with harvest crews in the wheat lands of eastern Washington, rode the rails in the hobo style to find work, fraternized with Chicanos, Indians, and Wobblies, the militants of the Industrial Workers of the World. Even while in college he would have at least two jobs going, principally one as a janitor and the other at a boardinghouse in return for his meals.

Because he was sickly as a boy, he took to studies, excelling and leading his class. As valedictorian at Yakima, he won a scholarship to Whitman College at Walla Walla, which otherwise would have been beyond reach. Because he was puny and picked on by tougher kids, he took to exercise and hiking, first in the foothills, then in the higher Cascades. He staked the wild country between Mount Adams and Mount Rainier as his domain, climbing most of the peaks, exploring the ridges, camping, and fishing for trout.

Following college he became a high school teacher, but decided to study law at Columbia. He rode the rails to the East, sleeping in hobo jungles en route and arriving in New York with six cents in his pocket. He worked his way through law school doing various and sundry jobs, including tutoring, for which he collected increasingly good fees. After graduation he worked for a law firm on Wall Street, taught law at Columbia, then at Yale. He was regarded as a brilliant comer and tapped for the New Deal, first as a member, then as chairman, of the Securities and Exchange Commission. In 1939 President Roosevelt appointed him to the Supreme Court (to succeed Louis D. Brandeis, the classic apostle of civil liberty), where he would serve until his retirement in November 1975, longer than any other Justice.

He had a lot of experience with the outdoors and outdoors people. His interest and involvement were unflagging. He became widely recognized in 1954, when he determined to save a little bit of nature in the backyard of the nation's capital. That was the year *The Washington Post* published an editorial favoring a plan to construct a parkway along the Chesapeake and Ohio Canal. It stirred Douglas's blood. In a letter to the editor he described the canal and its environment as a long stretch of quiet and peace "not yet marred by the roar of wheels and sound of horns." He challenged the author of the editorial to come out and hike the 185 miles of canal towpath between Washington and Cumberland, in western Maryland. The result was a gala protest hike. Douglas and thirty-six others took the train to Cumberland and started hiking down the towpath parallel to the Potomac River through rolling pastureland and Appalachian mountain gaps and past small historic towns. Some dropped out along the way. The Immortal Nine, eight men and a woman, including Bill Douglas, Olaus Murie, and Harvey Broome, completed the full journey, reaching Washington to cheers and a repentant editor who had learned his lesson and reversed his stand.

From then on Douglas was sought to support nature preservation efforts in all parts of the country. He responded to calls from Kentucky, Tennessee, Arkansas, Maine, Wyoming, Texas, not only with his person but with his pen, contributing a stream of articles to national periodicals and more books than most professional full-time authors would produce during the same period—all this plus his foreign expeditions and books about those exotic distant places. At the root of his passion was love of the earth, the American earth, as evidenced in *My Wilderness: The Pacific West* and *My Wilderness: East to Katahdin*.

I saw Justice Douglas in May 1977. He had suffered a stroke in December 1974 and retired in November 1975. Shortly after he left the court, legislation had been introduced in Congress to dedicate the Chesapeake and Ohio National Historical Park to him and it had lately, in March 1977, been enacted, commemorating the park to Justice Douglas "in grateful recognition of his long outstanding service as a prominent American conservationist and for his efforts to preserve and protect the canal and towpath from development."

Now it was time for a ceremony and the unveiling of a bronze bust beside the canal in Georgetown, the oldest part of Washington, the starting point of the canal that was intended to open commerce with the West. It was a bright and balmy day, with chairs for invited guests, who numbered, as I recall, about two hundred. The Chief Justice and almost all associate justices of the Supreme Court were there. So were a dozen members of the Senate and House. Presently, the honored guest arrived with Cathy, his attractive, personable young wife. The crowd stood and cheered as he was wheeled in; he, however, was frail, ashen, his face contorted with partial paralysis, wearing a gray tweed hat. In years past it was said that he looked like his close friend, Spencer Tracy, the Hollywood actor, for whom he was sometimes mistaken. Douglas himself recounted how once he was waiting to meet Tracy in Washington, when people stopped to ask for his autograph—not as a Supreme Court Justice, but as a movie star (in response to which he obligingly signed his friend's name). Now, however, he was a helpless shadow of himself.

Cathy unveiled the bust and speeches were made. She prepared to read the remarks that had been prepared for him, but Douglas stopped her. He intended to speak for himself and not from the text. Microphones were lowered to wheelchair height. He began in a high, disembodied voice, cracking a joke or two, thanking his colleagues on the court for coming (though he was never able, he said, to entice any of them to walk the whole distance with him), pausing between sentences in an unnatural speaking cadence. But the clarity of his mind was unquestionable. He reminisced about Justice Brandeis, who used to canoe on the canal. During one of the pauses, Cathy whispered something to him and he plunged ahead:

"What I've been trying to say is that many presidents and numerous public officials have helped with the canal project. I thank you all for coming. I thank all those who have no portfolio but who have two strong legs and like to hike, and to listen to the pileated woodpecker. I promise to get well, and we'll be able to walk it again."

I can't imagine that anyone present believed that he would walk anywhere again, except, perhaps, for Bill Douglas himself. During his lifetime he had conquered adversities, including the physical, and was powered by indomitable will. In 1949, while riding in the Cascades, a horse fell on him. He suffered broken ribs and a punctured lung, which led physicians to warn that his mountain climbing and high altitude days were done. But in 1951, as recorded in *Beyond the High Himalayas*, he crossed a series of passes up to 17,479 feet, spending more than a week above 15,000 feet without oxygen. In ensuing years only age, rather than lungs or diaphragm, curtailed his mountaineering, which led him to conclude: "All of which proves, I think, that given time and patience, the body can make great and profound adjustments if one chooses to live to the full."

His time was done, but he had proven the point by living his own life to the full. Shortly after his death *The Washington Post*, on January 20, 1980, paid him editorial tribute, beginning: "Perhaps more than any other public figure of recent decades, William O. Douglas followed only his own star. Whether sitting on the bench of the Supreme Court, where he served longer than any other justice in history, or before a campfire in a desolate wilderness, he knew what he believed and what he wanted. . . ."

Little wonder that he felt Goose Prairie and the Cascades were the places to call home and to recharge batteries, and that he enjoyed the company of Kay Kershaw and Isabelle Lynn at the Double K. They were the same kind of independent, outspoken, outdoors-oriented people, aging physically but not in the brain. They were free of pretensions, slender ladies dressed in simple, well-worn jeans they made look classy.

Kay was raised in the Yakima Valley and learned in girlhood how to get by in the wilderness, skiing cross-country on skis she made herself and climbing Mount Rainier because it was there. She purchased the property in Goose Prairie and built the Double K in 1945. Isabelle, a native Pennsylvanian working as an editor for the American Red Cross in Washington, came as a guest in the mid-fifties, and elected to throw in with Kay.

We sat in the combination kitchen-dining room, talking, while Kay occasionally fed the wood stove on which they cook. Why didn't they have a more modern appliance?

Kay: We get exercise cutting the wood. It keeps us young.
Isabelle: The food tastes better.
Kay: We do it different than anybody else.

The bedrooms on the second floor, furnished tastefully but spartan, accommodate ten or twelve guests at most, with two baths down the hall. The parlor adjoining the kitchen, however, was quite attractive and sophisticated, with stone fireplace, piano, easy chairs, and a lot of books: on flowers, birds, trees, philosophy, theater, and music. It was empty, a room with a past.

*   *   *

Kay: The front room would be jumping with twelve or fifteen people, coming in after riding all day. . . . Times are different. We retired gracefully.

Isabelle: Kicking all the way!

Kay: But that's the only way to go. Like a Bay steer. We have a lot of time to do the things we like to do. Hike, fish, ride . . .

There's hardly any wilderness left. We're all trying to save what little wild country hasn't been roaded or logged or tromped to death, and we have to have certain rules and regulations because it's hard to manage people. They all want to go there, with all the new equipment and the little stoves and everything to take with you. You want to make it like uptown. It would be easier to stay home.

Isabelle: I really would not want to go camping without an open fire.

Kay: It's no fun.

Isabelle: A stove is not my idea of going first-class.

Kay: On our trips we always have a stove to cook on, but we use wood. You need a stove to feed that many people, but then we have a campfire.

They disagreed on when they had quit leading horse trips. Kay said it was only four or five years earlier, but Isabelle insisted it was longer, that time goes faster than you think.

Isabelle: We cut down the trips ourselves. Horses cause damage. So do people, even without horses. The Sierra Club is very guilty. They have taken mobs into the wilderness.

Kay: You cannot go into the country without leaving some kind of mark. But you want to take care of it the best you can. So we finally decided to cut out the help and take only hikers. People hike, birdwatch, and enjoy the flowers. There are three hundred kinds of birds at one time or other. Lots of different kinds of warblers. . . .

We keep saying things are getting better, but there's less wilderness all the time.

Isabelle: Theoretically you have to get a permit to go into wilderness. Like the Goat Rocks. I asked our district ranger how they enforce it. He said, "We don't." It's stupid to have regulations if they don't enforce them. They ask you to take not more than X number of horses, four or five, but that doesn't mean anything. Why do they say, "Please don't." Why don't they say, "If you do it, we'll kill you, or we'll arrest you and give you a big, fat fine." The fines are just minimal sums of money. I don't understand why they don't want to offend the local people. They're always offending somebody.

Kay: I'm pretty skeptical. There's not much wilderness left and we're raising the kind of people who aren't going to visit it anyhow. Look at the thousands we have in this state with their ORVs [off-road vehicles] and motorcycles, and that's all they want to do. People aren't going to miss what they don't know about. They go to big ski resorts and are wrapped up in downhill skiing.

Isabelle: In the Bugaboos in British Columbia they go up by helicopter and ski downhill. Now they're trying to do it in the national forest at Wenatchee. They don't want to herringbone up those hills. They never see anything. They don't give a darn—it's a hill with snow on it. Those people don't know anything about wilderness. . . .

Kay: And they don't want any trees in their way. Downhill skiers, when it first started, didn't have any lifts, or any lifts to amount to anything. You had to work, to have time to know the country. People who go in droves want cross-country trails groomed. They go with nine hundred dollars' worth of equipment, come back in two hours, and think they cross-country skied. You say, "Well, what did you see out there? How was it? See any wildlife or birds? What kind of place was it?" And they have no answer.

Many wild areas these days are accessible and conquerable, wild forests to hunters and loggers, wild streams to kayakers, canoers, and fishermen, mountains to skiers and climbers. Some die, this is true, like Dr. Blackadar, the kayaker, who pressed his daring until he perished in the waters of the South Fork of the Payette River, and Willi Unsoeld, the Everest climber, philosopher, and teacher, who tumbled to his death on the snow slopes of Mount Rainier. Still the question remains: Do easy access and modern equipment make it difficult to sustain the respect, love, and reverence that nature deserves?

I weighed this question on the morning I drove from Goose Prairie across Chinook Pass into Mount Rainier National Park, contrasting my feelings with emotions that swelled within Philomen Beecher Van Trump on his first view of Mount Rainier in August 1867. He recorded them as follows:

"The first true vision of the mountain, revealing so much of its glorious beauty and grandeur, its mighty and sublime form filling up nearly all the field of direct vision, swelling up from the plain and out of the green forest till its lofty triple summit towered immeasurably above the picturesque foothills, the westering sun flooding with golden light and softening tints its lofty summit, rugged sides and far-sweeping flanks—all this impressed me so indescribably, enthused me so thoroughly, that I then and there vowed almost with fervency that I would someday stand upon its glorious summit, if that feat were possible to human effort and endurance."

Three years later he proved the feat possible. Van Trump and a single companion, General Hazard Stevens, were guided by Sluiskin, a Yakima Indian, to a point near the top of the peak. Though the Indian warned against going any higher, they persisted, going on without him to achieve the first recorded ascent of Mount Rainier. Even then, their lives were presently endangered by the cold and blustery weather of late afternoon, but they found sanctuary for the night in an area warmed by jets of volcanic steam blowing through the cracks in the rocks. "Strong men, stout hearts," Sluiskin greeted them, in the Indian tongue, on their return.

Rainier in our time has become a well-climbed mountain. In one recent year more than four thousand climbers reached the summit. Throughout the summer the mountaineering guide service conducts a steady stream of parties to the top. (Kay Kershaw had snickered at the idea of a guided trip; in her day it was something young people did without hoopla.) I myself wanted to be in one of these parties—it was the purpose of this visit to the park, a personal goal of the season. I realized that it demands conditioning of lungs and legs, and had trained for it, doing my daily stretching and bending exercises and lots of running. Only the week before, on a hot August Saturday, I had competed in a 9.25-mile road race; true, I had finished last, but I hadn't dropped out, as had two or three others, and my time was a hair under two hours, a respectable showing. Besides, all kinds of people, from eight to eighty, and even a man with one leg, had made it to the top of Mount Rainier. Why shouldn't I?

The schedule of the climb was as follows: first day, climbing school at Paradise, 5450 feet, the center of activity in the park, with training in the use of ice axe and crampons and assessment of participants to be sure they're up for the summit; second day, climb of four to five hours to Camp Muir, a rock shelter at 10,000 feet; third day, continue to the summit, at 14,410 feet, starting about one A.M., this time roped together, hoping to get to the summit and back before the sun brings icefall dangers, returning directly to Paradise by late afternoon.

I checked out my equipment (ice axe and crampons) at the stone Guide House and sat on the steps and waited. Others were doing the same. I was joined presently by John, a Denver physician with experience climbing in the Colorado Rockies. Like many others from all parts of the country, he was drawn by the challenge of the ice climbing of Mount Rainier. He was in his early forties, whereas most of our group, as I judged them after we assembled, were in their early twenties, all evidently well conditioned, good physical specimens.

We climbed a snow slope, about twenty of us, both hes and shes, with three instructors, or guides. The instructors were seasonal employees, accustomed to climbing Mount Rainier two or three times a week during summer, then studying at college or heading for beaches or ski slopes. One guide was said to be so proficient that he could climb from Paradise to the summit of Mount Rainier and back within five hours. Now, Kay Kershaw, what have you to say about that?

John, my physician friend, was encouraging and supportive. The equipment was new to me. So were the procedures of self-arrest and team arrest, of digging in to avoid disaster to one's self and to others of a team on the same rope. Younger members of the class took to it quickly and frolicked on the snow slope, while I plodded deliberately, conscious of each step. Near the day's end, as we headed downgrade, one of the instructors walked with me briefly. He was a handsome young Chinese-American, slim and trim, a graduate student in clinical psychology. He was very clinical: "Sorry to tell you this, but you are too slow and your reflexes are too slow. You might cause problems for yourself and others. We can't take you tomorrow." "How about to Camp Muir?" I asked. "No," he responded, walking away without a further word.

I was disappointed, but not about to cry or complain. If there was question about my ability, it was right that I not go. My friend John was surprised when I told him. He thought I had the hang of things. I suppose it takes old dogs longer to learn new tricks, while young people, on the other hand, are apt to be reckless and take chances.

That evening I had dinner at the cavernous dining room of Paradise Inn, the rustic, rambling old wooden lodge, with John and the park superintendent, William J. Briggle. Years before, when he was superintendent of Glacier National Park, I had sharply criticized Briggle in a magazine column. Then he had come to Washington, where I recognized that along with his weakness he had strengths as well. He was helpful in my planning to come to the park, and shared my disappointment.

John suggested I ought to take the class again the next day, confident that I would then be ready for the summit. Briggle vetoed the idea: "Let it go for now. We'll send you up next year with one of the rangers on patrol. You'll have more time to explore the mountaintop, camping a night or two, instead of making a rush for the summit, the way the tour groups do. There's a lot of pressure among climbers themselves. They want to get to the top—that's the main thing—they don't want anybody to jeopardize their chance or to slow them down."

Briggle stayed late with me in the bar discussing various options. He proposed that next morning I head up the mountain toward Camp Muir on my own. "See how it feels, how far you can go." That sounded like a worthy consolation prize possibly within my reach.

John and I breakfasted together to say goodbye. He personified fitness. Six years earlier, he said, he was still smoking and couldn't run two blocks. Now he was not only climbing, but running in mountain marathons.

"It gets to be an addiction."

"What's wrong with that?" I asked. "It sounds like a healthy addiction to me."

"Not exactly. I go to parties where the doctors are in one part of the room telling about their great achievements as marathoners, while their wives are in another part complaining that their husbands haven't been to bed with them for two months."

There must be some significant implicit psychological lesson, but for the present I was focused on Mount Rainier. I started early, climbing easily with a light day pack, at my own pace, free of stress or pressure to keep up with anyone. On the slopes of Rainier, Douglas fir yields to trim alpine fir and grassy highland meadows colored with wildflowers. The lower trails, unfortunately, were seriously eroded from too many feet, and not well heeded either, disfiguring the slope. The weather was cloudy and overcast, but now and then it cleared, so I could enjoy the presence of the long, narrow Nisqually Glacier beside me and the sight of the massive broad dome of Rainier calling me higher.

At Pebble Creek, about halfway, a signpost advised that Camp Muir was only 2.4 (or perhaps 2.5) miles, but it was steep, all on snow. I dug my feet into the snow and climbed, and climbed, following the steps made by others wherever I could, resting now and then and looking back, south across the Tatoosh Range to Mount Adams and Mount St. Helens. Climbers were coming down, some virtually rolling downhill and frolicking in the snow. Most of them had not made it to the summit, turning back in the face of lightning storms.

The climb to Camp Muir was steep and tedious, but I made the best of my own company and my determination to reach it. I arrived in a little less than five hours, feeling as though I could have gone another five hours. I found Muir a cluster of three stone shelters, one each for the park rangers, the mountaineering service, and the unattached public. I rested for a little while in the public shelter, to escape the wind and have my lunch, while two climbers who had been to the top, or near to it, slept in the bunks.

The downhill stretch was effortless, sheer pleasure. I hadn't been to the top, but getting to Camp Muir was pretty good for me, and I now knew what it would take, what preparations I must take to go all the way. On the way down I met my "classmates" going up, trudging in single file with full packs, resting on each step as we had been instructed. John came out of line to congratulate me and I expressed the wish that we might be together again.

Back at Paradise, I telephoned Briggle. When I mentioned that I had passed my climbing class, he said, "You should have told them you went all the way to the top—and what was holding them up!"

I felt pretty good about it, with business unfinished—the challenge of going all the way, of meeting and understanding wild nature with mind and body. Older people may not be able to do everything young people can, but I haven't found the reason to quit trying: given time and patience, as Justice Douglas put it, the body can make great and profound adjustments if one chooses to live to the full.

CHAPTER XI

✑

Magic of the Stanislaus Canyon—Can Numbers and Statistics Replace It?

Mark Dubois fell in love with the Mother Lode country in general, and the canyon of the Stanislaus River in particular, because he was fascinated by caves. He and his younger brother, Gar, would come out from their home at Sacramento almost every weekend while still in high school. They discovered a rich vein of caves, not all large, but plenty large enough to keep them busy. Like a pair of Huck Finns on the loose, they would rappel down cliffs to probe inside canyon walls for old Indian hideaways.

John Muir, to whom Mark bears strong philosophic and spiritual kinship, was acquainted with Mother Lode caves. In *The Mountains of California*, Muir described with admiration a guided tour he made to one of them (Cave City Cave). He and other members of the party entertained themselves by striking with a stick a series of stalactites that combined in size and tone like the strings of a harp. The sounds they heard were the music of fairyland:

"Here we lingered and reveled, rejoicing to find so much music in stony silence, so much splendor in darkness, so many mansions in the depths of the mountains, buildings in the process of construction, yet ever finished, developing from perfection to perfection, profusion without overabundance; every particle visible or invisible in glorious motion, marching to the music of the spheres in a region regarded as the abode of eternal stillness. . . .

"When we emerged into the bright landscapes of the sun everything looked brighter, and we felt our faith in Nature's beauty strengthened, and saw more clearly that beauty is universal and immortal, above, beneath, on land and sea, mountain and plain, in heat and cold, light and darkness."

Mark evokes equally emotional and moving images of wild beauty (though not in such polished prose), reflecting the mode and goals in his own life. "He takes a very idealistic approach," said one of Mark's opponents in deriding his heroic effort to save the Stanislaus, as though there could be some other approach more pertinent to our age.

In the spring of 1979 Mark demonstrated his commitment. He headed to a remote spot on the Stanislaus and chained himself to a boulder (after hiding the key in the brush). He threatened to stay until the waters behind the New Melones Dam covered him or until he received official assurance the Stanislaus would not be buried under two hundred feet of reservoir water. Newspapers carried such headlines as: PROTESTOR HIDING IN RESERVOIR MAY BE TRAPPED AS WATER RISES and FUTILE SEARCH FOR MELONES PROTESTOR. A CBS camera crew was rafted in and Roger Mudd talked about Mark on the evening news. *The New York Times* blithely dismissed him as "an angry vegetarian," noting that, "It happened in California, of course." Nevertheless, Governor Jerry Brown dispatched this telegram to President Carter: "I urge you to instruct the U.S. Army Corps of Engineers to halt the filling of New Melones Dam at the Parrotts Ferry Bridge. The beauty of the Stanislaus Canyon and the life of Mark Dubois deserve your personal attention."

Mark's readiness for martyrdom emerged slowly, over time. From caving and prowling around the limestone canyon bluffs, he took to river running, which meant that he could explore the floor of the canyon as well.

"The Stanislaus, which was only nine miles of unspoiled river, is the only place where I really explored lots and lots of wilderness. Sometimes I'm amazed at how few places I've been. I would find something new and discover new places and new things every time I was in it. I ran into friends who had run rivers all over and they would ask, 'How can you keep going back to the same little tiny river? I mean, don't you get tired of it?' I recognized that yes, there were times that I got tired or bored, but it was only when I wasn't putting energy out. I would ask, 'When is this trip going to be over?'—but only when I stopped being alert. Any time I tuned energy in I was always discovering a new little side creek, a new archaeological site, a new historical site, new vegetation, new plant life. All of these in the little wilderness of the Stanislaus."

It developed as we talked that Mark had been on other rivers, too: in the East, the Youghiogheny in Pennsylvania, and the New in North Carolina; the Middle Fork and main Salmon in Idaho; a handful of rivers in California; two or three rivers in Guatemala, and then, of course, the Colorado in Arizona, where we first met.

"Each river has its own personality. Getting to know the Stanislaus is like getting to know one person. It doesn't detract from getting to know other people. When I was on the Colorado I was blown away. I could never get to know all that place, and I would love to.

"I got interested in the Stanislaus because of the caves. Then I had always been interested in archaeology. So eventually I started finding all these sites, petroglyphs and campsites of the Miwoks. It was obvious people hadn't run across these sites before, they weren't recorded anywhere. I got turned on by the history of the canyon, and eventually to the Native Americans who fished and hunted along the Stanislaus in winter before migrating to the Sierra in summer, living on salmon, acorn meal, berries, and wild greens. I was fascinated by all these little plants and how they ate them, and which were edible. I did it through the seasons and it was amazing to watch the cycles of this place.

"I also learned that we're trained to tune things out. We're so used to neon that we stop seeing things. I recognized that it took me fifty trips before I started *seeing* the incredible magic in this canyon. There's so much stimulation in a river itself that it draws the excitement of people and they don't even see the canyon.

"One of the other things that was interesting to me was watching people. I was guiding little two-day river trips. At the end of those two days, all of those people who were city slickers—you knew that some little bubble had burst. They were just starting to smile in a way they had never smiled before. I recognized that I had been raised in Sacramento and I had never seen people smile like that. I knew there was another magic going on that I couldn't quantify or qualify, but I knew that somehow we were all getting in touch with something we hadn't been in touch with while we lived in all these cities and, despite all the nice things and the laughing we did in cities, there was something else going on out here that was magical to all of us.

"For me it was a place for personal growth, too. I was shy and couldn't talk to people. My family had done a lot of car camping when I was young and I thought I knew a little about the woods, and my dad knew a fair amount, so I felt pretty confident about being an outdoors person. Now I laugh at how little I knew.

"Several years before I started guiding I went down the river with several close friends. I had gotten pretty good at knowing how to read water. Finally I was going to be a river guide. I was trying to get to be like my brother and his friends. They were all outgoing, laughing and joking all around. I'd try and I'd get out one loud word and I'd go 'Oooh'"—here Mark sucked in his breath—"and I'd immediately get timid again.

"Well, in 1968 the first river trip came and, well, I lost all my confidence. Here I was going to be on my first commercial river trip and I freaked out, and sure enough at Death Rock I flip a boat. The whole raft flipped over. There was one old couple from Chicago who had never been down a river before and this young fellow. As soon as I poked my head up, I suddenly realized I'm responsible for them: What if they don't come up? They finally popped up and everything was okay. Next weekend I had to come back to prove myself. But I contracted mono and couldn't go back for six weeks. When I finally got back it turns out that the old guides like my brother and his friends had gone off to Idaho and all these other rivers, so all there was was all these new guys who were just as new as me, only I had a little more practice. Suddenly that one weekend was the most remarkable—I was the most outspoken, outgoing, joking around with everybody, jumping around in the water, acting as crazy as all these others had.

"The next Sunday, actually Saturday night, I was suddenly going, 'My gosh, what have I been doing? This isn't me, I can't be like this, I'm not that kind of person.' I said, 'Tomorrow I'll have to be me.' Well, the next day I did the same thing. Halfway through Sunday I said, 'You know, folks, you wouldn't believe it, but I'm usually not this way. I'm usually really shy.' And they go, laughing, 'Sure, Mark, sure, we know.' Just after we went past Death Rock—I couldn't say anything before we went through Death Rock; that was my menace, where I flipped—right after I said, 'You know, you wouldn't believe it, but the first time I came down this river I flipped on that rock.' One of them said, very jokingly, 'Yeah, that was the last time, right? Wasn't it?' I didn't tell him, 'You won't believe it, but it was.' I had so much confidence, and they were sure I was an old hand.

"So I did a lot of growing. I saw how rivers do this remarkable equalizing. One way is in terms of uniform. Everybody is stripped down to cutoffs or a swim suit and nobody has a blue collar or a white collar or tie or coat. Everybody is exactly the same. And the other amazing equalizer is that a river puts people through this incredible fear. 'Ooooh'"—here he sucked in again—"'are we going to survive this thing?' As they go through this fear it strips away—usually we not only have all these clothes façades, but we also have these mental façades to keep us from contacting each other. You go through fear together and all of a sudden it strips away all these façades. You get to laugh at each other. 'Wow, we survived. Boy, we made it!' So I watched, in those first years especially, this amazing connection of human beings. Not only was this place incredibly beautiful and magical, but that experience of the river stripping all those barriers away made people connect like I had never seen before."

The words rolled from Mark's lips, which led me to joke that for a fellow who professed shyness he sure could be talkative, though I realized he was venting deep inner feelings and personal revelations. Continually he cited how he "recognized" one aspect of life or another, particularly of "magical" qualities in the Stanislaus, or qualities stimulated by that little wilderness river for whose wildness he had fought and lost. We were driving back to Sacramento through the Mother Lode, Mark, Sharon, and I, feeling upbeat after canoeing the Stanislaus, or what remains of it, and camping a night on its banks.

I had met Mark and Sharon in the summer of 1981 on Martin Litton's flamboyant expedition down the Colorado River through the Grand Canyon, designed to attract attention to the government plan to restrict the flow of water (even more than it did already), and to turn public opinion against it. Mark had impressed me then as the earthiest boatman on the trip, a kind of quiet giant, six feet seven or eight, of slender build, more graceful than gangling, with a handsome brown beard and walking on huge bare feet (size 17 as I learned). Mark was a celebrity, the activist who had chained himself to a rock above the Stanislaus River and prepared for death by drowning, yet he was the busiest boatman on the trip, loading and unloading dories and rafts, quietly performing any and all chores. I had admired Sharon, too, slender and willowy, a shrimp alongside Mark; dark complected, rather quiet, but bright and perceptive. She was twenty-three, nine years younger than Mark. Lately Sharon had completed research and writing for a prominent Californian, highly regarded in fields of the environment and politics. But she felt he was too willing to compromise and to skirt the tough issues. That is often the way: Young people with hope and ideals want to look up to older heroes only to find the heroes playing things safe.

Mark is free of artifice. He wears simple clothes, shoes are a bother. Like a latter-day Jesus, he never loses faith or hope. In voicing sorrow and frustration over the Stanislaus, he said: "Every time we lost one campaign, people would say, 'Well, it's over.' I would say, 'No, it's only over when it's over.' I would always say, 'It's one more, one more, one more.' Had we won the last referendum we would have been able to bring this thing out starting right now, even though the river had been flooded."

The Stanislaus must have been a particularly lovely river. It was the setting of California's most popular white water, with more than a dozen outfitting companies guiding passengers on raft trips of one and two days. The guides were young women and bearded young men wearing scant clothing to obscure their tanned bodies, an adventurous breed of individualists. The rafting was all on the nine-mile section of the Stanislaus Canyon, the last undammed, free-flowing portion of the river; the rest of it, flowing 120 miles from headwaters in the high wilderness between Lake Tahoe and Yosemite, had already been tamed and transfigured by thirteen dams.

For Mark and Sharon the canyon was full of ghosts. Mark said later how he kept getting flashes, as we passed one point or another, of wildflowers and small animals he had known in years past. They talked of where they would sit on a sand beach and watch the fish jump, of where a pool turned gold in the evening, of where hawks circled high above the cliffs. To reach the Stanislaus we had driven through Placerville (once known as Dry Diggins, later as Hangtown) and Angels Camp, Mother Lode towns that came to life following the 1848 gold discovery. The ensuing boom brought stagecoaches, freight wagons, brick stores, saloons, and thousands of fortune-seeking miners, leaving in its wake ghost towns, old mine shafts, and legends. In the foothills we stopped to meet a friend of Mark's, Coyote, living a simplified but studious back-to-the-land life, and he had dropped us at Camp Nine, the put-in point.

It was November, but the weather was mild. Sharon and I traveled downstream in a canoe, Mark in a kayak. He barely bothered with a paddle, relying on his hands and body English. A child of nature, Mark, to whom appliances are mere encumbrances. Were I lost in wilderness with him, I would be free of fear. Wandering for forty days and forty nights would be more adventure than travail. "It took me three days to isolate one tiny sound, to focus on it and realize it was a little shrew poking under the leaves, skittering back and forth looking at me," said Mark after he came down from his chain-in. "I had a river otter who would come and play in front of the rock. Beavers were working across the way. Every kind of insect. Spiders. Once I was sitting there and felt this movement right behind me. I turned and saw this huge snake slithering past. It had the coloration of a rattler, but it was just a big gopher snake." And if it had been a rattler, the snake would have been as tranquil as Mark.

Wooded slopes rose back from the stream bed. The limestone cliffs, almost white, were pocked with caves and crevices. The river water flowed smoothly, carrying fallen logs and rotting driftwood. Treetops sticking above the surface signaled that a valley lay buried. Now and then the water quivered and swirled, a remnant of a current boiling underneath. A motorboater might find challenge and pleasure, without even knowing what makes a river or a riffle or a rapid. How can a man with a motor hear the wild music in a flowing river? Or perceive the mysterious upwellings, puzzling swirls, and unexplained eddies? Or lament the loss of boulders, chutes, and eddies?

Each of us had his own thoughts. Twilight overcame us, and then darkness. We paddled in the dark. Mark left us for a time to be alone in Rose Creek, a place of special sentiment to him, which I regretted not seeing in daylight since I had read of it as a significant mix of rock formations revealing the geology of the Sierra—a well-known field laboratory for geology students. I thought of something else I'd been reading, an excellent book titled *Stanislaus: The Struggle for a River*, in which the author, Tim Palmer, wrote:

"In October 1978, the Army Corps of Engineers finished the dam, bringing to a close 34 years of authorization, 20 years of planning, 10 years of hard opposition, and 10 of construction. The next step was to fill it. Delayed by historic preservation laws, the Corps' schedule called for impoundment in April 1979 to an elevation of 808 feet above sea level—somewhere near the old Parrotts Ferry Bridge. . . . For two weeks, a few supporters remained by the river, camping at the rising edge of the flatwater and moving upstream as the impoundment swelled. The Indian petroglyphs at Horseshoe Bend went under. Pendola Ranch, where Lorenzo Pendola had raised food for miners in 1870, and where his grandson continued to farm in recent years, went under. . . ."

We pulled ashore at a place that Mark knew, and camped for the night on rocky beds, continuing the next morning to Parrotts Ferry, where Coyote was waiting. The original Parrotts Ferry was established in 1860 to connect mining towns on opposite sides of the river in the steep, narrow gorge. The ferry yielded to a bridge in 1903, then to another, a sleek convex ribbon of concrete supported by two concrete pillars, an achievement of modern engineering constructed as part of the New Melones Dam project. Impressive, yet its need and social value?

The day, as it happened, was Thanksgiving. We felt a little festive, thankful rather than forlorn, and stopped at Angels Camp to buy home-baked biscuits and poke up and down the historic street. I watched Mark, pictured him with a white beard, and called him John Muir. He could have begun his adventures, as did Muir, with a thousand-mile walk across the Southeast, followed by a wide range of travels over the West, then focusing his interest on Yosemite, which lay close to us, possibly only an hour's drive from Angels Camp. Muir lived for six years in Yosemite, where he waged his own fight to save a wilderness river and lost.

President Theodore Roosevelt came to camp with Muir in Yosemite in 1903 and was deeply moved. "It was like lying in a great solemn cathedral," Roosevelt wrote, "far vaster than any built by the hand of man." Then he went to Stanford University, where he delivered a speech demonstrating concern for preserving both the giant sequoias of the Sierra Nevada and the coast redwoods:

"I feel most emphatically that we should not turn into shingles a tree which was old when the first Egyptian conqueror penetrated to the valley of the Euphrates, which it has taken so many thousands of years to build up, and which can be put to better use. That, you may say, is not looking at the matter from the practical standpoint. There is nothing more practical than the preservation of beauty, than the preservation of anything that appeals to the higher emotions of mankind."

Muir's influence was manifest in Roosevelt's attitude toward redwoods, but not toward the Tuolumne River flowing through Hetch Hetchy Valley in Yosemite. As early as 1882 city engineers of San Francisco had scouted the possibility of damming Hetch Hetchy's narrow lower end to make a reservoir for water storage, then of using the fall of the impounded water to generate hydro-electric power. Establishment of Yosemite as a national park in 1890 appeared to head that off. But San Francisco politicians pressed the issue for years, from one national administration to another. Muir foresaw a frightening precedent in the destruction of a beautiful valley, warning, "It behooves us all faithfully to do our part in seeing that our wild mountain parks are passed on unspoiled to those who come after us, for they are national properties to which every man has a right and interest."

Yosemite's proponents looked to Theodore Roosevelt, when he took office in the White House, to defend the integrity of Hetch Hetchy, but he accepted other counsel (principally from Gifford Pinchot) that the greatest good for the greatest number would be to furnish water to hundreds of thousands rather than to save a scenic valley for a few hundred. In 1913 the battle was resolved in Congress: The dam was built, flooding a valley that many have said compared in beauty with California's treasure of the Sierra Nevada, Yosemite Valley.

Most California rivers have been sacrificed. From 1900 to 1940 the cities of San Francisco and Los Angeles constructed water-supply systems on rivers located hundreds of miles away from them. The Central Valley, flat and dry, is kept fertile and productive, supporting vast corporate agriculture enterprises by a web of dams and canals. Once there were twenty-five thousand miles of rivers and streams in California, flowing downhill from the Sierra mountain wilderness during the spring runoff, but now there are less than five hundred miles. Water has been put to work, for better or for worse, by thousands of major and minor dams, irrigation canals, aqueducts, and levees, a testament to modern engineering, leaving most rivers polluted, flowing as trickles during the dry season, devoid of fish life.

"Hey, I hear they're going to build a dam," someone said while Mark was sitting on the limestone bluffs of the Stanislaus, but it didn't register as an impending disaster. Sure, it would be tough to lose the river, but he had been raised going to dam overlooks and to regarding dams as part of progress.

"After two years of commercial river running, a friend came up with the idea of doing free river trips. So we started doing free river trips with kids, mostly inner-city kids, delinquents, kids that don't get out very often. We worked through the Sacramento Children's Home, Sacramento Free School, California Youth Authority, drug rehabilitation centers, just a wide variety. At first we were just Ron, Fred, and Mark; then Ron, Fred, and Mark, Et cetera. When a lot of people joined in doing it, we became simply Et cetera. Besides, we did not only river trips, but backpacking, caving, environmental education, et cetera.

"We didn't get paid, it just felt good doing it and we needed

215

just enough for gas and minimal expenses. We taught stars, edible plants, and how to identify the critters. We would lead the blind into caves, switch off the light, and let them lead the way out. It's amazing how much you can learn from the blind.

"At the end of that first summer we gave a five-day river trip and realized that's what we wanted to do all along, that there was too much to see even in those nine miles. When we put in the first day the kids weren't helping at all. We hiked a couple of those ridges and they were moaning and groaning the whole way. We had nine kids on that trip and at the end the lives of two of them were totally turned around. We recognized if we had had a few more days—two did complete somersaults, two others came really, really close.

"We recognized that out on the rivers there isn't such a thing as a delinquent. Not in these wild places. The only reason there's delinquency is when you don't have anything to do and you break a window, where out in the wild places all of a sudden quote delinquents unquote and quote normal kids unquote, you can't tell the difference anymore, because there are so many things to occupy their attention that they're all the same.

"In the winter of 1973–74, Proposition Seventeen happened, the first referendum initiative for the Stanislaus. We did a lot of helping out. The Environmental Defense Fund had been conducting legal action and had purchased a full-page advertisement on behalf of the Stanislaus; it all cost an amazing amount of money. So the outfitters were going to have a thing called Stanislaus Week and they all agreed to donate their boats and guides for one day. Because we lived up there, right on the river, we became the coordinators, sort of assigning people and getting them in place; when they were short a guide, we'd row a boat for them, things like that. The Stanislaus battle slowly took more and more time. After the third year I found myself spending a third of my time doing Et cetera and two thirds doing river-saving."

Friends of the River was formed to pursue the referendum on the 1974 election ballot in California. The river people in the leadership did not object to a smaller dam that would solve any flooding problem, as long as the upper gorge was spared. Volunteers collected half a million signatures to get the initiative on the ballot.

Their campaign gained strong support, but pro-dam forces, notably the Central Valley agricultural producers, had more money to invest in voter appeal. The River Initiative lost by a narrow margin, 2,576,000 to 2,891,000. The volunteers, free spirits of the river family, were crushed and turned elsewhere. Tim Palmer, in *Stanislaus*, wrote that they followed a variety of options: "Go kayak the Salmon, bum in Mexico, make money, smoke some grass, guide on the Tuolumne, graduate from college, take a job with the state, enroll in law school, raise a family, raise a garden."

As for Mark:

"First I felt the pain. Then a greater hurt came for those friends, many people who were never involved in the political process before. It was an era of cynicism and they didn't want to bother, they didn't believe their effort would make a difference, but they did it anyway. They said they would try working through the system and they poured themselves into it. They worked their hearts out. They gave all they had, then saw that the winning was bought by money. It was somehow a rip-off of the human spirit.

"Last night when I went up Rose Creek, it was interesting to— to start sobbing, to keep wondering where that pain came from. After crying a fair amount, the silence of all that life, all those years of evolution all those little plants and critters have gone through. Somehow the frustration of the absurdity—the point where we have to burn our cathedrals for firewood. 'Why did that fellow do that crazy thing in the canyon?' a little child asked. 'Well, that's that man's temple, it's his church.' I recognized that partially fits. For me the Stanislaus has been both. It's been a combination of friends: lover, a combination of both parents, a religious teacher, a spiritual guide; it's been a close friend, it's even been an enemy at times; it's been every kind of friend I ever had.

"That canyon has been each and all of those things to me. An amazing teacher. I guess when I cried a couple of years ago I recognized I felt the tears came from losing a friend, but it was much more: losing a place you belong, all of those things and everything I ever touched. It's not just a friend, it's somehow part of my spirit. I recognized when you get a cut you can eventually see the scar from that cut. It's much more difficult to see the scars on our spirit, but I somehow knew they're there.

"You asked what wilderness is to me. I've watched how much I've spent the last few years of my life talking numbers and statistics. When we started on Prop Seventeen, 'Sign this initiative to save the river!' 'Well, don't we need the power?' 'Well, oh . . . uh . . .' Eventually I had to learn some facts. 'Oh, no, this isn't going to reduce power. This is only going to produce—why, they're only going to need all the power from this to pump the water, so it's not a power plan.' 'Oh, okay, I'll sign.' 'But don't we need it for irrigation?' 'But we don't *need* more water, only if they subsidize it.' So I started learning this amazing repertoire of facts, not because I cared about numbers or facts at all. They're the antithesis of what this river tells me; but I recognized because these people hadn't touched the magic of the canyon they had to relate to it how they could relate to it. They had to relate to the numbers.

"'How many species live in the canyon?' The Corps of Engineers just distilled in their impact statement: 'We will destroy sixteen miles of new river canyon, twenty-three miles in all. We're going to destroy about thirty-five caves. We're going to destroy twelve thousand acres of wildlife habitat.' They had it in numbers. 'And we're going to gain X amount of dollars in power, water, blah-blah.' They tried to mitigate the white water, but they found all the other rivers were crowded. The reason there are no other places to go to white water is they're used already. You can't find a new river. I remember Dave Brower's classic line about Glen Canyon. Sure, we'll let you build a dam on Glen Canyon as soon as you build us a new canyon equally as beautiful.

"I found out how much it cost to build a quarter mile of white water one time and we calculated that out. We found it would cost them about two hundred fifty thousand dollars just to build the nine miles of white water stretch of the Stanislaus. That didn't include building the canyons and the caves. Disneyland would never tell us how much it cost them to build a cave and we didn't figure how much it would cost to take the little blind cave critter that evolved over ten million years and how much it would cost to plant all those trees.

"There's something that—I've watched how few of us have taken time to talk about that magic of the canyon, that magic of wilderness. It seems like it starts to border on the spiritual because we don't have any other words for it. Other life on this planet? I find myself saying often that if they had put a fence around it and I would never be able to go for it, I would have fought just as hard to save it because somehow I knew that all the critters of that place had a right to be there whether I ever got to see it again or not. It was always funny to hear people say, 'Oh, they're just fighting to save their own white water.' Yeah, folks, call it recreation, but that word comes from re-creation and I recognized that's where a lot of folks' spirits got re-created down there. That place deserved to be saved even if none of us had the chance to re-create our spirits and get back in touch. That place needs to be here."

The wilderness of the Stanislaus Canyon was lost, but not for want of effort to save it. In 1976 Friends of the River (of which Mark was then executive director) supported a bill in the state legislature to preserve the upper canyon. It was narrowly defeated. In 1978 the New Melones Dam was completed, a structure the equivalent in size to a sixty-two-story building, but the river people still would not quit. They cited the precedent of the Cross-Florida Barge Canal, which President Nixon had called to a halt in 1971 when it was one third completed. I know that area along the Oklawaha River in the lush central Florida subtropics, and how the project was undone. Marjorie Carr, a woman of mature years, the wife of a well-known biology professor at the University of Florida, was like Mark, clinging to a vision of wilderness saved to the point that she and others of like mind never quit. Sometime after Nixon called it off, John Ehrlichman, the presidential assistant for domestic affairs, who had some understanding and sympathy for the environment, let out the intelligence that he had taken the action on his own in the President's name. Which illustrates the thin line of power in the decision process. There was also the case of the Tellico Dam across the Little Tennessee River at the edge of the Great Smoky Mountains. The dam was nearly completed when an aquatic biologist discovered the snail darter, a small spotted fish only two inches long, but a whole species nonetheless, and enough to bring construction progress to a halt under terms of the Endangered Species Act. Ultimately, in 1978, Congress cast aside its own laws and directed that Tellico be completed and filled. President Carter, the last hope, who had spoken in support of wilderness and

219

wild rivers, signed the bill in return, it was said, for something he wanted from Congress. Which illustrates the gloomy fickleness of politics.

After New Melones Dam was in place, Friends of the River still campaigned to keep the reservoir from being filled completely. It proposed filling sixteen miles above the dam, as far as Parrotts Ferry, while saving the upper nine miles. In May 1979 legislation was introduced in Congress to add the nine miles in question to the National Wild and Scenic River System. It was defeated in committee on a vote of twenty to nineteen.

Through early 1979 the reservoir filled. River people conducted Witness Encampments, bidding goodbye to their cherished bits of nature. On May 17 Mark Dubois dispatched a letter to the district engineer of the Corps of Engineers in Sacramento, Colonel Donald O'Shei. He wrote that he had been doing some serious thinking:

"While the dam may have seemed a good idea in the 40's and 60's, when it was first authorized, we have acquired much new information since then. I believe we should have the courage and maturity to admit a mistake has been made and stop the blind momentum of this 'public works' project which will cost us and future generations so much. All the life of this canyon, its wealth of archaeological and historical roots to our past, and its unique geological grandeur are enough reasons to protect this canyon just for itself. But in addition, all the spiritual values with which this canyon has filled tens of thousands of folks should prohibit us from committing the unconscionable act of wiping this place off the face of the earth."

The letter concluded as follows: "I plan to have my feet permanently anchored to a rock in the canyon at the elevation of Parrotts Ferry the day the water reaches that elevation. I urge you to do all in your power to prevent the flooding of the canyon above Parrotts Ferry."

When Mark secured himself to the rock, he had only a sleeping bag, a poncho, some books, and a cup for scooping water from the reservoir, the level of which was two feet below him and rising. He had no food, but was planning to fast. Only one person, code-named Deep Paddle, knew his location. Mark was well hidden, beyond the sight of officially dispatched search parties, including five boats, a helicopter, and a light plane, all of which he later said traveled too fast to find him, and eighteen men combing the river-banks. His dramatic act made him a celebrity, at least for the moment, and Americans who had never heard of the Stanislaus now knew that one man was prepared to surrender his life in its behalf. Six more protesters appeared on the rocks near Parrotts Ferry Bridge. Other river people staged a rally on the steps of the state capitol at Sacramento. Governor Brown responded with a wire to the President and by publicly calling the river "a priceless asset to the people of California and the nation." After a week the Corps of Engineers yielded. It pledged to maintain the water level at 808 feet, as Friends of the River had sought, and the state of California promised to monitor the level until Congress and the courts resolved the issue once and for all.

Mark came down, still hopeful. However, Congress ruled against the wild, or semiwild, river. Interior Secretary Cecil R. Andrus ordered the reservoir filled to 818 feet and his order was upheld in federal court. In January 1981 Friends of the River petitioned President Carter, then in his last days in office, to exercise executive power and declare the upper Stanislaus a national monument. Though the plea was emphasized by a group of handicapped protesters who chained themselves to rocks along the river, it was denied. Even after the reservoir was filled, a coalition rallied behind Proposition 13, the Water Reform Initiative, and collected 350,000 signatures, more than enough to get it on the 1982 ballot. The coalition cited the vast waste of water resources, particularly in cropland irrigation, and the need for conservation as the long-term course, but Proposition 13 was defeated—the vote this time was not even close.

That 1982 vote was only about three weeks old when I was with Mark and Sharon. They were still in the process of recovering from this seemingly ultimate defeat. We returned to Sacramento and had an interesting vegetarian Mexican Thanksgiving dinner at Mark's house. It was in a pleasant neighborhood. Mark's mother had given it to him and he, in turn, had made it Friends of the River headquarters during all the battles, with assorted river people camping in and trying to match penniless enthusiasm against moneyed power. Now the house was being converted to Mark's again,

Mark's and Sharon's. It was simply furnished; I can't think of them ever living lavishly. As Mark said:

"Recognizing again that—about my need for things. I'd always been raised to think I needed all these things that make people happy. Material things. Like clothing and buying a game and a new car, whatever those things were. So here I was living on this river and I was wearing tennis shoes and cutoffs and the good old Sierra Club cup and, of course, I had to have all these things, but eventually I recognized that I didn't even need these things. I recognized we were having far more smiles without all these things than I'd ever had in a city with all those abundant goodies that I'd been raised to think I needed to have. That was one of the first, most powerful lessons that the river taught me.

"The word *need* to me is really a funny word. Everybody uses it, but I more and more question what you really need. Gandhi has a quote that says, 'There's enough in this world for every man's need, but not for every man's greed.' I somehow feel that greed is too harsh a word. It's not just greed: There's an ignorance of thinking these things are going to give us happiness. Wild places teach people, ohahhh, you don't need all those things.

"When I go to backpack stores I see so much bright new plastic and nylon—we're trying to get away from it and we're still so much a part of this culture. We still take all our little goodies when we go. A couple of years ago a bunch of my friends got together and they actually bought me a pair of cross-country ski boots, which I didn't believe possible. One friend had been looking for a year till he found a pair large enough. They also bought me skis. They knew I had never gone out and I was pleased they got me these waxless skis. In the old days people had to play with waxes to the weather. I recognized that I missed something. I said that, and yet that's something I complain about. Now I don't have to learn the different textures of snow. Now I don't have to be sensitive to that. I can just scoot off and never be conscious of what kind of snow I'm on.

"I talked to a kayaker. 'Now we have fiber glass. Boy, when we first started we had cloth boats and boy you had to watch everything you did.' Now people say they'll have plastic boats, and new people won't even have to be sensitive to rocks. Now they can bump over a rock and never even notice it. I'm aware that there is that factor: that people don't have to be sensitive, they don't have to learn. There's a good and bad to all of that. It's a tradeoff, but maybe we ought to learn by doing it, learn by going slow.

"One of the things I recognized after I came out of the canyon on my little camping trip, I was blown away by all the coverage I got. I recognized, ah, for three months the lower canyon had been flooded and we took reporters up. We told them all about it and they said, 'No story, kids, it's just too—a few inches a day are getting flooded and it's just trees. What's the story?' When I was ready to go down, all of a sudden they were ready to cover me. I said, 'Look, I'm going to join my friends in the canyon. They're suffering the same fate.' 'Oh, they're just going to fill it with water, that's all that's going to happen.' I recognized how homocentric our society is. Most folks don't understand that other life has a value. Everything else is for our benefit. . . ."

Sharon had been listening thoughtfully. Not that she lacked her own ideas or ability to express them, far from it, but when Mark gets talking—listening becomes a treat. Now, however, she felt moved to interject: "Last night when we were paddling on the river and after we were going over all that I kept thinking, *Why aren't more people as devastated about this as I am?* When I watch television and I see what happened in Nazi Germany I can't believe that the rest of the world just sat back and watched. As the river was being flooded, I asked, *Why aren't more people screaming and saying, 'No! This is absurd and this can't happen!'*"

I commented that in Hitler's time some of the best people allowed themselves to be intimidated. They would say, "He's too powerful. We have to work with him." It was the same with slavery in the United States, abundantly evil but too powerful an institution, socially and economically, to thoroughly oppose and bring to an end. Little wonder that those who stand on principle and speak for direct action are viewed as more of the problem than the problem itself. Mark didn't deny this, but had his own view:

"I was actually amazed at how much support I had. I was equally amazed a month later when I got a bunch of clippings from the Central Valley and I found how angry the farmers were, how much anger and hatred they had. Eventually I recognized I was a nice target for all their frustrations, a scapegoat. They had anger toward the government and the middleman and the pests out there on their fields, and I was sort of a nice target. But I mostly got support.

"There were also a lot of people that I didn't hear from. 'No, no, no, you can't do it that way. We'll lose all our credibility within the system. People will never believe us.' There were strong individuals I respect a lot who were convinced the organization couldn't support or condone such actions as mine, that they had to be individual statements. The whole speaking out—when I came out of the canyon I ran into a quote from Margaret Mead: 'The trouble with this country is there's not enough people ready to die. Nobody believes in anything anymore.'"

We discussed that point. I knew a lot of people who believe with passion in wilderness and wild things, though it isn't always easy. Martin Litton has always insisted that Glen Canyon was sacrificed in order to save Dinosaur National Monument when dam projects in *both* could have been stopped, and he would assert with ridicule that members of the board of the Sierra Club, on which he served, didn't even know where the Grand Canyon was located. I've heard stated many, many times—principally from people on a regular payroll, or with professional or academic reputations to sustain—the importance of doing what is "politically feasible . . . settling for half a loaf . . . being pragmatic . . . reasonable . . . realistic," while wild nature continually disappears from the landscape.

"Developing an ethic takes a long time," said Mark. "After the Civil War slavery didn't stop. Now it is socially unacceptable. . . . 'Look, folks, we can exploit all this wilderness now; you'll have it, but your great-great-grandchildren will never have anything.' If we can take the time to explain, most people would say, 'No, leave it. I'm going to have to do without.' Most people are not so selfish. We are ignorant, but not that selfish. Yes, there are selfish people and we get selfish at times, but collectively, when forced to take responsibility for our actions, I don't think—when we act as a whole, we're not that selfish. But that doesn't happen because decisions are made by advertising, PR boys, the quickie vote—they buy the answer, instead of it happening out of consciousness.

"How do we develop an ethic? It takes that individual commitment. I feel so much better knowing that I at least gave it every ounce of my energy, trying to protect that place. That doesn't help the pain of it being gone. We're just not mature enough. Not enough people are ready to take responsibility. I know that we could have done it and that we didn't do it because of where we are at collectively. Enough people are still hooked on the belief that they might need more, and that's why it was easy to confuse the voters. People are still afraid; they're not sure of what they're afraid of, but needing more is one answer.

"Enough people are not ready to take responsibility. 'But we can't! Mark, what are you trying to do? We can't do that. That's impossible!' Or, 'Gee, Mark, I can't do that. I'm just one bureaucrat in the middle of this agency.' Or, 'I'll give it a try, but I don't really think that—'

"When I cried last spring, after I cried for the river, I again once more cried for our lack of—we're just not smart enough; we're just not mature enough. I think one of the things that's made me survive is I recognized how slow evolution is, what an incredibly slow process.

"My analogy for the human race is that we're very, very similar. We're at the state of teenagers driving around in a very fast car. We aren't quite taking responsibility for other people out on the highway. We're not taking responsibility for those in the car with us. We're not quite taking responsibility for our own lives or for the future generations that we have produced. And we keep going around these corners, like an environmental disaster, or the other corner of health, while all these little blips of conscience are coming up. Most youths survive that and I hope we're going to survive it, too. But not all youths do survive—they often go over those cliffs and they don't make it.

"I feel we're at that point where we're going around a lot of hairpin corners in some pretty amazing terrain and we don't know it's nighttime and it's dangerous and we can't see how dangerous it is, but we're getting all these little flashes—oil spill, nuclear waste dump polluting ten square miles of the Snake River drainage—and we're cringing at these things, but we haven't throttled down yet. Individuals are trying to take that responsibility. Are we going to do that fast enough before the whole world goes poof?"

In September 1983 Mark and Sharon were married on the shore of the American River a few miles outside of Sacramento. For their honeymoon they departed for a year to look at rivers and other wonderful places around the world. It had to be an adventure on a shoestring. They didn't want gifts, but suggested donations to either Friends of the River or two or three other groups. Nevertheless, a committee made a mailing offering friends the opportunity to "provide a surprise dowry for Mark and Sharon's honeymoon, so they can splurge a little, and get to wherever they want to, and home again."

As stated somewhere else in these pages, wild nature evokes lofty, noble thoughts and words. Perhaps the question should be asked, who lives fully to the measure of the words? "As just about everyone knows, money has never been of much importance to Mark," the committee's letter continued. "Many of us want to tell them not only how much we love them, but how inspiring it has been over the years to see Mark give himself, all of himself, and at times a great deal more, to protect the Stanislaus, the Tuolumne, and wherever rivers flow, or wilderness still remains, in this lovely state of ours."

CHAPTER XII

Up the Delaware: Wilderness Consciousness and Connection

I continually discover singular perceptions and descriptions of wilderness, written and spoken by many different kinds of people, just as I discover actual wilderness in different parts of the country where, logically, it should no longer be. Wilderness is a persistent and relevant influence.

A headline on page two of the Diamond Jubilee Edition of the *Union-Gazette* of Port Jervis, New York, on July 1, 1982, caught my eye: WILDERNESS TO CITY. Below the headline was this charming literary fragment written at Port Jervis in 1892 by Stephen Crane, best known as author of *The Red Badge of Courage*:

"In the wilderness sunlight is noise. Darkness is a great tremendous silence accented by small and distant sounds. The music of the wind in the trees is a song of loneliness. On the ridge-top a dismal choir of hemlocks croon over one that has fallen."

Crane, I assume, drew this mood-picture from experience in the Delaware Valley, just above Port Jervis, the upper Delaware, shaped by the Catskills of New York, the Poconos of Pennsylvania, and the river flowing between them. For the retrospective article beneath the Crane quotation began as follows:

"It must have been like that many years ago before white men came to this valley. Vast tracts of virgin woodland: pine, hemlock, beech, maple and oak; sturdy, silent forests carpeted with pine needles upon which the woodland creatures and the red man moved without a sound.

"And before that there was the river, always the river; sacred to the Indians, they held secret ceremonies on an island in midstream and buried their venerated dead along its banks."

The Indians are long gone, but the wilderness may not have perished. UP THE RIVER: STILL A FEELING OF WILDERNESS—so headlined the main article of the travel section of the *Philadelphia Inquirer* on June 7, 1981. A strong feeling, I would say, considering the corridor of the upper Delaware is one of the few places in the East to see eagles, osprey, herons, migrating Canada geese, diving kingfisher, and outsized pileated woodpecker in their natural surroundings.

Zane Grey drew a lot of inspiration from the Delaware. He had been a practicing dentist in New York City, but decided that life was not for him. He wrote his first westerns, baseball stories, and fishing tales while living, from 1905 to 1918, at Lackawaxen, Pennsylvania, a few miles upstream from Port Jervis. "My years in Lackawaxen represented to me more than a struggle to become independent through writing," he would later recall. "Here I gained my first knowledge of really wild country."

Grey nurtured a generation of young believers in wild country (myself included) who devoured his novels—*Riders of the Purple Sage, The Thundering Herd, To the Last Man, The Vanishing American*, and all the rest—as he cranked them out until his death in 1939. Of course, they've been well read since, but there was something specially sweet about the fruit when new. As to his motivation and goal, a foreword written by his daughter, Loren Grey, to a 1982 edition of *The Vanishing American* states:

"This book contains some of my father's most magnificent descriptions of the desert, the mountains and the wilderness—where Nophaie finally resolves the conflicts between his Indian heritage and his white upbringing. I believe that to my father, Nature, even in its harshest manifestations, was akin to God, and perhaps the only God he could wholly relate to during his lifetime."

Though he frequented many wild places to pursue fishing, his favorite sport, and find settings for adventure novels, like *Rogue*

River Feud, Zane Grey was most attached to this relatively tame eastern stream. He lived and wrote (and fished, of course) where the Lackawaxen River—named by the Indians for its "swift waters"—joins the Delaware; when his days were done, he returned here for burial. Once, after he had become famous and left for California, he wrote a friend:

"Just to get your letter made me see the old familiar places as vividly as if I had been there. I could see the October colors of the hills and the old Delaware winding down from the mountains and the purple asters blooming along the trails, the smoky Indian summer colors and the smell of the pine."

I spent a year close to the Delaware. Between the summers of 1981 and 1982, I lived in Milford, Pennsylvania, a dozen miles downstream from Port Jervis. I came for other reasons, but in odd times I would explore the river, its valley, and the mountains rising above it. I never realized there could still be in our time such natural charm, variously pastoral and wild, left in the populous Northeast. The fact is that Pennsylvania has more black bears in its woods than any other state, and bigger bears, too, and an abundance of them in the Poconos, less than three hours by car from Times Square. Little wonder the Poconos are honeycombed with summer camps for kiddies, hotels featuring heart-shaped bathtubs for honeymooners, and assorted retreats and hideaways.

The first weekend Jane came to visit, we hiked the trails in High Point State Park, where a Washington Monument-like obelisk rises to the highest elevation in New Jersey, all of 1803 feet. Not very high, as compared with the Rockies or even the southern Appalachians, but we were both overwhelmed by the vistas of unbroken forests in neighboring New York and Pennsylvania, as well as the Kittatinny Range at our feet in New Jersey, and by the river flowing between the ridges like a strand of silver.

The extreme northeast corner of New Jersey I found as different from Newark and Atlantic City as the Adirondacks are from mid-Manhattan, or the High Sierra from Los Angeles. The Appalachian Trail, the wilderness footpath of the East, extends the length of the Kittatinny Range through forty-two miles of Jersey forests and parks, landscaped with pine, hemlock and oaks, laurel and rhododendron, waterfalls and glacial lakes. Portions have remained unchanged down through the time of the Indians, the Lenni Lenape, whose antecedents came into the valley ten thousand years ago, and the Dutch, who began settling these environs before William Penn founded Philadelphia.

The river winds and bends through its valley, with natural terraces, rolling hills, and the mountains rising above it. About forty miles downstream from Port Jervis, the Delaware Water Gap stands as one of nature's distinct landmarks, a long, mile-wide notch in the Kittatinny Range of the Blue Ridge, carved by the river. During the nineteenth century, as I learned, the Gap was considered almost on a par with Niagara Falls. Stylish hotels were built overlooking the river to capitalize on the view. The entire region was a popular summer resort, with abundant taverns and boarding houses enabling New Yorkers and Philadelphians to escape urban heat and humidity.

Milford became one of the fashionable retreats. Early movie studios moved from Fort Lee, opposite upper Manhattan, to do a lot of shooting in pre-Hollywood days. Tom Mix made westerns and Pearl White recorded various episodes of the celebrated *Perils of Pauline*. David W. Griffith brought Mary Pickford, Lillian Gish, Lionel Barrymore, H. B. Walthall, and Harry Carey to Milford to make a 1912 epic which preceded by three years his *Birth of a Nation*. In 1918 a film was made here on the outdoors life of Theodore Roosevelt, the ex-President who generously endowed his royalties to the American Red Cross.

I learned these bits of social history by looking, listening, and reading in my spare time. I had come to Milford to complete a book about the Forest Service—its history, organization, policies, a review of what it does, and why and how it got that way. I wasn't making headway at home, just outside of Washington, with all its distractions. Now it would be much simpler to see Jane, who lived a little more than two hours away in Bucks County (though she worked in Philadelphia).

Milford was a convenient happenstance. The Forest Service invited me to work at Grey Towers, a forty-room mansion, which it administered and which it called the Pinchot Institute for Conservation Studies. The building and surrounding estate came under the agency's aegis as a logical bequest. Grey Towers had been the

home of Gifford Pinchot, the first Chief of the Forest Service and
later two-term governor of Pennsylvania, a man born to wealth who
never had to work, but who allied himself with Theodore Roosevelt and others of means in the cause of social justice, notably the
conservation of natural resources. His parents had built the mansion in 1886 on a design by Richard Morris Hunt, architect of Vanderbilt castles at Newport and Asheville and of the Fogg Museum
at Harvard. The Vanderbilt mansions are larger and more regal, but
for a country summer place, Grey Towers in its day doubtless was
the showpiece of the Poconos: built of stone, in the style of a
French country chateau with three circular towers, a handsome
pedestal on a landscaped hill, reached on a driveway of a quarter
mile from the gatehouse (pretty fair digs in itself), with far views of
the Jersey forests. Pinchot was long a bachelor, till after his mother
died, then he married a flaming redhead, Cornelia, spirited, a femi-
nist, committed to social justice like himself. Regardless of their
philosophy, they enjoyed fine living. In the 1920s Gifford and Cornelia built the South Seas Patio just outside the Grey Towers dining room with a stone mosaic from the private yacht they owned
and had sailed to the South Seas. The patio was bordered by huge
Italian urns, but its centerpiece, the stone "Finger Bowl," was
more showy. It was filled with water and designed for outdoors
dining with a flair; guests (possibly as many as twenty) ate from
stone ledges, passing the food by floating large bowls on the surface.

Pinchot's heart was in forestry and conservation, in which fields
he influenced Franklin D. as well as Theodore Roosevelt; at the
time of his death in 1946 (at the age of 81), he was promoting the
idea of a world conference to conserve natural resources. Cornelia
lived on till 1960. I missed knowing her personally, but heard
many stories about her vigorous, unorthodox personality. Once,
while she was entertaining a group of foresters at her Washington
home, an industry man suggested the discussion consider means of
keeping the labor unions of loggers in their proper place. Mrs.
Pinchot rose angrily. "To think such talk against the workingman
would take place under this roof!" she exclaimed. "Gifford Pinchot
is turning over in his grave at this very instant." She banished the
antilabor forester from the house forever.

At Grey Towers I was privy to a large, comfortable office on the third floor of one of the towers, enhanced by curving book shelves well fit into circular walls. The room was hot in summer and cold in winter, but there was always some way of making out. Nobody bothered me; it was an ideal place to work. There wasn't much research or conservation study of consequence going on—foresters not being the breed to generate new social ideas—but the house was well kept. Tourists would be guided through rooms on the first floor, be told the story of the Pinchot family, and wander off to the terraces, patios, and lawns, thinking that something significant might be under way upstairs.

I saw a lot of nature, if not exactly wilderness as we define it, in the Delaware Valley. While the Forest Service provided working space, I was responsible for living quarters, which I fortuitously found at a nature reserve, called the Milford Reservation, three miles away. The setting was superb: sixteen hundred acres of forest, second or third growth mostly, surrounding a quiet lake, roughly circular and about a mile around. There were five cottages on the lake, but only two permanent residents, Tom Smith, the program director, occupying one of the cottages, and I in another. It was a curious kind of place, having passed through various hands, private and nonprofit, and was now intended as a nature study center for urban school groups. To house them adequately, a modern, solar-powered brick building, with composting toilet facilities, had only lately been completed. The building was in place on a wooded bluff at one end of the lake, with dormitory accommodations for one hundred, but there were no school groups. Mostly there were Tom and me, sometimes only one of us. On weekends his roommate, Gayle, would come up from their place near Princeton, but she, although a trained biologist, didn't care for the isolation. Sometimes Tom's brother and his roommate would come up, or other friends, all lively people. Or Tom would go down to Princeton. Jane came now and then, and sometimes I would go to Bucks County. As the year passed I had a lot of time, a lot of weekends on my own. It was lonely, especially in winter, but in retrospect not so bad after all, for I learned a lot about the Delaware and its valley.

Compared with the Mississippi, Ohio, Colorado, or Columbia,

the Delaware might be dismissed as a modest stream. But it should not be. When Henry Hudson arrived on the scene in 1609, he described it as "one of the finest, best and pleasantest rivers in the world," and that description is still apt. The heavy industries of Trenton, Philadelphia, Camden, Chester, and Wilmington have treated the downstream Delaware—the estuary where the current mixes with the ocean tide—like a sump, destroying the sources of striped bass, sturgeon, shad, and oysters that Indians and early settlers knew. Above the estuary, however, the river is one of the liveliest, loveliest, and cleanest in the East. It flows about 330 miles from its source on the western slopes of the Catskill Mountains southward in three gigantic zigzags, forming the boundary between New York and Pennsylvania, then between Pennsylvania and New Jersey, before reaching its outlet at Delaware Bay, below Wilmington. Through underground conduits, the river provides half the water supply of metropolitan New York City and all the water supply of greater Philadelphia. East and west branches of the river and upper tributaries have long been dammed, filling reservoirs that store eighty-five billion gallons of drinking water. However, below Hancock, New York, where east and west branches join, not a single dam blocks the main river. That is unusual—rare—for any river of any length in our time.

The entire Delaware plays a singular role. The upper forested stretches come closest to meeting the accepted definition of wilderness. But even so, one section and another affords pleasure and inspiration for people of all kinds: fishermen, canoeists, kayakers, bicyclists riding the towpaths of old canals, birders, artists, students of history and archaeology—all these and more. Below Wilmington and the industry blight, the river opens into a broad saltwater bay, shores dotted with farms and villages, and the water with boats.

I explored portions of the river and its corridor, not all the way to the mouth, but enough to recognize and appreciate its values. Driving to Bucks County to visit Jane, I followed the river. On both sides, farmlands and towns filled much of the shoreline flatlands. I might take an old byroad, for a shortcut (or a long cut) leading to lakes and waterfalls, passing an occasional eighteenth-century stone house with rough wood framing, built by Dutch or German settlers. At Easton, the Lehigh River, once the West

233

Branch, joins the Delaware. From here down, Roosevelt State Park, sixty miles long, embraces the Delaware Canal and towpath, where mules once pulled barges loaded with coal bound for Philadelphia. The Delaware has always been a well-used and useful river. Rafting pine logs began before the American Revolution; by the mid-1800s, rafts were twenty-five feet wide and two hundred feet long, manned by a steersman and four or five hands. Then came the canals (after most of the usable timber was cut), moving hard coal to the cities until the 1930s, when their day was done.

A lot of history and abundant historical vestiges trace back to the Lenape Indians, sites revealing where they hunted, fished, gathered edible plants, and lived in harmony with the land. They spent growing seasons in small, unfortified villages near river-bottom clearings, then moved to higher camps for fall and winter. They considered game animals gifts provided by the Creator for work properly done and conducted in a precise, correct manner. There is a lot of colonial and revolutionary history, too, sometimes intermingled with the Indian sites. Point Pleasant, for instance, just a few miles above New Hope, in Bucks County, was a Lenape fishing and trading encampment, later an English settlement, and then a major stopping place along the Pennsylvania Canal.

Jane and I would visit such points in Bucks County, including Washington Crossing State Park, and the other Washington Crossing State Park on the opposite shore in New Jersey, where General Washington pulled ashore in the dead of winter. We'd have dinner or a drink at country inns and restored stagecoach stops along the river road at New Hope or Lumberville, or at Riegelsville in a more rural setting. Whether she wore jeans or a dress or slacks and sport jacket, she always seemed sleek and stylish to me and she would insist that I take off my tie and loosen up. Bucks County, Pennsylvania, resembles in a way Marin County, California, attracting upscale kinds of people who live well, dine well, and collect art, good books, and records. She had that air about her, although struggling to support three children, a house, and a large dog. She was a native, descendant of an old Swiss or Swiss-German farm family. So the places that were "points of interest" to others had been part of her growing up.

The farther upstream, the wilder the river becomes. The Delaware Water Gap National Recreation Area, covering the corridor between the Gap and Port Jervis, may not be as large as Yellowstone, but it serves its purpose in the East. I'd canoe sometimes with a friend into a little cove or to one of the islands and feel isolated from civilization, or hike to a waterfall splashing over rock ledges through green jungles of hemlock, pine, and rhododendron and feel no envy for Yosemite.

North of Port Jervis, the Upper Delaware National Recreation Area was established in 1978 to protect seventy-five river miles. It is not a national park in the ordinary sense, since the federal government administers only the river portion while encouraging the states of New York and Pennsylvania and their counties to safeguard the shorelines in their relatively natural, sometimes wild, state.

Tom Smith, my landlord, imparted to me a degree of his uncanny sensitivity to nature. He was a Rutgers graduate in biology, a handsome, dark-haired, third-generation Irish-American in his mid-thirties, who seemed to have cataloged in his mind all the birds, insects, plants, flowers, and mammals. He had refined his skills as a high school biology teacher and naturalist working for the Boy Scouts of America. Normally he was considerate and generous, but sometimes moody and gloomy, as the Irish can be. Once he and his brother were arrested for violating some insignificant fishing regulation. At least *they* felt it was insignificant and argued with the game warden, who slapped them with a summons to court. I saw them just before they went to trial, both resentful and rebellious, and I feared they might raise a ruckus before the judge; fortunately, they calmed down and got off light. Tom and Gayle had their chronic ups and downs, but they outlasted them. It wasn't so much that he was Catholic and she Jewish as it was that he wanted to get married and she was reluctant. Once pregnant she finally agreed, but that stirred the pot as to whether they would be married by a rabbi or priest. Tom opted for one of each, but Gayle's mother insisted on a strictly Jewish service. A week before the wedding Gayle had a miscarriage, but went through with it anyway. (A child came later.)

Around the reservation we would see signs of beaver, where they had cut aspens and willows along the stream bank or in muddy backwaters, and signs of bear; we saw otter swimming and diving, different kinds of turtles, lots of deer, groundhogs, raccoons, porcupines, skunks, and orange butterflies. Canada geese would rest on the lake while heading south in autumn, north in spring. One in particular that had trouble flying stayed a long time. It returned early and hatched three chicks, which made us feel like godparents, but one by one the chicks were lost to predators.

Tom and I (or Jane and I when she came up) went to see waterfalls in the river valley, cool and moist, little self-contained ecosystems carved by glaciers out of ancient rock. I observed waterfalls through the seasons. In spring the water is fullest, at maximum flow, and freshest—even before spring takes hold, the first breakup of ice on a stream yields the purest, clearest water dancing with promise. In summer the waterfall ravine is shaded with mountain laurel, smaller than in the southern highlands, luxuriant rhododendron showy with blossoms, and hemlock, though turtles still manage to sun themselves on moss-coated rocks out of water. In autumn the scene is colored with brown, gray, purple, and red. The water flows softly, quietly. The valley is quiet. Camps have closed, tourists don't come for weekends anymore. They miss completely the wonders of winter, crisp and stark, the sight of the waterfall frozen like a polished candelabra.

One day late in autumn I drove to Port Jervis and north along the river on the New York side. It was a cloudy, soggy day, but there was little traffic and I could easily pull off on the shoulder where the road climbed high above the upper Delaware and observe the contour of the river and the layout of the hills. On a summer weekend the water would be covered by a flotilla of canoes moving downstream by the hundreds. Now there was only the river, a flowing liquid gray.

I stopped for beer and lunch at the Minisink Inn, perched on a cliffside at the Minisink Ford, a strategic site along the river. It was a simple country pub serving country food, never seeming very busy, though I can picture it otherwise in its earlier life. Perhaps it was built sometime during the resort heydays, though there might have been some kind of structure in the canal era or even earlier. Rafting pine logs on streams flowing into the Delaware, such as the Lackawaxen, Minisink, and Neversink, began during the colonial period. There were certain disruptions to that activity, such as the American Revolution and the Indian uprisings. On a wooded bluff a mile or two from the Minisink Inn, I visited the site of the Battle of Minisink, really a skirmish, in which Joseph Brant, the Mohawk Chief, and his warriors massacred a company of militia in 1779. That word *massacre*, I thought while following the trail over the rocks and along the ridgetop, is a white man's word. So is *savage*. Joseph Brant was educated in an English school, converted to Christianity, and visited England, where he became a favorite of society and was painted by Gilbert Stuart. His goal was simply to ensure historic rights of the Six Nations and to protect Indian lands from encroachment by settlers—a sound reason for influencing his people to side with the British. Following the Revolution, he moved to Canada, continuing work as a missionary and endeavoring to gain new lands for the dispossessed Native Americans.

With the British and Indians out of the way, it became possible to concentrate on wilderness, civilizing and settling the wild, or at least extracting raw materials from it and transporting them back to the cities. Rafting logs was an early method, but it was a cold, wet job, demanding men of strength and endurance, and it generally took a year for water-soaked lumber to dry. Canals became the answer to the demand for greater speed and convenience.

Pennsylvania alone built 1200 miles of canal, much of it along the Delaware, or on streams feeding into it or flowing from it. All told, 4000 miles of channeled, controlled waterway extended as far as Illinois, carrying settlers and supplies to the western frontier, returning products of forests, mines, and farms to eastern cities. Canals were costly to build, but they made transportation smooth and dependable. They removed the trials and uncertainties of running the rivers with their waterfalls and rapids, raging spring torrents, and difficult if not impossible upstream travel. Locks and aqueducts easily conveyed the canal over a stream or deep depression. When porous soil caused trouble in maintaining an adequate water level, canal builders compensated by installing a water wheel to pump supplies from the adjacent river. Mules provided the main source of power, pulling the canal boats while walking surefooted and uncomplaining along the towpath.

The Delaware and Hudson Canal was constructed from Honesdale, Pennsylvania, to Kingston, New York, a distance of 108 miles, in order to facilitate the transport of hard anthracite coal ("stone coal") to New York City. An entire family lived aboard and operated the canal boat, taking ten days to travel the route. The first twenty-five miles followed the Lackawaxen to its junction with the Delaware at Minisink Ford, where an early problem involved the occasional collision of timber rafts, coming down the main river, with canal barges. This contributed to the decision to build a suspension aqueduct to carry canal traffic above the water, for which project John Augustus Roebling, a Pennsylvanian of promise, was engaged as architect.

I walked across the Roebling Aqueduct, or the Roebling Bridge, which he completed in 1848 as part of the practical training for his later, larger work, the Brooklyn Bridge. It was roughly forty yards across and was supported fifteen yards above the water by three stone buttresses. Originally it was a long trough with two thick sides, wide and deep enough to hold a canal boat in flowing water, then an auto bridge, and finally a footbridge covered with planks. I found walking across the Delaware into Lackawaxen a pleasant experience, but learned the locals were unhappy about their bridge being closed to cars because it meant an extra few minutes of travel via another crossing upstream or downstream.

Zane Grey would like it as it is, a hamlet undisturbed. When the author returned alone to Lackawaxen for a visit in 1920, he wrote to his wife, Dolly: "This is home. This will always be home for you and me . . . this hard, barren, lonely place." The white-framed wooden house in which he lived stood five hundred yards above the bridge, facing the river. The day was gray, damp, and dismal, yet four or five fishermen, all in high waders, were in the stream. I watched them for a few minutes, casting patiently without any sign of action. They might have all been spending their Sunday afternoon in comfort somewhere else, but Zane Grey would be pleased they were here.

At the house I met Mrs. Helen Davis, a lady of seventy-plus years, who occupied a part of it with her husband and maintained the rest as the Zane Grey Museum. The author was a friend of her father, a New York journalist. She mentioned how the two of them once attended a lecture by Colonel J. C. "Buffalo" Jones, an eccentric frontiersman who invited Grey to his ranch in Arizona. The visit spurred him to write frontier tales and to become the author who, as they said in his time, "made the West famous."

Zane Grey, after graduating from dentistry school in Philadelphia, opened a practice in New York City. But he was drawn to the outdoors and began visiting a resort lodge in New York State across the Delaware from Lackawaxen. He returned often to camp and fish. Inspired by this eastern wilderness, he began to write, first magazine stories, then novels, but without success. In 1903 he bought five acres in Lackawaxen and quit dentistry. In 1905 his brother built the big white house and Grey moved in with his new wife. He wrote furiously, scribbling on plain white paper. By the time he moved to Hollywood in 1918 he was a celebrity, destined to become "the most popular author on the planet."

Mrs. Davis displayed a lot of memorabilia: his old foot-driven dentist's drill, Indian sand paintings, Navajo rugs, photos taken by Grey himself of canyon and desert country, book jackets, movie posters with stars of Zane Grey films, such as Richard Dix (who came before Joel McCrea, who came before John Wayne). As a guide, she was almost painfully frank about her subject. Even at the height of fame, with all his movies, books translated into many foreign languages, and wealth to cruise on his own yacht and fish wherever he wished, Grey suffered depression, largely because he was scorned by critics who considered his work more corny than literary.

Possibly so, but Grey had something. It was more than a talent to grind out a hundred or so adventure novels that ultimately would sell more than one hundred million copies. He had a perception of wilderness as relevant to human life and growth and universal truth, as evidenced by this passage from *The Vanishing American*:

"Nophaie wandered on and on over the sage hills, proud and fierce as a young eagle, aloof and strange, dreaming the dreams conjured up by the wise men of his tribe. At seven years of age he had begun to realize the meaning of a chief, and that a chief must someday save his people. What he loved most was to be alone, out in the desert, listening to the real sounds of the open and to the silent whispering of his soul. In the shadow of the hogans, among the boys and girls there, he was only Nophaie. They were jealous.

They resented his importance. But out on the desert, in the cold rosy dawns and the solemn hot noontides, and the golden sunsets, when the sunlight stole down softly and white stars smiled at him from the velvet blue—then Nophaie could be himself, could listen and feel, and know the four winds of heaven whispered of his future, of how he would make the medicine to save his people.

"Nophaie did not walk alone. Innumerable spirits kept pace with his light steps. The sage was a carpet of purple, fragrant and sweet, through which breathed the low soft sigh of the wind. The shallow stream of water, murmuring and meandering in the red sandy wash below, lined white along its margins, spoke to Nophaie of winter snows now melting on the heights, of water for the sheep all summer, of Utsay's (the god of Indians) good will. To east and west and south heaved up the red gods of rock that seemed to move with Nophaie as he moved, shadow and loom over him as he halted, watch him with vast, impassive faces. Though they were far away they seemed close. In their secret stony cells abided the soul of Indians—many as the white pebbles along the stream. The flash of a swift-winged canyon bird was a message. The gleams of melted frost, sparkling and pure, were the teardrops of his mother, who forever hovered near him, wandered with him along the sage trails, in spirit with his steps. The sun, the moon, the crag with its human face, the black raven creaking his dismal note, the basking rattlesnake, the spider that shut his little door above him, the mockingbird, singer of all songs—those held communion with Nophaie, were his messengers. And all around him and above him, in the great silence, in the towering barriers of stone, in the vast flare of intense sunlight, there seemed to be life in harmony with him, a voiceless and eternal life that he felt but could not see."

Such natural rhythms and cycles are accessible only with patience and away from crowds. Primitive peoples, including Native Americans, free of impersonal, artificial instruments, have sensed the connection and continuum that bind the hours of their lives with the centuries of time. We tend to dismiss dances, lustrations, ceremonial hunts, new fire-making, and new-moon feasts as manifestations of superstition; the Indian, however, believes in mysticism and power of the ceremonial emerging from supernatural forces that build the growing earth in spring, drench it with rain, or tear it apart with lightning. Among the Lenape, the Masked Being, or Masked Spirit, was guardian of wild animals of the forest. He was sometimes seen riding on the back of a buck or herding the deer. The hunter learned that he must be on friendly terms with this spirit who had the capability of "breaking the hunter's speech," thereby causing him to stammer or, worse still, bring death through psychoses.

The medicine man, or shaman, could frighten away sickness and death by use of secret formulas and herbal remedies, dancing around his patient with incantations and rattling gourds. "Witchcraft," still powerful medicine, enabled the patient to become one of the Holy Beings, in harmony with the infinite, free of ills and evils. The power of Indian medicine is now better defined as psychosomatic therapy, directed at the whole person—mind, body, and faith—the natural remedies being enhanced by varied paraphernalia and ritual, which makes him believe in the efficacy of the cure and the authority of the shaman, the intermediary between the afflicted party and supernatural world.

The Indian system is akin in greater or lesser degree to folk medicine, psychic healing, herbal treatment, acupuncture, yoga, biofeedback, massage, and reflexology; however, it is fundamentally nature-based and requires commitment and extreme patience, and concern for the individual's relationship to earth and sky, sun and moon, sacred mountains and vegetation, rains, dark clouds and mist, and inner forms of the cardinal points. It is powerful medicine, perhaps the ultimate in holistic health.

Jane wanted me to visit the Himalayan Institute (actually, the Himalayan Institute of Yoga Science and Philosophy) at Honesdale, about forty miles north of Milford. She had attended a program or two and told me of the medical unit following principles of holistic health. I was curious to learn about health care beyond prescriptions and pills, and self-care of my own ecosystem. I didn't get to it for months, until one day while visiting a dentist in Milford the technician took my blood pressure and told me it was elevated—not seriously, but serious enough to indicate the time was right. When I phoned Jane that evening she was solicitous. "I don't care whether you go to the Himalayan Institute, but please get yourself checked by a physician." I told her that I had already made an appointment at Honesdale.

My doctor's name was Larry Cohen, the youngest of three physicians on the staff. He looked and acted like a doctor, wearing thick eyeglasses and asking the standard questions to record on a form, but the office didn't look very medical to me, perhaps because it lacked the right magazines, potted plants, deep carpeting, and sanitized nurses and secretaries answering busy telephones. The Himalayan Institute just wasn't that kind of place. The main building was a solid brick structure, formerly a Catholic school or seminary, with a four-hundred-acre campus around it, a tranquil setting designed to encourage "learning, introspection, and psychological growth." Larry evidently had lots of time and asked lots of questions, which made me wonder: *Why doesn't he look at his watch? Why doesn't he give me the subtle signal to go? Where are all his patients? What the heck kind of doctor is he anyway?* Whatever it was, when I left the office I gave up salt, sugar, canned food, fried food, preservatives, red meat, and hard whiskey (a subject in which I had been an A student for years) and was headed down the road to grain, legumes, and tofu. Larry introduced me to relaxation techniques, abdominal breathing, exercise, and walks to cope with stress and hypertension. Much later I asked him why this happened. "Because you were ready. You just wanted me to give you the okay to do that. You must have had it in your heart of hearts, to feel it consistent with the life you should be leading." As a consequence of changing eating and drinking habits, I lost weight, about twenty pounds in two months. I had to discard clothing or have it altered. I felt fine, but the people at the Pinchot Institute thought I would die. Live without meat? How in the world would I keep my blood red?

I kept coming back to the Himalayan Institute. I would stay for the evening meal and sometimes overnight. I attended various lectures and short courses in yoga and meditation. Tom Smith joined me in the meditation class; he was troubled with high blood pressure, but after a time found this practice brought it down. The people at the Himalayan Institute were classed as residents and students, including some serious long-term students in Eastern philosophy and in Buddhist and yoga psychology. Some of the women took Sanskrit names for themselves. They spent their days in group meditation, yoga, attending classes and seminars, and always with time for walks across the grounds with views of the mountains. In the dining hall one large table was reserved for those who chose to eat in silence, and on Monday evening at dinner everyone was silent. It struck me that some of those I met were trying to withdraw from everyday life because it was too much for them to handle; they wanted a sanctuary to shelter them from harsh reality, to achieve peace for themselves away from cities and wars and nukes and social problems others cannot escape. When I saw a group feasting on cheeseburgers and milkshakes at a fast-food parlor off the reservation, I realized they weren't all wedded to tofu and lentil loaf.

The best ideas are idealized, institutionalized, and then corrupted. Through Jane I met professionals and amateurs in humanistic psychology and "human potential," some of whom were deeply into paradigms and dialogue full of jargon. She took me to a workshop that began with talk about everyone loving each other, but many attendees were self-centered gurus, focused on themselves, hardly listening or caring about what anyone else had to say.

I felt, however, that my physician and friend, Larry Cohen, was for real. He was bouncy and bright, self-assured but not pushy, a psychedelic kind of character; he was raised in Texas, where his father, a pharmaceutical salesman, introduced him to Ouija boards, séances, and psychics. Larry had been into grass and hard drugs, peddling some of it through medical school. He had been married briefly in his early twenties. He worked in emergency rooms in Texas, at a government hospital on the Navajo reservation in Arizona (where he and another physician were both tempestuously involved with the same woman, a Baptist missionary), and on the Cherokee reservation in North Carolina. He had spent a year traveling solo around the country in a camper van.

Larry was thirty-three. We celebrated his birthday when he came to visit the Milford Reservation. We rowed around the lake, had a glass of wine at my pad, and went to dinner. I could see that he had his own hang-ups. He ate too fast and seemed knotted by some internal problem. But he was a good companion and conversationalist, free of fraud and put-on. Another time we drove to

New York in his camper. We were headed separate ways, but first, when we arrived in the city, he insisted that we each get a cup of Italian ice from one of the street vendors. "But, Larry," I protested, "that's exactly the kind of stuff you told me not to eat! What are you up to?" "Oh, I have to have my buy-ins now and then." So we enjoyed the Italian ice with a clear conscience.

One day in early June we rented a canoe and spent a day on the river. Larry, in the stern, proved an experienced, competent steersman. It was a bright day, free of pressure, demand, competition. We were headed for Skinner's Falls, rated a Class II rapid, rather tame, but not to be taken lightly. The river was broad, lazy in the eddies, the silence punctuated only by the splash of paddles. Even so, I put mine up now and then to listen to the rustle of grass along the banks. Like a moving mirror, the river reflected the light of the sky and the colors of the hills and trees. I watched a great blue heron in the shallows poking its sharp beak for a fish, possibly a frog or salamander. Drops of water on a nearby spiderweb glistened in the sun. That spider might trap its quota of flying insects, but it would be fair game to fish, along with crickets, beetles, ants, and grasshoppers, any time they fell, hopped, or crawled into the river.

We went through mild riffles, then a calm, glassy eddy, listening to the roar of Skinner's Falls around the bend. That roar was the sound of water at work, tumbling boulders and pebbles against each other and against the bottom, grinding it down. We eased into a rocky cove and scouted the rapid. We had been cautioned at the rental shop, told of several reckless daredevils who had been killed and seriously injured. The water was churning, boiling, tumbling; the waves plumed and fumed. We watched another canoe make it through, then took off. The river's gathering momentum swept us around the rocky bend into roaring white water. We zigzagged between boulders down a twisting course, with Larry doing most of the heavy work, and made it in good form.

"I was glad to be out on that river with no bullshit," Larry said that evening at dinner. "With people, they're demanding. Being with nature makes me be in touch with a more dynamic free flow. I mean, being pulled along by the river without battling it. That was nice."

I asked him about his experiences as an emergency room physician and on the Indian reservations, and how they led him to holistic health.

"I learned the limits of what I could do in the emergency room. I learned not to be concerned with whatever rolled in the door. I worked five twenty-four-hour shifts a month and learned to deal with twenty-four hours of constant craziness, including intense sleep deprivation. I was a surgeon in one room, a psychiatrist in the next room, a plastic surgeon in another room, a medical doctor, an optometrist. From one room to the next I learned to deal with families about sudden deaths. People would crash in front of me. I saw incredible scenes. I mean, *incredible* scenes. At the hospital in Abilene, in West Texas, we had two good emergency rooms to work with. One night we had a cardiac patient in each room; one man was dying, another was throwing up, in full cardiac arrest. And another man was sitting in a chair, obviously having a heart attack. We didn't know where to put him, so we put him in the same room with the guy already having a heart attack. This guy is sitting not two feet away with a little wet towel over his face so he doesn't have to see everything, but he *hears* everything.

"I learned to predict the sense of the city. When I worked at the hospital in the barrio at San Antonio, it could be dead quiet. Then a kid would come in, shot in the head. He lived but lost an eye. Dead quiet—then in ten minutes it was full. Like another world. I would treat a sore throat, *anything*. I saw forty people in eight hours. I was constantly running. I learned that emergencies are almost always made. People are under tremendous emotional stress. They're angry, something is wrong, so they do things in a hurry. In the barrio you were *the* doctor. People didn't have doctors, or they were aliens. They would come in at five A.M. because of crotch itch. I treated lots of Friday night stabbings, gunshot wounds . . .

"The Navajo I saw are part of a pure culture. They haven't had inbreeding. A large percentage speak their own language. They live in a poverty situation, but they have their own rites and treatments. But the North Carolina Cherokee have mixed with whites for two hundred years. There are very few purebloods. The majority were marched west to Oklahoma in the 1830s. There is very little culture left.

"In Cherokee we were meeting the social structure needs of the community. They came for everything. They drank, smoked cigarettes, had no place to go, nothing to do. They're psychosexually at about the twelve-year-old level. There is a lot of macho—at an adolescent, sexual level.

"The Navajo had malnutrition and diseases of poverty, but they only came in when they were sick. They are very pleasant people. No evidence of fetal distress, no heart disease. The Cherokee are not happy; they are angry. The people we saw at the hospital were very dependent. The Navajo when they had their babies were very quiet, they didn't need any narcotics at all, they just had their kids. The Cherokee!—They were just young girls, fourteen or fifteen. They were frightened in labor. Some would scream and go crazy. They had a kind of low-key field distress. People would come in with abdominal problems, ulcers, lots of migraine headaches. They were in constant distress, upset, a very unpeaceful people—because the culture was lost. It showed how their emotional life played on their physical life. I'm talking about the hospital population, the ones we saw. There were many good people, too.

"The Navajo were still having problems with the interface of culture and alcohol, but it wasn't to the same degree. The people weren't demanding or hostile. I knew there was something more than medicine. The difference between Navajo and Cherokee was so sharply defined, I couldn't deny how people's mental state affects the physical. I couldn't go back to the old way full time."

He felt the influence of his father ("My dad was kind of weird, but the words, concepts, and potentials of unexplainable other approaches were in my home as reality"), and the experiences in the emergency rooms and on the reservations guiding him to the Himalayan Institute to explore the unknown scientifically.

"Harmonious functioning of the body stems from consciousness of unification, understanding how it works so it can work better. If you're a very sexual person, try to channel it, rather than work against and suppress it. Use that kind of energy, then work on it. Listen to your body, don't work against it. We expect things to revolve around us, but observing the system, learning how to get it to respond, trying to find out who you are and where you fit in, being able to cope—all that takes time. You have to visit and hang out, it takes years to understand. Most people don't want that responsibility, they want somebody else to count on.

"The Plains Indians have a ceremony called the Vision Quest. I've only read about it. Basically every man, and I think woman, too, took a period for it at the age of twelve or thirteen. They were given a name when they were born, but went on a Vision Quest to get another name. They prepared for it carefully, then went out and fasted and prayed and had these visions. They returned to the elders, people who understood, and told their stories. The elders would tell them who they were spiritually, what their 'path' was, and they were given a spiritual name. People who didn't have visions could buy other people's, but everybody had to have some meaning to their lives.

"This sort of sums up what we've been talking about. You have to get your own vision and meaning for yourself and life. Or accept that you don't and go along with somebody else's. Once you found out where you were it was your goal in life to complete yourself. The Plains Indians had the medicine wheel. It had stations, with different colors that meant different things. If you were born here, you might be called Black Elk of the North, but you had to learn South, West, East, and to know Green, Black, White, Yellow, and different animals that run in their own spaces. You started somewhere and had your given and had to experience life to become complete and know each place and understand the marriage to that place."

My time at Milford neared its end. Jane came to canoe the uppermost portion of the Upper Delaware with me. Actually she had been staying for a week at a hostel in the Poconos as part of an accelerated psychology course in her doctoral program. She was ready for two or three hours on the river; I thought it would take about five, but it proved to be more like seven. We started with the canoe rental at Hancock, at the junction of the two branches. The river was peaceful and quiet, deserted except for an occasional fisherman wading in hip boots. Now and then we passed a hamlet with clapboard farmhouses and cottages clinging to the banks, looking like a transplanted New England vignette. Jane, paddling in the front, said she was pushing the houses out of her mind and felt like the Indians in their time here. Hawks and vultures glided and swooped in graceful spirals. These ridges and valleys are favored by migrating birds: warblers and tanagers, possibly bald eagles, in spring; great blue heron and osprey in summer; and hawks, on some days hundreds sailing by every hour, in autumn.

We paddled through a few rifts—shallow spots with rough water—but the river generally was calm and low, so low that we sometimes had to get out and pull the canoe. After a time the trip became an exercise in endurance. I didn't mind, but Jane said later that she lost interest in the river and became painfully aware of the hours.

That was unfortunate, considering that our little canoe excursion was virtually our farewell. Not quite then, but shortly. Jane came to Idaho to visit for a week at the end of summer. I wanted to fly back to be with her at Christmas, but she resisted. She didn't want me, but didn't want to lose me either. She sought guidance through counseling. I came east the following spring and we were together, quite pleasurably, but all too briefly, after which she wrote me a letter calling it off—for keeps. She had blessed me with tenderness and loving, a lot of loving, and had helped me to a new perception. Little by little, I became aware of mind-body connection, the way to reach deeper levels of consciousness, the flow of energy between myself and a parcel of earthly wildness, the sense of the Indian who regards procedure as important as purpose. Our romance began, fittingly, in the Yellowstone wilderness, in a blue and gold spaceship that is still out there, orbiting the cosmos.

CHAPTER XIII

⁓

Wild Desert: Those Magic Lands of Little Rain

Theodore Roosevelt was pleased and proud when he came to Arizona in 1911 to dedicate the mighty dam named for him at the confluence of Tonto Creek and the Salt River. The Reclamation Act of 1902, adopted early in his administration, had launched the Salt River irrigation project and would launch many others to follow. At 280 feet, Roosevelt Dam was the highest dam in the world. It impounded as much water as the world's previous three largest reservoirs combined.

Aboriginal Indians, the Anasazi, tapped the rivers to irrigate their dry lands. Their methods of working with soil and water were primitive, but they met the desert on its own terms, living for more than ten centuries without altering the balance of nature. The same was true, to some extent, of the first Spanish and Anglo settlers, who built long ditches to move water to their food and forage crops and to their homesites. But Roosevelt Dam and reclamation were much grander in concept. The Apache Indians had fought for their land and lost. Now serious development of the arid Southwest wilderness could begin.

Roosevelt as a historian essentially was a chronicler of expansionism, and no less so as a statesman, for all his good deeds in natural-resource conservation. He described the frontier days as "the winning of the West" by heroic pioneers specially chosen "to conquer the wilderness and hold it against all comers." Like many others, he regarded the Indians as strangers, intruders in the path of national destiny.

Nevertheless, in dedicating Roosevelt Dam, he exclaimed that the vast wild country spread before him presented the most sublimely beautiful panorama nature had ever created. He was given to such sweeping pronouncements. As when he went to the Grand Canyon in 1903 and advised the people of the country: "Do nothing to mar its grandeur. Keep it for your children and your children's children, and all who come after you, as the one great sight which every American should see."

Roosevelt likely thought there was so much desert in Arizona and its neighboring states that dams and development to eternity would scarcely make a dent. For most Americans, Arizona was as distant as the moon, harsh and fearsome, where Indians practiced strange medicine—when they weren't on the warpath. There was, for instance, the Rainbow Bridge just north of the Arizona-Utah border, a symmetrical salmon-pink sandstone arch curving upward to a height of 309 feet, almost 30 feet higher than Roosevelt Dam. To the Navajo shamans, it was *nonnezoshe*, a sacred destination for religious pilgrimage. Zane Grey in *Tales of Lonely Trails* wrote:

"Rainbow Bridge was not for many eyes to see. The tourist, the leisurely traveler, the comfort loving would never behold it. Only by toil, sweat, endurance and pain could any man ever look at *nonnezoshe*. It seemed well to realize that the great things of life had to be earned."

Today the Indian medicine men are gone from Rainbow Bridge. The impounded waters of Glen Canyon Dam have made painless visits possible, via boat on the reservoir called Lake Powell to the Bridge Canyon landing, then walking about one mile. The desert once so abundant, in other words, now desperately needs to be saved.

In the early 1960s I went to the Desert Botanical Garden at the outskirts of Phoenix, which the Arizona Cactus and Native Flora Society had established so there would always be someplace to observe and study desert plants. I interviewed W. Hubert Earle, the director. He was a man who had come to Arizona some years before on his doctor's orders. He knew nothing about plants, but began working around the botanical garden as a volunteer. When I met him he was an international authority on cactus and succulents.

"A few years ago you looked across Paradise Valley toward the mountains and saw one light," he told me. "The fields were filled with meadowlarks and wildlife. Now our one hundred fifty acres are surrounded by the city. Of course, there's plenty of desert remaining in Arizona, but some plants are becoming extinct. A little cactus, *Navajo peeplesiana*, has vanished under the pressure of grazing. The paper-pined pincushion is fast disappearing. Hungry rodents are destroying the saguaro, since man has killed the foxes and coyotes that used to keep them in balance." And that was more than twenty years ago.

The wild desert cries to be saved. Those who wish it saved cry, too; sometimes they cry in anger, often in despair. The desert stands in the way, like the Indian, an intruder in the path of national destiny. But it is a way in itself, a place to be alone, where the individualist finds release from the crowd, a place to touch magic and mystery. The desert inspires eloquent writing in its behalf, as in *Desert Solitare*, by Edward Abbey, and in *The Monkey Wrench Gang*, his fictional counterattack against a system unresponsive to the needs and wants of nonconformists who prefer to walk alone.

Sometimes I think the inspiration of the desert is in its flora. Cacti and succulents have adapted through long periods of evolution to survive with little water, rather a marvel to contemplate. From late March to May, the seemingly barren, grayish desert floor bursts into bloom with short-lived wildflowers of many colors. The sundrop opens delicate yellow petals at night and closes them soon after sunrise. The lavish poppy covers wide areas with a cloth of gold. The misty green-branched paloverde, the Arizona state tree, blooms in pale yellow. The ocotillo, formed of slender wandlike stems, shows scarlet clusters at its tips. Penstemon, usually on rocky hillsides, flames in color from violet to deep red.

Cacti long ago surrendered their leaves in order to reduce transpiration, shifting the function to the green outer cover of the stem, while also developing tissues that enable them to retain water through prolonged drought. The many related members of the cactus family range from tiny pincushions, small as a thimble, to the towering giant saguaro, which emerged from the rose family. The saguaro, the largest tree of the American desert, stands like a primitive pillar, gnarled and grotesque, until it bears its creamy white spring flowers, like a rose in bloom. Following soaking rains, a saguaro's widespread root system draws in immense quantities of water to store for long dry spells—though some greedy saguaros may drink so much they split open at the seams. Some kinds of cactus, like the hedgehog, are easy to raise in home gardens. Others, like the organ pipe, grow fifteen feet tall and are used as fences in Mexico. The fruit of the prickly pear cactus has plentiful juice, which Indians and early white travelers found a refreshing substitute for food and water in the desert.

When vegetation is considered useful it becomes defensible. Along the few streambeds of arid Arizona, a particular class of plants called phreatophytes clusters densely, with roots reaching deep into the water. Tamarisk, the salt cedar, lush in contrast to most others, grows twenty feet tall, bordered by shrubs such as the mesquite, greasewood, willow, and baccharis, and by streamside and valley-bottom trees such as cottonwood, mountain ash, alder, and sycamore. For years Arizonans thought the phreatophytes were utilizing water that rightfully belonged to them, and public agencies did their best to uproot the miscreants. They never were successful and in due course the dawning came that the unwanted weedy shrubs actually stabilize stream banks, enrich the landscape, and furnish food and cover to many birds and small animals. So the efforts at eradication have tapered off.

Anyway, it's not really the flora that makes the desert. It's the whole space of which plants are a part, and the vibes the individual receives in a quiet hour of contemplation. The Indians cultivated their receptive inner antennae. Zane Grey appreciated their system, as evidenced by these lines from *The Vanishing American*:

"Before Nophaie could walk he had begun to learn the secrets of the life of the open. Birds, lizards, snakes, horned toads, packrats and kangaroo rats, prairie dogs, and rabbits—these, and all the little wild creatures of the desert, were brought to him to tame, to play with, to study, and to learn to love. Thus the brilliant and intense colors of desert life were early stamped upon his brain. The

love of natural beauty, born in him, had early opportunity for evolution. The habits and ways of all desert creatures became a part of
his childhood training. Likewise the green covering of the earth, in
all its beauty and meaning, soon occupied its place of supreme
importance in his understanding—the grasses, green in the spring,
bearded and seeding in the late summer, bleached white in the
fall; the sages with their bittersweet fragrances and everlasting
gray; the cactus, venomous yet fruitful, with their colors of ver-
million and magenta; the paintbrush with its carmine; the weeds of
the desert, not without their use and worthiness; the flowers of the
deep canyons; the mosses on the wet stones by the cliff-shaded
brook; the ferns and lichens; the purple-berried cedars and the nut-
bearing piñons of the uplands; and on the mountains the great
brown-barked pines, stately and noble, lords of the heights. . . .

"Nophaie wandered on with his sheep, over the sage and sand,
under the silent, lofty towers of rock. He was unconsciously and
unutterably happy because he was in perfect harmony with the reality and spirit of the nature that encompassed him. He wandered
in an enchanted land of mystery, upon which the Great Spirit
looked with love. He had no cares, no needs, no selfishness."

Mary Austin perceived enchantment and mystery, too, which
she expressed in her own distinctive style. As in *The Land of Little
Rain*:

"The desert floras shame us with their cheerful adaptations to
the seasonal limitations. Their whole duty is to flower and fruit,
and they do it hardly, or with tropical luxuriance, as the rain ad-
mits. It is recorded in the report of the Death Valley expedition
that, after a year of abundant rains, on the Colorado desert was
found a specimen of Amaranthus ten feet high. A year later the
same species in the same place matured in the drought at four
inches. One hopes the land may breed like qualities in her human
offspring, not tritely to 'try,' but to do."

Mary Austin, who gave voice to the wild arid West and the wild
arid Southwest, is little read or remembered, though she as an individual and her work deserve not to be forgotten, certainly never to
be forgotten by those who champion the desert. She was born in
1868 on an Illinois farm, came west to discover the charms of mes-
quite-covered ranges and sky-reaching mesas, lands beyond human

occupancy. Her land of little rain, celebrated in her book of 1903, was the California desert east of the Sierra Nevada, which she explored while living with her husband in the Owens Valley. She later left him to pursue her own career, writing novels and nonfiction books, short stories, poems, and plays, championing the rights of women and of Indians and Hispanics. She moved to Carmel, on the coast, where she pioneered a literary colony whose members included Lincoln Steffens, Jack London, and Ambrose Bierce, then tried New York, finally settling in Santa Fe until her death in 1934.

"Go as far as you dare in the heart of a lonely land, you cannot go so far that life and death are not before you," she wrote in *The Land of Little Rain*. "Painted lizards slip in and out of rock crevices, and pant on the white hot sands. Birds, hummingbirds even, nest in the cactus shrub; woodpeckers befriend the demoniac yuccas; out of the stark, treeless waste rings the music of the night-singing mockingbird. If it be summer and the sun well down, there will be a burrowing owl to call. Strange, furry, tricksy things dart across the open places, or sit motionless in the conning towers of the creosote. The poet may have 'named all the birds without a gun,' but not the fairy-footed, ground-inhabiting, furtive, small folk of the rainless regions. They are too many and too swift; how many you would not believe without seeing the footprint tracings in the sand. They are nearly all night workers, finding the days too hot and white. In mid-desert, where there are no cattle, there are no birds of carrion, but if you go far in that direction the chances are that you will find yourself shadowed by their tilted wings. Nothing so large as a man can move unspied upon in that country. . . .

"For all the toll the desert takes of a man it gives compensations, deep breaths, deep sleep, and the communion of the stars. It comes upon one with new force in the pauses of the night that the Chaldeans were a desert-bred people. It is hard to escape the sense of mastery as the stars move in the wide clear heavens to risings and settings unobscured. They look large and near and palpitant; as if they moved on some stately service not needful to declare. Wheeling to their stations in the sky, they make the poor world-fret of no account. Of no account you who lie out there watching, nor the lean coyote that stands off in the scrub from you and howls and howls."

Another of my heroes of the desert, Joseph Wood Krutch, has also been lost in time. But what a message—in his words and life—for our time or any time! In an article published in *Wildlife Review* in 1971, the year after his death, Krutch set down this admonition:

"Something is fatally lacking in the concept of conservation and the thing lacking is the feeling for, or the love of, the natural work of which man is a part. It is the failure to realize that this is not only one world, but one earth. Mankind is not only an island in respect to other men, but also an island in respect to nature as a whole. He must come to some kind of terms with it. But without the glad appreciation of our relationship to nature, without the idea of living with nature, we must end sooner or later living—or I think more properly dying—in a world where man has paid the penalty for doing what he cannot do successfully; namely, thinking only of himself."

Krutch wrote these words based on his own experience and growth. He was born in Knoxville and studied science at the University of Tennessee, but gave it up to pursue a literary career in New York. During many years at *The Nation* (while also teaching at Columbia) he wrote hundreds of book and drama reviews, essays, and editorials for *The Nation*, and books of his own, establishing a reputation as a highbrow social and literary critic. He epitomized sophisticated urbanity, believing that wild things must be antithetical to culture and civilization. (As his colleague, Lewis Gannett, wrote: "He felt that the lush vegetable growth of the country was stifling; he was eloquent in proclaiming the superiority of civilized to wild life.")

Yet, he was not a happy man. Afflicted with assorted ailments of body and spirit, Krutch recognized that he must be missing something important. At his Connecticut retreat he became a diligent observer and chronicler of squirrels, newts, rabbits, butterflies, katydids, and wrens, recording changes in temperature and dates when spring flowers bloomed and birds and other animals returned from winter retreats. He discovered and described the whole new world that lay beyond politics, economics, and literature. In 1934 he wrote: "No one totally ignorant of natural history has any right to call himself a modern. The difference between a person to whom a cockroach is merely a bug and one to whom it is *Blatta orientalis*, and thus a representative of one of the very oldest families of this earth, is the difference between one to whom man is a unique creature and one to whom he is merely the latest stage in nature's vast experiment with life."

After annual visits to the Southwest, Krutch and his wife moved permanently to Tucson in 1952. Now he was surrounded by the lower Sonoran desert, studying and admiring its distinctive flora and fauna. In Connecticut they had kept at various times a crow, geese, fish, salamanders, a goat, and as many as fourteen cats. In Arizona he made friends with lizards, scorpions, horned toads, coyotes, tarantulas, jackrabbits, and roadrunners. As he wrote in *The Voice of the Desert*, published in 1955:

"In Connecticut the chickadees came to see me when I did not go to see them. In Arizona the desert birds do the same, though the attraction—which was certainly not me in either case—is water rather than food. A curved-bill thrasher, his threatening beak half-open like the mouth of a panting dog, approaches defiantly, scattering the smaller birds as he comes. A cactus wren, the largest and boldest of the wren tribe, impudently invades my porch and even jumps to a window sill to peer at me through the glass. And as I know from experience, he will invade even the house if I leave a door open and will carry away for his nest any material available. Only the large white-winged dove does not seem to notice that summer is over and now, when the temperature in the sun must be at least 120 degrees, he seems to be saying, 'But we don't call this hot in Campeche.'"

Krutch puzzled over his observations, marveling at how the Sonoran spadefoot toad survives in a world largely without water; how tadpoles mature in the brief time that puddles last; how *Dipodomys*, the diminutive desert kangaroo rat (which gets its name from outsize hind legs that enable it to escape enemies) never drinks, yet converts carbohydrates into water, and how bats, when leaving a cave at dusk, invariably fly in a counterclockwise spiral.

Krutch's biographer, John D. Margolis (whose specialty is

teaching English at Northwestern, rather than conservation), describes the process of transformation in the man in *Joseph Wood Krutch: A Writer's Life*: "His life had ceased to strive for effects. In his life he had also ceased straining, and at last was living authentically. No elaborate psychosomatic theory is required to see a connection between emotional distress and physical illness. The uneasiness Krutch felt with his New York career had its counterpart in a chronic malaise. It was hardly coincidental—and a result of something more than the Arizona climate—that Krutch in Tucson enjoyed more consistent good health than he had since his youth in Knoxville. . . . The desert became a temple, where the former agnostic, now a pantheist, went to worship."

With large straw hat, baggy trousers, shirttail flapping behind him, Krutch traveled countless miles of untrod desert. He would carefully avoid stepping on some small plant struggling to make a life for itself. Between 1949 and his death he wrote seven nature books. Krutch became the voice of the desert, as well as the voice of the Grand Canyon. Though he perceived more of nature's meaning than many trained natural-resource professionals, he avoided posing as a professional naturalist. He had a little fun along the way, as with one of his last books, *The Most Wonderful Animals That Never Were*, an intriguing inventory of unicorns, mermaids, dragons, and other legendary creatures of "unnatural history."

His outlook enabled him to write works of what I consider lasting value. In his earlier days Krutch had snobbishly sought to portray himself as an intellectual elitist. In Arizona his goal in nature writing was to show that all men could enjoy experiences like his if only they would open their eyes and ears, consult a few books, and turn their minds to contemplation.

"By contact with the living nature we are reminded of the mysterious, nonmechanical aspects of the living organism," he wrote in 1960. "By such contact we begin to get, even in contemplating nature's lowest forms, a sense of the mystery, the independence, the unpredictableness of the living as opposed to the mechanical. And it is upon the recognition of these characteristics that he shares with all living creatures that any recognition of man's dignity has to be based."

Krutch was an individualist. Throughout his life he enunciated principles of individual rights and individual dignity. He considered America's problems basically philosophical and spiritual. We must find the answers inside ourselves before looking for a political solution, he believed. "Real success or failure comes only from within and society cannot impress it from without," he wrote. "Only the individual succeeds, for only self-realization is success." He wrote of his biography of Thoreau: "The true moral of the book and perhaps one which Thoreau would have accepted is not that men should do as he did and society attempt to compose itself of Thoreaus but that every man should lead the kind of life that seems best for him."

He was not a joiner and not an activist, but he was plainly concerned. *Grand Canyon: Today and All Its Yesterdays* (1958) ends with a plea for conservation characteristic of his approach to things: "The wilderness and the idea of wilderness is one of the permanent homes of the human spirit." That was the same year, 1958, when he called space travel "the most grandiose escape mechanism yet elaborated by the ingenious but self-defeating human mind," declaring himself a member of "that minority which would prefer to have nobody at all get there."

I never met Krutch, although I visited in and around Tucson during his life there. However, I clipped an article by him from the travel section of *The New York Times* of February 22, 1959, which I still have in my files. The article was datelined from Baja California, that unusual peninsula of southern Mexico where he traveled several times. The four-column headline reads as follows:

INVASION OF BAJA CALIFORNIA

SPORTSMEN LEAD WAY AS PENINSULA'S HISTORIC ISOLATION

BEGINS TO YIELD TO A NEW TYPE OF CONQUEST

It was the invasion of tourism to which he referred, following the beachhead of fishermen and hunters. Baja California for most of its eight-hundred-mile length is desert, down which runs the spine of a mountain range rising to more than ten thousand feet. Little of Baja is arable. The desert as Krutch saw it was empty except for a few tiny villages so primitive they made the occasional strangers who saw them rub their eyes. It was a land where time stood still.

"Because it has stood still, the conservation of wildlife and of unspoiled natural grandeur was, until recently, no problem at all. They conserved themselves. Here is a land pretty much out of this world; and that, for certain people, is one of its charms."

While acknowledging the blessings tourism is said to bring, Krutch cautioned about the potential damage to human person- ality. He cited the tropical village of San Bartolo, with a population of some three hundred, where water from a large spring creates an oasis surrounded by desert hills, with irrigation extending for sev- eral miles and sugar cane growing lushly.

"There is one store and an old stone chapel. Surely—although I did not happen to see him—there is also a guitarist. But as I stood by the spring watching the women carrying water, they did not appear to feel put upon. As for the vaquero loitering there on his horse, a good deal more could be said. Held erect in the saddle by the last vestige of Spanish pride, he was certainly not longing for the tourist trade. His son may very well get it whether he wants it or not—but it is not certain whether he will be better off."

The closest Krutch came to activism was through his involve- ment with Arthur N. Pack and William H. Carr in the Arizona- Sonora Desert Museum, an outdoors educational facility estab- lished in a fitting setting fourteen miles west of Tucson. Carr, a pioneer in the field of outdoor museums, had been on the staff of the American Museum of Natural History in New York, before moving to Tucson for his health in the early 1950s. Because he had brought with him a reputation for having organized and operated the Museum of Natural History's trailside museums and nature- trail network at Bear Mountain State Park, he was asked to prepare a survey for the proper use of Tucson Mountain Park and an old building waiting for a new mission. This led to liaison with Pack, a quiet millionaire who supported nature preservation causes. Krutch joined the Arizona museum board as secretary-treasurer and was intimately involved with its affairs.

The Arizona-Sonora Desert Museum has been operated as a different kind of place, displaying desert animals in conditions sim- ilar to their native habitats. Instead of signs warning Do Not Feed the Animals, they would politely admonish, Do Not Feed Your Fingers to the Animals, Their Diet Is Carefully Supervised. The underground tunnel was designed to answer the question of

"Where do desert animals go when the sun is so hot?" by showing prairie dogs, ferrets, badgers, pack rats, and foxes burrowing about the cool underside of plants. Once a visitor congratulated the staff on the lifelike rattlesnake in the middle of a nature trail, but it was an actual gate-crashing snake attracted by the water and greenery.

With due credit to such facilities, with their professional interpretive naturalists at work, I lament their studied avoidance of critical issues in the world across the fence. Or, as the director of the Palm Springs Desert Museum—an oasis filled with lovely natural science exhibits, yet surrounded by a deteriorating and polluted environment—told me in 1978: "Our board doesn't want us to be involved."

Krutch observed and was distressed by degradation of the desert and by the urbanization of Tucson, but an urge to do something about it in an organized way lay beyond him. Throughout his life he championed freedom of the individual and the right of self-expression, but as an individual right. While covering the Scopes trial for *The Nation* in 1924, he commented on efforts of the Daughters of the American Revolution to prevent performance of W. Somerset Maugham's play, *Rain*, in his hometown of Knoxville:

"Tennessee has a state university so pure or so cowardly that when the governor signed the anti-evolution bill not one professor dared protest. From such a center, radiating not light but visible darkness, the supercensor might well be expected. . . A book disappears from the shelves of a public library, a theatrical manager modifies or withdraws a play, and the process of censorship comes to be, by mere repetition, accepted as a normal practice."

Krutch's works are no longer found much on the bookshelves, but they will be back. He has too much of substance, of red literary meat that individualists need, to be kept out of circulation. Following his death, *The New York Times* paid this rare editorial tribute:

"The current wave of concern for the environment, the contempt for materialism voiced by so many youthful Americans, and now perhaps their growing rejection of nihilism as well—these should turn a generation unfamiliar with Joseph Wood Krutch to a reading of his books with delight to themselves and profit to the world."

Or as he himself wrote in the last lines of *A Krutch Omnibus*, the

260

edition published following his death: "Only human beings, not machines, can become heroes. Or at least that was true for my generation. Perhaps the generation now growing up has already developed an opposite reaction. Perhaps its members will admire computers and group technology more than human resource and courage. Perhaps its only hero will be those abstractions, Science and Technology, rather than human enterprise, but I hope not."

Human enterprise holds different meanings. To hike the desert after dark in order to watch the night-blooming plants and to feel close to stars, or to spend a day in the desert studying a single saguaro, or the trunk of a saguaro, and of how it provides shelter for spiders and lizards, niches for woodpeckers and flickers and hummingbirds where they can lay eggs and rear young—that is one form of enterprise, the Thoreau or Krutch form. Then there is that other form, of what practical people would call *real* enterprise.

When enterprise came to the Southwest, grass was "as high as a cow's back," or "belly deep to a horse." River bottoms, forested with giant mesquite, were the homes of beaver. Herds of antelope and elk roamed the plateaus, feeding on nutritious grama grasses. Deer, turkey, buffalo, quail, and dove filled woods and plains. Enterprise brought change. Beaver were trapped, their dams destroyed. Valleys were stripped of mesquite, while ironwood was cut from the hills to furnish fence posts and feed lime kilns. Wildlife, deprived of vegetation and water, retreated to higher ground or to extinction.

Then came the post-Civil War "beef bonanza," when fortunes were waiting to be made all over the West by those of true enterprise, fortunes greater than in the California gold rush. Unfortunately, the severe winter of 1886–87 on the northern plains changed many plans. Fortunes were lost instead of made and cattle perished by the tens of thousands. Still, the Southwest was considered ideal for stockgrowing, with mild climate over its vast wilderness, lush grasses for cows and horses, and broadleaf herbs for sheep. But the Southwest in 1893 suffered much the same fate as had the northern plains a few years earlier.

The effects on land and landscape over time proved drastic and long lasting. Valuable grasses and forage plants thinned and disappeared. In some places they were replaced by cheat grass, the fiery flash fuel, in others by invading weeds like Russian thistle. Trampling hooves stripped the protective layer of decaying plant materials from the soil, which then dried and rose in the wind, swirled in dust, or washed in unchecked flood waters, leaving bare gravel and sand, otherwise known as "desert pavement."

That is the process of desertification, whereby juniper, mesquite, and cacti multiply where grass once grew. But even the saguaro today plays a fading role in the desert community. Around Tucson, saguaros grow in their greatest size and concentration; but rodents, avoiding the spiny armor, chew into succulent tissues unmolested. Snakes, hawks, and owls formerly kept rodent population in bounds, but now the hunters are the hunted, vanishing themselves under human pressures. Old saguaros stand on bare soil, so that only an occasional tree produces a new plant. The decline of the saguaro is felt on birds such as flicker, wren, woodpecker, and hummingbird.

The California desert has some of these problems, plus others besides. The desert is crisscrossed by roads, power lines, and pipelines. Large blocks are under military administration. Mining interests, ranging from corporate giants to lone and lonely prospectors, are exploring or exploiting oil and gas, phosphates, sodium salt, sand and gravel, potential geothermal sites, borates, and other minerals. New cities are sprouting in the desert, demanding water where there isn't enough. Off-road vehicles have made inaccessible areas easy to reach. Geologists say that damage by ORVs in even the least vulnerable areas will require periods for recovery measured in centuries or millennia. Losses of soil and changes in land surfaces will be long lasting, and certain natural life systems may never recover from intensive ORV impacts already sustained.

The West is enriched by its desert. Some portions have been set aside as wilderness, while other portions with luck may still be. It takes a lot of desert to get the feel and mood of it. We can never have too much to meet the needs of human enterprise.

The Great Basin Desert covers most of Nevada and some of Utah, with fringes in Oregon, Idaho, Washington, Wyoming, and Colorado. This "high desert" is an arid upland of broad basins and plateaus, shut off from the moist Pacific by the Sierra Nevada. The Great Basin is marked by the remnants of Pleistocene lakes, like

Lake Bonneville, an ancient inland sea in northwest Utah, and Great Salt Lake, ancestral nesting place of pelicans, cormorants, and terns—birds not normally seen so far from the sea.

The California desert, covering nearly one fourth of the state, is filled with strange, subtle, and spectacular aspects of nature—flats and dry lakes, limestone caves, mountain ranges, remote valleys, old volcanic craters and lava flows, alluvial fans formed by rain-storms rushing down steep channels. Ages ago the Mohave desert of southeastern California and Nevada was covered with rivers and lakes, though now it is one of the driest areas in the world.

The Chihuahuan desert lies mostly south of the border, with prongs into southeast Arizona, New Mexico, and West Texas. It is nearly as extensive as the Great Basin, spreading across ancient lava flows, lost rivers, an ancient inland lake, and dunes of white sand.

The Sonoran desert, reaching from southern California across western Arizona into the Mexican state of Sonora, receives only ten inches of rainfall yearly. Western portions get less than five inches, distributed between summer and winter—a striking arid land of little rain. Steep, rocky slopes, scarred by centuries of erosion and exposed to the heat of the low desert, provide an environment that only the toughest species of plants and animals can endure.

Yet these deserts are rich in life-forms, different forms in different settings. Approaching the southwestern borders of the Great Basin, for instance, sagebrush bows to the Joshua tree of the Mohave desert, *Yucca brevifolia*, which grows to heights of forty feet, with densely clustered, sharp-pointed leaves, and long green-ish-white blossoms from March through May. A survey in Death Valley National Monument has revealed 608 different kinds of plants, growing everywhere except on the salt flats, while about 160 species of birds have been recorded in the hottest, driest areas below sea level, and 230 species in the entire monument.

I hadn't thought of it till now, but I've been to substantial areas of desert wilderness, some already legally protected and others wanting protection.

Twice I've been to the Superstitions, the land of the Lost Dutchman, an elusive and probably illusionary mine hidden some-where in the mountains. Southeast of Phoenix, beyond Roosevelt

Lake and Roosevelt Dam, the Superstition Wilderness, a unit of
Tonto National Forest, survives as an unconquered vestige of natural history. Like a reddish, bold landmark of the desert, the Superstitions rise abruptly above the desert floor, with sheer canyons and
stark rocky formations.

Even this seemingly forbidden country turns into a flower
garden of desert plants and shrubs. These include the slender-
stemmed, night-blooming cactus, *La Reina de la Noche*, with exotic
large white flowers that open but once a year—and then from sunset till early morning; the barrel cactus, a stocky, five-foot-high
water tank of the desert, which blooms with yellow, pink, and
orange flowers; and the fuzzy-spined cholla cactus. I learned
sharply and unforgettably why one variety is called "jumping
cholla" when I stepped on one. Two or three cactus sections detached from the plant, their spines plunging through the canvas
shoe I was wearing. I jumped. I tried to extract the cactus, but it
stuck to both hands. Finally, my companion pulled out the cactus
spines with a pair of pliers.

The Weaver's Needle vicinity of the Superstitions supposedly
is the location of the legendary Lost Dutchman Mine, which receives its name from Jacob Waltz, the "Dutchman." He would arrive in Florence and Phoenix on occasion with sackfuls of gold
nuggets and mysterious murmurings about his hidden mine, and on
his deathbed in 1891 gave vague directions to locate it. Prospectors
have been relentlessly hunting after the Dutchman ever since. Several have died in the process, particularly those who tried in summer when temperatures reach 115 to 120 degrees and water is so
scarce that even the cacti must grow thirsty. While approaching
Weaver's Needle on horseback, the ranger with whom I was riding
warned of a dangerous prospecting party camped ahead. Its leader
was a black woman, believed to be well financed in her search for
the Dutchman, protected by at least two armed guards. Shots had
lately been exchanged with a rival camp and one man had been
killed. We came to her tent at the edge of the trail. The lady was
youthful, buxom, wearing a white blouse and dungarees. At the
moment one guard was evident, a slender, grizzled buckaroo. A
shotgun lay propped against the tent. Seated in a camp chair, she
seemed friendly, glad to have company. I asked if I could take her

picture, scarcely knowing what to expect, but she reacted flattered and flustered, agreeing to pose providing she could make up her face—with thick layers of lush, red lipstick. I never learned the ultimate outcome of her expedition, but the search for the Dutchman goes on. At the end of 1983, except for valid existing claims, mineral prospecting was terminated in classified wilderness (as stipulated by the Wilderness Act), but I imagine a few hardy, defiant souls will be out there anyway.

"The palpable sense of mystery in the desert air breeds fables, chiefly of lost treasure," as Mary Austin wrote. "Somewhere within its stark border, if one believes the report, is a hill strewn with nuggets; one seamed with virgin silver; an old clayey water-bed where Indians scooped earth to make cooking pots and shaped them reeking with grains of pure gold. Old miners drifting about the desert edges, weathered into the semblance of the tawny hills, will tell you tales like these convincingly. After a little sojourn in that land you will believe them on their own account. It is a question whether it is not better to be bitten by a little horned snake of the desert that goes sidewise and strikes without coiling than by the tradition of a lost mine."

In 1978, during the period I was writing a weekly column for the *Los Angeles Times*, I spent a little time exploring the California desert and reporting what I learned. Two years earlier Congress had adopted legislation establishing the California Desert Conservation Area, requiring that desert lands be managed "in a manner that will protect the quality of scientific, historical, ecological, environmental, air and atmospheric, water resources and archaelogical values." The Bureau of Land Management (or BLM) was directed to prepare a detailed plan by September 1980 and to inventory roadless areas for possible inclusion in the National Wilderness Preservation System.

This mission represented a departure for BLM, whose activities have centered on the disposal and commercial uses of public lands. Though working in a region of astounding variety and striking beauty like the California desert, BLM personnel had little background in fields such as wilderness or endangered species, and some of them had little appreciation for these resources.

National forests and national parks have been identified and protected, but public domain, the leftover lands that embrace most of our western desert, have largely been forgotten. They've been left to miners, ranchers, squatters, the military, ORVs, and free-lance vandals. Reversing course doesn't come easily.

Nevertheless, I discovered outstanding wild desert. In all my travels I had never seen or conceived of anything like the giant white sand dunes of Eureka Valley, part of the desert landscape near Death Valley. They made me realize anew how little we know about our own land. Extending a mile in width, three miles in length, and rising nearly seven hundred feet high, those dunes comprise a scenic spectacular, but an ecosytem, too, of rare plants and animals, and a library of human history, with traces of early Americans possibly reaching back ten thousand years.

I camped one night in north Saline Valley, on the east side of the Panamint Mountains from Death Valley, one of the pristine portions of the desert, especially singular for both its natural warm springs and fresh springs. Then, at the north end of the Argus Range, near the old mining town of Darwin, under a hot desert sun, I walked only a half-mile up a dry wash into a cool Shangri-la, complete with thirty-five-foot waterfall and freshwater stream. Another choice place I visited was the Desert Tortoise Natural Area, covering more than twenty thousand acres north of California City, which BLM had selected for protection because of its prime habitat for tortoise, Mohave ground squirrel, and desert kit fox. I must have seen at least half a dozen tortoises, cousins to the celebrated giant tortoises of the Galápagos Islands, moving slowly over the desert on blunt, club-shaped feet. Until recent years the tortoise was considered common in California, though its decline seems traceable to heavy sheep grazing and ORV use.

Species such as the tortoise ought to be assured of their place. They enrich the environment. Yet, the widely admired desert bighorn sheep is threatened by game poaching and competition from burros; the shy, gentle, little kit fox by indiscriminate shooting and habitat destruction by ORVs; and the amazing pupfish, the "desert sardine," which feeds on insects and algae in warm saline ponds, by pollution and drainage.

It doesn't have to be this way, given a change in social values. Wilderness can be restored as well as preserved. "Every plant ei-

266

ther sticks, stings, or stinks," the stockmen along the Rio Grande in West Texas would say; and when Big Bend National Park was established in their wake in 1944, there wasn't much vegetation left on the plains and slopes. Since departure of the large livestock herds, plants of a thousand different species have returned, and with them, life-systems they support. Birds range from the road-runner, that cuckoo-like weak flyer but speedster over the ground, to the elegant Scott's oriole found among yuccas and agaves, cactus wren, heron, teal, cliff swallow, golden eagle, and the rare colima warbler, sparrow-size, with lovely lyric trill, which divides its time between south central Mexico and the Big Bend.

Comanches in their time rode through the Big Bend to raid isolated Spanish settlements along the Rio Grande. Following annexation of Texas by the United States, a military troop arrived in 1856 with more than thirty camels, dispatched by Secretary of War Jefferson Davis as a revolutionary mode of transport across the desert. Altogether, some eighty camels were imported, but the whole idea was scrapped with the Civil War, and the last of the animals were turned loose, never to be seen again. That desert, so far as we know, was not meant for camels. Following the Civil War, the cavalry was in and out of the area to protect cattlemen from Indian raids. The last wild flurry occurred in 1916, when Mexican revolutionaries invaded the United States via the Big Bend.

Nowadays, smugglers of narcotics crossing the border through the national park play hide-and-seek with the law, and so do Mexican laborers, the "wetbacks." One day, in Boquillas Canyon, the longest and most spectacular of Big Bend's gorges, my friend Elmer and I happened on a candelilla camp. It was a delightful discovery of Rio Grande lore that frightened us a little, considering that candelilla workers are alleged to be tough hombres resentful of company, like mountain moonshiners or marijuana farmers. The candelilla is a tall-growing wax plant that these men boil in huge vats along the river in order to sell the residue for use in making polishes, paper coatings, pharmaceuticals, and cosmetics. They apparently cut the plants on the American side and process them on the Mexican. They were not the least bit hostile. Their labor, I thought, is elemental and hard, tougher than moonshining.

That evening I walked the desert at twilight. It was the witching hour, when mule deer leave the arroyos to feed on open hill-sides and coyotes begin their nocturnal serenade, when nighthawks swoop low to feed on insects and great horned owls alight on long-stemmed ocotillo to await nightfall. The wild desert needs no people to be filled with life—it is richly filled with the interwoven lives of insects, lizards, snakes, tortoises, tarantulas, mountain lions, and javelina. The lives of plants of this arid land are better known to Mexicans than to most Americans: the lechuguilla, an agave (little sister of the century plant), from whose fibers Mexicans weave ropes, harnesses, and saddlebags; the dropping juniper, which grows from Central America to the northern limit of its range at Big Bend; the sotol, or desert spoon, which produces tall white blooms every other year in June and July; and the Spanish dagger, the yucca, with bell-like creamy blossoms in March and April.

Desert is not a wasteland. It needs no "reclamation." As wilderness reached with some effort, it becomes anew what it always has been, one of the great things of life to be earned.

CHAPTER XIV

On the Idaho-Montana Frontier: The Foresters' Wilderness

The last stronghold of wilderness in the country outside of Alaska lies in the region known as the Inland Northwest. In the first lines of the introduction to *The Nez Perce Indians and the Opening of the Northwest*, historian Alvin M. Josephy, Jr., sets the scene for entry to it:

"One of the most spectacular and least traveled parts of the United States is the so-called Inland Empire of the Northwest, a ruggedly majestic 150,000 square miles of interior land lying between the Cascades and Rocky Mountains and extending southward from the Canadian border for about 300 miles. It encompasses present eastern Washington, northeastern Oregon, the northern panhandle of Idaho, and Montana west of the Continental Divide. Topographically it is a stupendous country of wide open spaces and unspoiled scenery. Much of it is a high plateau, cut into precipitous up-and-down terrain in which climate and temperature vary abruptly according to altitude."

The valleys, prairies, and plateaus for thousands of years were home and hunting grounds of Indian peoples, including the Nez Perce in north central Idaho and adjacent Oregon and Washington, and the Flatheads across the mountains on the Montana side. Into their country came Lewis and Clark and other explorers, followed by fur traders, missionaries, soldiers, settlers, miners, and loggers. New generations took riverbanks and benchlands in the valleys, raising cattle, sheep, grass, grains, dairy herds, beets, and truck crops. "From the valley centers," as Josephy writes, "miners, timber men and recreation-bent sportsmen have sent groping fingers into the surrounding mountains and high meadows. But they have only probed; the untouched wilderness is still immense."

I was wondering one day how large is immense. It was the summer of 1983.

"Tom, how much wilderness do we have out here?"

"Out where, Mike?"

"I mean, just out here down the ridge between Idaho and Montana—or on both sides, in the two states."

"Oh, I see what you mean. I don't have the figures on the top of my head, but I'd say there is a lot of wilderness. There must be five million acres already in the wilderness system. And then the roadless areas being studied for possible addition to the system. So I would say five million acres easily.

"But it could be ten million acres, too, depending on how you figure it."

"Well," I asked, "how would you get to a total of ten million acres? Considering the whole wilderness system covers eighty million acres, that would be one eighth of it."

"If you wanted to include Yellowstone and the Absaroka-Beartooth on the north side of it in Montana, and maybe the Tetons, the Washakie, and down to the Bridger in Wyoming. And then across the Snake River to the Wenaha-Tucannon Wilderness in Washington State and the Eagle Cap in the Oregon Wallowas. Alaska has more, that's for sure, but outside of Alaska no other region of the country has as much as the upper Northwest."

"I was thinking of just the western Montana-Idaho country."

"What you mean is from Glacier National Park south. A great concentration of wild country, which you would have a tough time matching wherever you go. Right around Glacier, you've got the Bob Marshall—that's over a million acres right there—plus the Great Bear and Scapegoat; then there's the Mission Mountains, and the Rattlesnake, just outside Missoula, like an urban wilderness; and the Anaconda-Pintler, on the Montana side.

"Now here where we are you've got the Selway-Bitterroot, Gospel Hump, and the River of No Return Wilderness right through the heart of Idaho, and then the Sawtooth Wilderness outside of Sun Valley. Idaho has more wilderness than any of the lower forty-eight states. But you know ,that; that has to be why you came here."

We were just turning in, lying in our sleeping bags at the bunkhouse at the Selway Falls station of the Nez Perce National Forest. The station had once been a backcountry patrol cabin. Now it was a gateway to the Selway-Bitterroot Wilderness, where we were headed for a weekend of backpacking and camping. My friend Tom Kovalicky was the supervisor of the Nez Perce National Forest, which includes 560,000 acres of the Selway-Bitterroot, or more than half of the wilderness (the remaining being administered by the Clearwater National Forest, adjacent to the north in Idaho, and the Bitterroot National Forest, adjacent to the east in Montana).

A forest supervisor holds a pretty fair rank. He gets paid more than forty thousand dollars; he administers two or three million acres, with a staff of sixty or seventy people (many more in summer), including five or six district rangers who exercise substantial authority on their own. Most forest supervisors I know are desk-bound and some are hidebound. But not Kovalicky. He made excellent company because he was casual, easy, and open, a backpacker's backpacker, who programmed his time to be outdoors. It might be that he was still a new supervisor, only a year in the job, but I doubt that was it. Most foresters, by the time they get to be supervisors (or even rangers), are well broken into a bureaucratic system, almost all in their mid-forties or older, an age when men are cautious and don't deviate far from the norm. Kovalicky came up through the system and understood it, and was loyal to his outfit, but was different. In fact, his selection as supervisor had surprised a lot of people; he was too much of a non-bureaucrat, gregarious, outgoing, who identified himself with wilderness, rare indeed for one who advances through the ranks of the Forest Service. He was forty-seven and divorced, about six feet tall, athletic in build, with a full head of hair down to his forehead, spectacles, and a salt-and-pepper moustache that spread across a frequently smiling face. He was well prepared for the trip, with all the right equipment. He had brought along dried fruit, including apples, bananas, and strawberries, which he had prepared himself, to mix with the gorp I had bought on the way down from Moscow to his headquarters at Grangeville.

We were in our sleeping bags in the bunks. I was about to turn over.

"You know, Mike, of the wilderness we've been talking about, subtract Glacier National Park and all the rest of it is in the national forests. I think we've done a pretty darn good job for the American people."

Well, maybe so. Then, again, maybe no. To say that we have five million acres of wilderness, or fifty million acres, or whatever the number, may be impressive, but only as far as numbers go. What about parcels of wilderness that have been needlessly lost? What is the quality of the wilderness? The quality of the protection given it?

I got to thinking about the disputed issue of some years back involving the Magruder Corridor, a steep mountain area embracing the headwaters of the Selway River, which flows from the Bitterroot Range westward into Idaho to join the Lochsa River and form the Clearwater, which flows into the Snake, which is the main tributary of the Columbia.

For three decades or longer the rugged land abutting the Magruder Corridor had been part of what the Forest Service had established administratively as the Selway-Bitterroot Primitive Area. Then, in 1961, the northern portion was given more secure protection as the Selway-Bitterroot Wilderness and the southern portion was redesignated as the Salmon River Breaks Primitive Area. The presence of an unimproved road with a couple of short and minor spurs in the Magruder Corridor was held by the Forest Service to be inconsistent with criteria for wilderness, and, consequently, about 200,000 acres—a strip eight to ten miles wide—was left for "general forest administration," which can mean anything, and often means logging. So it happened that a plan was prepared to upgrade the old road and lay out new roads for timber sales.

Those new logging roads were to accommodate hunters, picnickers, and other recreation seekers, constituting a veritable network to replace the one lone road held as justification for withdrawing the Magruder Corridor from its long-term protected status.

People in Montana and Idaho, who lived with wilderness and learned to love it, protested. So did game and fish departments of the two states. Orville L. Freeman, Secretary of Agriculture in the Kennedy-Johnson administration, appointed a special advisory committee of natural resource experts to review the Forest Service plans. The committee found the agency was not such a good guardian after all. It questioned the need of a logging road and the economic feasibility of logging. It stressed, instead, the importance of protecting from erosion the watershed and fishing values in the upper Selway River drainage, the spawning ground of Chinook salmon and steelhead trout that make their way inland from the Pacific. "The Forest Service was preparing to initiate timber road building and timber cutting in this area," the committee noted, "without clearly stated limitations to this use or to other values." It also noted that wildlife resources had not received consideration commensurate with roads and timber cutting and recommended caution in any development in order "to maintain high quality primitive-type recreation for limited numbers of people."

I like to think, or perhaps to hope, that forest administrators in their decision-making process weigh the value of trees as trees and the value of wilderness as a means of protecting soils in the watershed, as habitat for wildlife, as a source of recreation, inspiration, and scientific research. Often, alas, they have let me down, showing they have timber foremost on their minds.

Yes, the western Montana-Idaho country is still largely unspoiled, essentially because it has been protected in national forests. In the 1890s and early 1900s these lands were withdrawn from the public domain, which meant they no longer would be open to claim or settlement. Henceforth they would be administered for the public good as forest reserves, later to be called national forests, with rangers in charge. Those men were the spirit of the Old West. They hadn't been to forestry school, as there were none to attend, but they were woods-wise and adventurous. Some were in-

competent (as some are today), but most worked hard. The ranger
had no automobile, no telephone, few trails, and few boundaries.
Perhaps the first official ranger station, certainly one of the oldest,
was built by H. C. (Hank) Tuttle and Than Wilkerson, on the
west fork of the Bitterroot River in Montana in 1899. These men
received sixty dollars a month and were obliged to provide their
own horses and feed in patrolling 300,000 acres of the newly created Bitterroot Forest Reserve. Their only shelter was an old
wagon sheet, their only equipment axes they had furnished themselves. With materials at hand they erected a one-room cabin,
which still stands as a restored historic landmark of the Bitterroot
Valley.

What we call wilderness today was then just "backcountry,"
and there was a lot more of it. In 1919 when young Norman Maclean looked outside the Elk Summit ranger station of what was
then called the Selway National Forest, he saw mountains in all
directions—oceans of mountains. It was twenty-eight miles to the
nearest road, fourteen miles to the top of the Bitterroot Divide,
and fourteen down Blodgett Canyon to the Bitterroot Valley only a
few miles from Hamilton, Montana. Maclean, seventeen at the
time, was the youngest summer employee on the district. Later he
became a professor of English at the University of Chicago. When
he retired in 1973, he set down recollections of the early days in a
book titled *A River Runs Through It*.

The backcountry across the Bitterroot Divide in northern
Idaho, as depicted by Maclean, had no four-wheel drives, no bulldozers, no power saws. The twenty-eight-mile trail from Elk Summit to the mouth of Blodgett Canyon was a Forest Service trail and
therefore marked by a blaze with a notch on top; only a few other
trails in the vast Elk Summit district were so marked. Otherwise,
there were only game trails and old trappers' trails that gave out on
open ridges and meadows with no signs of where the game or trappers had vanished. Young Maclean saw a world powered by strings
of pack horses and men who walked alone—a world of hoof and
foot, and the rest done by hand. He writes as follows:

"Nowadays you can scarcely be a lookout without a uniform and
a college degree, but in 1919 not a man in our outfit, least of all the
ranger himself, had been to college. They still picked rangers for

274

the Forest Service by picking the toughest guy in town. Ours, Bill Bell, was the toughest in the Bitterroot Valley, and we thought he was the best ranger in the Forest Service. We were strengthened in this belief by the rumor that Bill had killed a sheepherder. We were a little disappointed that he had been acquitted of the charges, but nobody held it against him, for we all knew that being acquitted of killing a sheepherder in Montana isn't the same as being innocent. . . .

"In the early Forest Service, our major artist was the packer, as it usually has been in worlds where there are no roads. Packing is an art as old as the first time man moved and had an animal carry his belongings. As such, it came ultimately from Asia and from there across Northern Africa and Spain and then up from Mexico and to us probably from Indian squaws. You can't even talk to a packer unless you know what a cinch (*cincha*) is, a latigo, and a *manty* (*manta*). With the coming of roads, this ancient art has become almost a lost art, but in the early part of this century there were still few roads across the mountains and none across the 'Bitterroot Wall.' From the mouth of Blodgett Canyon, near Hamilton, Montana, to our ranger station at Elk Summit in Idaho nothing moved except on foot. When there was a big fire crew to be supplied, there could be as many as half a hundred mules and short-backed horses heaving and grunting up the narrow switchbacks and dropping extra large amounts of manure at the sharp turns. The ropes tying the animals together would jerk taut and stretch their connected necks into a straight line until they looked like dark gigantic swans circling and finally disappearing into a higher medium. . . .

"As head packer, Bill rode in front of the string, a study in angles. With black Stetson hat at a slant, he rode with his head turned almost backward from his body so he could watch to see if any of the packs were working loose. Later in life I was to see Egyptian bas-reliefs where the heads of men are looking one way and their bodies are going another, and so it is with good packers. After all, packing is the art of balancing packs and then seeing that they ride evenly—otherwise the animals will have saddle sores in a day or two and be out of business for all or most of the summer."

Over the years I've spent some little time in this country, hiking and riding in wilderness, talking with supervisors, rangers, other Forest Service personnel, and various kinds of citizens. The Bitterroot Valley certainly is one of the loveliest parts of America. In spring, orange-yellow masses of flowering balsamroot sweep across the valley slopes, the vanguard of hundreds of kinds of wildflowers. To the west the Bitterroot Range thrusts saw-toothed peaks and ridges skyward; to the east are the rugged Sapphires in the Anaconda-Pintler Winderness, with elevations up to nine thousand feet on the crest of the Continental Divide. The vast high country for many miles is composed of national forests: the Bitterroot, Lolo, Nezperce, Clearwater, Deerlodge, Beaverhead, and Salmon—with high mountain lakes bordered by sheer cliffs and snow and pine, and lots of wildlife, including elk, deer, black bear, mountain goat, mountain lion, species for hunting and species for saving in shrinking sanctuaries.

One of the oldtimers I met here, the late Charles McDonald, known as "Ranger Mac," began his career in 1919 as a summer employee in high school. During his working career he was a ranger at various locations in Utah, Wyoming, and Idaho, but for his last twenty years he was in charge of the Stevensville district of the Bitterroot National Forest. His field experiences were touched with raw adventure, the kind that make western novels and movies. "I had to deal with real killers, men who would shoot their neighbors in the back," he would recall in the late 1970s of the time he had spent in Jackson Hole, Wyoming, fifty years before. "They were from families of outlaws and fugitives who had moved to that country a hundred years ago." He was slight of build, but serious and deliberate in carrying out his duties and following his conscience.

In 1966 I met Ranger Mac when he showed up as a more or less uninvited participant on a survey trip of the proposed High Uintas Wilderness in Utah. The Forest Service had invited Stewart Brandborg, executive director of the Wilderness Society, Clifton Merritt, western representative of that organization, and me to have a look at that area and consider what the wilderness boundaries should be. There were two forest supervisors (of the Wasatch and Ashley National Forests), two or three rangers, two representatives of the regional office, and Carl Hayden, a gutsy one-legged reporter from the Salt Lake City *Tribune*. And there was Ranger Mac, already retired, showing up with two horses and a desire to learn what was going on.

I had known nothing of the High Uintas until our week on the trail. The Uintas comprise the major mountain range of the country, following an east-west axis instead of the usual north-south. They include the five highest peaks of Utah, rising to an elevation over thirteen thousand feet, and epitomize the natural marvels of the pioneer West that greeted the early settlers—high broad basins, green meadows, and rocky canyon walls of bold and unusual colors. For myself, I was taken mostly by the scenery; the Wilderness Society representatives, by the search for appropriate topographic boundaries; the foresters, by the chance to ride horseback in macho style; and McDonald, by the pursuit of what the wilderness actually contained. He would examine the smallest of plants for its individuality and rarity, pondering why it grew on a particular site. With due credit to the others, he alone seemed to focus on the wilderness life.

McDonald was ally and henchman of his old boss, Guy M. Brandborg (father of Stewart Brandborg, mentioned above), who for twenty years was supervisor of the Bitterroot National Forest. I knew him intimately as a two-fisted populist, who in the scary 1950s defied accusations and investigations that had tried to smear him with a Communist label. In 1914, at the age of twenty-one, he joined the Forest Service to follow the banners of a social crusade unfurled by Gifford Pinchot. Although the first native-born American trained in forestry (at the École National de Forestière in France), Pinchot saw forestry not as a technical end in itself, but as a wedge in the fight "against the control of government by Big Money." When "Brandy" joined the Forest Service it was led by idealists determined to halt destruction of the forests by timber barons and to rescue the grasslands from powerful cattlemen. Through forty years in the agency, and in the retirement that followed, he was imbued with the idea that wealth, all of it, comes from the earth, and committed himself to leaving the land in better condition than he found it.

He retired in Hamilton, the heart of the Bitterroot Valley. Presently, however, his old outfit launched a program of extensive logging and roadbuilding in areas characterized by shallow soils, slow-growing trees, and steep slopes, but with high recreational and scenic values. Brandborg became the leader of citizen protest, conducted with such vehemence that a local newspaper, the *Missoulian*, carried a series of nine articles on the issue. Brandborg had a lot to do with that coverage; in fact, he had an uncanny touch with writers. Among them was Bernard DeVoto, who had come to Montana in the late 1940s for his articles in *Harper's* defending the national forests from the cattlemen; then, twenty years later, correspondents from *The New York Times*, *Washington Post*, and CBS, who came across the country for his guidance on the logging debacle, and Dale Burk, of the *Missoulian*, his closest disciple. In my own case, his ideas run like a thread through columns I wrote in *American Forests* and *Field & Stream*. From one end of the country to another, everywhere I looked in the 1960s and '70s, forestry was on the wrong side, destroying wilderness without reason or science—from Admiralty Island in Alaska, down through the redwoods and Mineral King Valley in California, the Big Thicket in Texas, the Bitterroot in Montana, the Monongahela in West Virginia. Old Brandy helped me to evoke protest against squandering the heritage of our forests for greed and gain.

He was insulted and abused by Forest Service leadership—which tried to put him down as "a disgruntled ex-employee"—but men in the ranks cheered him. The Forest Service, after all, earned respect in its early years for taking care of the land in its trust. But in our age, government run by politicians and bureaucrats finds it difficult to respond to public will; the people can demand, protest, and demonstrate, but without results unless asking for something that benefits a commercial enterprise, be it a logging mill, an aircraft plant, nuclear power, or the highway expansion favored by the local chamber of commerce. Brandborg had a way of linking little issues to big ones and issues to principles of social and economic consequence. Like Pinchot, the pioneer of modern conservation, he felt that exhaustion of resources leads to war and poverty of nations, while protection of resources, land, health, and peace begins with the forests. "There is no reason," Pinchot preached, "why the American people should not take into their hands again the full political power which is theirs by right

and which they exercised before the special interests began to nul-
lify the will of the majority." Brandborg preached the same message: that society must be born again, out of an economy of
exploitation into an economy of conservation.

That idea, you may think, would be the foundation of forestry
and of the technical forester's view of wilderness. True enough,
the River of No Return Wilderness, which lies just south of the
Selway-Bitterroot, covers an area larger than Yellowstone, and perhaps wilder, with a greater variety of fish, plants, and wildlife. It
has its weaknesses and deficiencies (with concentrated use and
overuse at key areas, privileged private landholdings inside the
boundaries, and airplane access to disturb the wild environment),
but its champions consider the River of No Return Wilderness the
most fabulous piece of land anywhere on earth because of its jagged peaks, mountain meadows, glaciated jewel lakes, and clear
streams such as the Middle Fork of the Salmon, which is passable
only by floatboat. But what else is it good for? Such lands are lovely
to view but difficult to exploit. Most of Idaho's wilderness lies
within the geological sphere called the Idaho Batholith, where
coarse-grained granitic soils are highly susceptible to erosion. The
very qualities that make these lands unsuitable for development
make them valuable to enjoy. Protecting the watershed protects
the streams for trout and anadromous salmon. The same is true of
protecting the forests for elk, deer, mountain goat, wild sheep,
cougar, wolf, and all the wildlife species. You don't have to do
anything to enhance natural beauty; on the other hand, it's difficult
to restore it from consequences of erosion and siltation induced by
logging, even with time and massive outlays of money.

It isn't that somebody said wilderness is the foremost value of
much of the national forest land of western Montana and central
Idaho—essentially it hasn't been good for anything else. The same
is true everywhere in the country. You don't find prime, luxuriant
forests set aside as wilderness, except in a few isolated sites.

In addition to which, in the country at hand, large repeated
fires in the years 1910, 1919, and 1934 burned for weeks beyond
control. In the great fire of 1910, flames engulfed three million
acres in a vast semicircle 160 miles long and 30 to 50 miles wide
across the Montana-Idaho border. The Forest Service commanded

a force of ten thousand men in the northern Rockies, armed with axes, mattocks, and shovels, but they couldn't make a dent in the backcountry districts of the Clearwater, Flathead, and Selway rivers. The 1934 fire, started by lightning in July, burned the major portions of the lower Lochsa and Selway river drainages, despite a fire-fighting force of nearly five thousand men; that fire was not fully controlled until the autumn rains came.

As a result, there is scant timber. This became clear when Tom and I started to hike into the wilderness from the Fog Mountain trailhead. The shrub fields were extensive across the slopes, which wasn't bad at all. Tom and I saw a lot of lovely plants: bear grass in mass, flowering white on tall slender stems; shootingstar, with distinctive, flared rose-purple petals; Indian paintbrush, brilliant red; yellow aster and marsh marigold; wild rose; ceanothus, or snowbrush, the brushy, glossy-green shrub with clusters of white flowers that look like fresh snow; and sticky geranium, with leaves that look like larkspurs and broad, pinkish-purple flowers. Tom mentioned that sticky geranium makes good feed for elk, deer, and bear, while ceanothus is favored as browse by elk, deer, and moose, especially during winter and early spring. There were trees, too, it wasn't all shrubby: aspen, lodgepole pine, ponderosa pine beyond its normal limit, Douglas fir, white fir, and Engelmann spruce—scattered survivors of the fires, and pioneers providing the start of new forests. We didn't see much wildlife—a blue grouse, a hummingbird, and several jays, or camp robbers, but we heard a lot of birds and saw elk and deer tracks, bear diggings, and coyote scat.

We didn't see another human either, perhaps, I reckoned, because the trail was tough and the weather poor. We hiked a steep route down and up; down for a mile and a half, then upgrade for a mile or so, gaining and losing elevation four times, with two streams to cross (the forks of Canteen Creek), where we removed our boots and waded barefoot. Our pace was slow, scarcely a mile an hour. Tom could have traveled much faster, I'm sure, but my speed is limited—my theory is that if I keep putting one leg in front of the other, ultimately I'll get there. He was patient, unrushed, and uncomplaining, which always helps.

We wore rain pants to cope with moisture in the brush and in the air. The weather was gray and overcast, not the best of days, but the point about backpacking is that one never knows for sure; however, once the decision is made to begin the only choice is to keep going. Winter is not likely to be like summer, but summer can be like winter, while fall and spring can produce the weather of all seasons on the same day. In October, two months after hiking with Tom, three students and I joined a group for a weekend in Long Canyon, a beautiful cedar forest just below the Canadian border near Bonners Ferry in north Idaho. We began in snowfall and hiked out through mud. But mushrooms glistened across the forest floor—it was *their* kind of weather. When that trip was over we had no complaints.

Tom and I climbed through snow banks on the cool side of the mountains. Then, as we approached Jesse Pass, clouds in the basin below us billowed like smoke or steam in some huge earthen bowl. The clouds suddenly rose and moved aside, revealing a lush mountain panorama: melting snow banks, high green meadows, the gray steep peaks forming the gateway to the area fittingly called the Crags. Several hundred feet below us the two Cove Lakes were cradled in a lovely basin, with a sheer rock wall rising above them. That setting was our destination.

It was the shank of the afternoon, raw and chilly. We located the best, more or less level site, pitched the tent I had brought, and gathered slim pickings of twigs and branches to build a fire. Tom cooked dinner, a concoction of dry veggies, simmered Ramen noodles with spices, and biscuits. Plainly, he enjoyed cooking on the trail. Just as we started to eat, the clouds turned upside down and the rains came. They started slowly so that we could finish dinner, but then grew downright dictatorial. Conditions were too miserable to fish or to walk around the lakes.

The rains fell all night, hard and steady. The tent was warm—from the heat of our bodies—but water kept intruding from one corner or another. At five or six in the morning, Tom asked, "Should I go out and add some water to the scene?" which would be the normal thing for a man ready to relieve himself at that hour to do. But as he was sleeping without clothes and it was so miserable, I counseled, "No, don't do it." And he didn't.

We were slow to get moving in a morning of fog, wind, and

rain, which gave us a chance to talk about a lot of things, including his forestry career and outlook.

Tom was raised in New Jersey, where his father operated a family-type tavern in the days when a shot of whiskey was twenty-five cents with the old-fashioned free lunch on the side. He became interested in forestry through his experiences with the Boy Scouts and reading a Zane Grey novel, *The Young Forester*, about fighting timber thieves and game poachers. When he saw the Hollywood film *Red Skies of Montana*, about forest fire-fighting smoke jumpers, he decided to enroll in the forestry program at the University of Montana. He started in 1953, but it took eight years to finish, including two years out for the army, plus time to live and work on a ranch, and to work in Alaska. His grades were marginal, but then some of the best outdoorsmen feel handcuffed by indoor education. Said Tom: "I balanced grades with other things in life. When I discovered the freedom of the West—hunting, fishing, wilderness, glaciers—grades became less important. Who wanted to be in a library on weekends?"

In 1962 he began as a junior forester in Wyoming, with occasional opportunity to ride with the packer hauling supplies to work crews in the Bridger Wilderness. In three years he was promoted to assistant ranger on the district covering the largest area of that wilderness. In eight years on the staff of the national forest he traveled the entire length of the Bridger, almost one hundred miles along the Continental Divide, on the east and west sides of the Wide River Range, sometimes alone and sometimes with others. Then he became a district ranger in Idaho, with responsibility for part of the Sawtooth Wilderness and the Idaho Primitive Area, which later became the River of No Return Wilderness. As ranger he had other responsibilities, but he was clearly developing as a specialist in wilderness.

Thus, in due course he was assigned to a position as wilderness coordinator at the regional office in Missoula. The job is considered nowhere near as important as timber coordinator, but in a region with so many millions of acres of wilderness, it is not to be ignored. An industry like timber can bring a lot of power to bear on the Forest Service, but wilderness advocates and citizen groups such as the Montana Wilderness Association need to be dealt with, too.

Few foresters are able to communicate effectively with such individuals and groups because few comprehend and appreciate wilderness as a public resource, but Kovalicky proved the exception who could and did.

I asked whether he ever expected to become a forest supervisor, considering that wilderness is out of the mainstream. "Yes," he said, "when they made me a deputy supervisor, I felt sure they were getting me ready."

He worked as deputy supervisor on the Flathead National Forest in northern Montana, which includes the Mission Mountains Wilderness, Great Bear Wilderness, and a large part of the Bob Marshall Wilderness; then, in 1982, he came to the Nez Perce.

I commented that he was one of the few people, or perhaps the only one, I know in the Forest Service to make his career in wilderness and advance successfully through the ranks. When I encouraged him to express his formula for administering national forest wilderness, he responded as follows:

"First of all, wilderness is not synonymous with recreation, though people equate it with recreation. Wilderness is the resource Congress set aside with the Act of 1964, recreation being one of the uses that are allowed and encouraged. But wilderness means a lot more. It's more sensitive and I get a little upset with people who promote wilderness for the wrong purpose. Even in terms of recreation, I can't see the point of describing every particular feature of a wilderness. To me wilderness represents surprise—surprise and discovery. I don't want that to be denied to me.

"From the standpoint of remoteness, wilderness is difficult to get to, difficult to administer—and costly, too. 'Wilderness management' as a term sounds like a paradox, but it requires educating people who are going to use wilderness, understanding and training our clientele not to do unnatural things: recreationists, miners, researchers, outfitters, private landowners, cowboys, and sheepmen, and the U.S. Geological Survey conducting mineral surveys. How can they use wilderness without destroying it? How can we be sure they don't, with the limits of authority under the law? The manager determines transportation, getting trailheads and trails in the right locations, distributing users properly to avoid concentrations and overuse at a few popular points. We need people doing outreach work in schools and communities, selling wilderness like the Forest Service sold Smokey the Bear, with lectures and demonstrations on proper use and understanding of wilderness on its own terms.

"A lot of people need to prepare themselves better. You have to have confidence, faith, and trust in your equipment, or you better stay home. I personally use Gore-Tex products as much as possible. I'm sorry I didn't take my Gore-Tex tent, you would have seen how effective it is and how dry we would have been. I've put together my collection of equipment over a period of time—to ensure my comfort and confidence: the Gore-Tex tent, Gore-Tex parka, Gore-Tex rain pants, boots that are so good I've had them resoled once, lightweight cooking gear, and flashlight.

"Good equipment costs more, but I'd rather have my little lightweight ten-dollar flashlight that saves me fifteen ounces than a dollar-ninety-eight flashlight that costs me fifteen ounces. Mine takes more abuse, it's tougher. The kind you buy for a dollar ninety-eight or three ninety-eight just don't take the abuse. Let's say in a crucial moment you drop your flashlight and it hits a rock. You bend over, pick it up, and start using it again. It's better than picking it up and having pieces in your hand. What do you do then?

"Yes, equipment is kind of a hobby with a lot of people; it's freaky, almost like a cult that says, Let's go for the lightest, best, and toughest, regardless of cost. My Gore-Tex pants cost one hundred forty dollars, but I've never regretted spending that money. You don't backpack all these years without learning a few lessons the hard way. With cheap equipment, or the wrong kind, in the wrong situation or the wrong location—that's how people die.

"One time in the Bridger we woke up with thirteen inches of snow on us on August first. Here you are, on a hot August night at eleven thousand feet and have a meal, campfire, and the whole bit, and lie out there with no tent, just your horse blankets (because we had horses), and you wake up in the morning with twelve or thirteen inches of snow. Your hands are numb and your sleeping bag soaking wet and you look around you and you're not prepared for that kind of weather. That will kill. At practically no extra expense in weight, a person could have had some of that emergency equipment.

"That was a frightening experience. We had to regroup and shake things out that were wet and pack the horses and get out of there. We were not equipped to stay in the mountains with twelve inches of snow. I remember climbing some peaks one time with poor equipment, poor ropes. The rope parted and left me standing on a ledge with no way out. Luckily, I was able to have help from the top, where people above were able to come down and get me to come up.

"You get away from your tradition and life-style in a wilderness and you find out in a helluva hurry who you are and what you're capable of, what are the real issues of life. What really frightens you will come to the surface.

"Wilderness is my life-style. Wilderness is necessary. It represents that part of America that once was and always will remain. Wilderness is forever. We should be lucky enough to be smart enough to set it aside. We don't have to be like the Europeans. We don't have to *wish* for that type of land representation. We'll have it. I think we're smart in doing it."

I recognized that a weekend, while better than nothing, was hardly anything when it comes to knowing the Selway-Bitterroot. The Crags were one stupendous fragment of mountain country, but only a fragment attached to other stupendous fragments that make wilderness whole and enrich it with discovery.

Tom wanted to plan another trip so that I could visit Moose Creek. One possible route would be a two-day hike along the Selway River from the end of the road at Selway Falls. We discussed various possibilities for autumn, but they never matured. Still, Moose Creek had its particular appeal as the site of the ranger station in the only all-wilderness ranger district in the National Forest System. While the ranger himself no longer spends all his time at Moose Creek, Emil and Penny Keck do, which I believe makes them the only Forest Service personnel living full time in wilderness.

I had heard and read about Emil and Penny as a colorful and gutsy couple more committed to wilderness than to bureaucracy.

Actually, I had first learned of them from a young man back east, Steve Wright, of the Sterling Institute in Vermont, who had worked at Moose Creek. "From the volunteers on up to the district ranger, there was an energy and commitment far beyond that required by job descriptions," he wrote on returning to Vermont. "These people believe in hard work and commitment to a wilderness ethic." The Kecks were at the heart of it.

One day early in 1984, the ranger, Barry Hicks, telephoned me from Grangeville. Winter prevailed but the weather was clear, and the next day he was to fly into Moose Creek to check on various items. He invited me to drive down (about two hours) and fly in with him for the day. It took no time at all to accept.

The light plane was equipped with skis for landing on the snow that lay in the mountains. It was a short flight of about thirty minutes following the steep-sloped Selway River canyon. The pilot, Frank Hill, circled sharply in the clearing over the ranger station in order to lose altitude, and landed easily on the long airstrip. He'd been doing it for years.

The Moose Creek facility consists of a cluster of log and wood structures: the office, ranger's residence, Construction and Maintenance residence (for Emil and Penny), two bunkhouses, warehouse, toolshed, and corral. During summer there would be a whole crew, but now only the Kecks.

They were, like wilderness people, tough stock, simply dressed, with emphasis on wool and good boots. Emil was outspoken and uninhibited:

"Life at Moose Creek should be down to its basic moments. My philosophy of wilderness is really very goddamn simple. I am really disturbed by how wilderness is regarded by a helluva lot of people: 'What can I get out of it for myself?' The land, which was here long before man, is being manipulated—when it should not even be touched.

"I don't want a transfer. This is the most important thing in my life. At least it's a chance to think clearly and straight, because there's nobody around to change your thinking. I don't give a fuck what they do with me. I say fuck it, let it come. I got nothing to lose. They could put me on a helicopter and fly me out, but tomorrow night I'll be back in.

"There isn't anybody except an old goat like myself that comes out of the land—that crawled out of the land, you might say—meant for this work. I don't think the computer has anything to do with management of wilderness. It's a reflection of man's intention to get away from hard work and brain work. They come in with a helicopter and harass the animals and then trap them and put radio collars on them so they can track them. The land ought to be raw and naked. If you buy one thing today, tomorrow you buy something that adds to it. So you keep on doing that until you have only a make-believe wilderness.

"You don't have to go to computers to find the answers. If you can't find the answers by yourself you don't belong in here. They brought a computer last summer to measure the weather to transmit it back to Grangeville. What a crock of shit. Out there is fine. In here it don't belong. See, I don't think nothing belongs in here except a guy standing in a clean and fairly well-knit jockstrap. And that's just about all.

"This piece of land should reflect no human being's presence. My God, it's sacrilegious to even think about mechanical contrivances within a wilderness. The only things Daniel Boone had were a stone axe, a dog, and some tobacco. No social security, no nothing.

"You identify with the land, with every rock, with every piece of stick and stone that's in here. You identify with every sonofabitch that comes in here. You find out there's a guy crawling into the back of your district and you go and find out what the sonofabitch is doing. You spend all of your time and energy seeing that the land is left completely alone. Get rid of the improvements as much as you possibly can. But if you go out there you become part of the 'management team,' or some other goddamn thing.

"Wilderness is a place where there is nobody at all. But the way we've got it constructed we have to go see it for ourselves. Once you take that first step that wipes it out. Just like that.

"We have to bring people in to show how we're spending their money. That forces you to split your thinking. The demands of the land are simple, to be left alone. It screams. When you come close to the boundary stand and listen, you can hear the wilderness screaming: 'Don't go any further, buster. Far enough!' You say,

'Goddamn wilderness, how do I know what you've got?' 'It's none of your goddamn business.' It's one of the toughest assignments there is in the world—especially if you're tormented by knowing that progress stands out there with a sharp sword, all the time."

Emil and I sat at the large table in the combination living-room-dining-room-kitchen. Their whole place actually was only one large room, with their double bed on the other side of the stove. The sleeping part also had space for Emil's exercise bike, which he rides at least an hour every day. The room was full, but not cluttered. "It's no goddamn fun working for your old lady and all," Emil groused, noting that in the old days he had only one notebook, whereas now, with Penny in charge, there were all kinds of papers, forms, books, and magazines. But his bark was easily more serious than his bite. He drank coffee and I Postum, though five years earlier it would have been whiskey with or without chaser for us both. The pilot sat on the bed with his coffee, while Penny and Barry, the ranger, walked across the snow to the office for some paperwork. There was no electricity. At first I looked for an outlet to plug in my tape recorder, but there was none and we laughed a little.

Emil had a large, square head, short-clipped hair, and penetrating, inquisitive eyes. He was built with a full-barrel chest, but was only medium in height at most, hobbled by what he decried as "christly sonofabitching arthritis." He arrived at Moose Creek in 1963, when he was fifty years of age, to work on fire control strictly for the summer, but has been there ever since (except for occasional trips to town for supplies). His whole working career has been spent in the woods of the Northwest, first as a logger: topping trees, setting up camps in remote places, keeping machinery and equipment working. He struck me as a living throwback to the days when woodsmen called the crosscut a *misery whip*, the dinner bell the *gut-hammer*, and those who used both knife and fork to feed their faces *two-tool men*. Emil married and joined the Forest Service as a technician, working on the ranger district adjacent to Moose Creek, until he feuded with the ranger and quit.

Penny arrived in 1967, four years after Emil. She was twenty-five, an Oregon farm girl used to hard work in the fields, and had been active in sports at high school and college in Portland. She

288

came to work as summer lookout on Shissler Peak, four miles from Moose Creek, but Emil, in charge of construction and maintenance for the whole ranger district, objected. There hadn't been any woman in such jobs and he didn't want any. His wife had died early that year and he was morose and boozing. Penny got the job, refused to be intimidated, and they got off to a stormy start. Before summer was out, however, they both saw things differently. She restored Emil's belief in himself. He proposed, but before she accepted Penny defined her terms: "If you think you're going to crawl in bed with me and then dump me in that house at Moose Creek while you go through this beautiful land by yourself, screw it. You can stop right here."

Since then they have hiked and horsebacked together on four hundred miles of trail, cutting windfalls, blasting rock, maintaining suspension bridges and lookout towers. Penny was the unpaid volunteer until 1980, when Emil retired. Then they traded places, with her in charge as the GS 9 forestry technician (which pays more than $21,000) and him as the volunteer. People who know have told me that Penny can hike to Selway Falls, twenty-six miles away, in about seven hours; that she works with her trail crews in the brush and in the dirt; that she stays in condition by running five miles before breakfast, skiing cross-country, or taking to the exercise bike. Nevertheless, when Emil has to stop on the trail to rest his arthritic ankle, she rests with him.

Time and again Emil has been recognized and honored for his work in the wilderness, but he remains unyielding to the system, critical and independent.

"I do what the old lady tells me. I'm working for her. I don't take orders from the ranger or the Forest Service. She don't give a shit whether the ranger accepts her way or not. She has to satisfy herself.

"Barry is the fifth ranger since I came. He's okay, they're all okay, but I think rangers as a class should be eliminated from the face of the earth. They use their job here as a stepping stone to a position of power."

Barry and Penny returned from the office; her tousled auburn hair and broad forehead reminded me of pictures of Amelia Earhart, the pioneer woman pilot. Penny stood two or three inches taller than Emil, quiet, thoughtful, choosing her words carefully.

Her upper lip curved, above a large set of teeth. Emil wanted her to express herself and so did I. After insisting that Emil was the vocal spokesman of the family, she opened up, with this dialogue ensuing:

Penny: Wilderness is an area where you let nature play its own role, where the ecosystems still have the upper hand. At this time we unfortunately must allow a variety of *Homo sapiens* to dash about in here. If you want to come and not make your presence known I think that's terrific. What we have is commercialism in the wilderness—outfitters bringing people by raft, horse, and plane in numbers the land cannot absorb.

The further away from the land base, the more you lose touch with it. I don't think there is one person in the Washington office of the Forest Service who knows what wilderness is about any longer. You're so wrapped up in policy that you have no time for anything else. On the reverse side of the coin, is the higher bureaucratic system in the Washington office good for wilderness?

Emil: When you're searching for answers, everybody in the room is looking around to make sure he says the right thing, instead of addressing the problem. That happens all the time.

Penny: Unfortunately, as an organization we're swayed by politics and nothing else. Ground people such as Emil and myself, we don't care to go out to the podium where it might do the most good. You [lecturing Emil] sit right here and moan and groan forever and ever, but that's not helping anything. If you're interested in wilderness as a whole, not just the Moose Creek district or the Selway-Bitterroot, then you should try to express your ideas further.

Emil: If you are doing your job, you don't have time.

Penny: How do you know, without analyzing yourself, whether you're doing it correctly? You and I completely disagree! You want a lousy bridge up there and I don't because a bridge is not part of wilderness. How can you call yourself a wilderness buff when you want bridges across every stream?

Emil: I'm getting old and fat and feeble and I want to cross it whenever I can cross it. . . . And I don't give a shit about anything else because this is more than I can handle here. This is more than anybody can handle.

Penny: Certainly wilderness takes a backseat in the Forest Service, but that has been a plus for us in a way. They leave us alone. The ground people, or Barry, or whoever, can make a decision and not have a decision made for us in Washington because it's no big political issue for them.

Emil and Penny showed me a lot of wisdom, fundamental and unalloyed, and clarity of purpose. They could afford to be outspoken; they felt no peer pressure, no need for promotion or higher pay. They were free people, who had earned their freedom. "According to the founding fathers," said Emil, "you're supposed to do the things your intellect tells you. If you haven't the experience, or desire, or guts, you don't belong. The founding fathers were talking about a society where people were able to cope with things as they came up, and to hell with the university degree or the status symbols. Those are completely secondary."

He groused about the improvements the rangers continually sought to install, such as a light plant or a new loading platform, and wondered aloud whether wilderness protection was really gaining ground:

"When I first came they had tons of crap in here, cans and glass in the lakes and streams. If we pulled out, in ten years it would be right back. You know that you haven't changed the human being. The minute you turn your back, there lays the crap. There's nothing in the goddamn world that tells them, 'Hey, look, you sonsofbitches, the only thing that separates you from the goddamn Russians today is that you are making some attempts to hang on to some of your natural lands.'"

We flew out just before dark. I observed the mantle of snow covering the slopes. When Barry pointed to Big Fog Mountain, the trailhead from which Tom Kovalicky and I had begun our weekend backpack trip the summer before, I thought of Penny and Emil watching the wilderness through the seasons, watching it from within the wilderness, coping without strain. "You never know how things are going to turn out," Emil had said, "so you better stick to your basic way of living." He and Penny had a grasp on their priorities and purpose, and no reason for envy of anyone.

CHAPTER XV

❧

Promised Land

Wilderness is where I find it, whether in the whistle of the wind, the feel of the rain, the mood of the sky, the mystery of darkness, the rhythmic heaves and sighs of the sea, the shrill song of birds flying free, or the softer song of the leaves and limbs of an old tree that takes more listening when it calls me to pause on some city street. Wilderness is a state of mind, which means it can be anything I conceive or imagine it to be. But I am able to picture it as I wish because I know that somewhere it exists in fact.

I see wilderness as a place and a process. The place is a cathedral without walls, though *cathedral* is the wrong word for it, being something made by men for their own clearly defined purposes. Wilderness is a different type of shrine, an object of pilgrimage beyond comprehension or fully known purpose. Wilderness is a religious encounter, though of a completely unstructured denomination, without benefit of Bible, Koran, or dharma. It is spiritual and personal, an intimate, individualized search for the spirit with which all of nature is endowed. As the Nez Perce father of time past told his son in preparing for the boy's Vision Quest among the rocks, strong in spirit power, atop the mountain:

"You know that spirits of the grass and of the plants make them grow. The spirit of the wind makes it blow; its whistle is its way of speaking. Every tree, every bird, every animal has a spirit. We thank the spirit of the salmon every year for guiding the salmon up the river. We obey the rules for cleaning and cutting the salmon, so that we will not anger its spirit.

"You know that every Indian wants at least one of these spirits of nature to be his own special guide, his guardian spirit. Each of us prays to his guardian spirit, that it will help us in our need. Our faith in the spirits of nature is our religion."

The father instructed the son, at the age of ten, to find his own spirit that he could summon whenever needed, to find it now because it was essential to his full growth. The body is related to the mind, as I learned from my holistic physician, Larry Cohen, and my friend Jane, and the body and mind are related to the spirit, which joins me with everything in wild nature.

This appreciation has come through conscious study and subconscious absorption over a long period of time. Just being there has helped. So has being with friends I trust, who have been on their own quests longer and perhaps more successfully than me.

"It's something you can't really understand until you get into it and practice it. It's a way of looking at yourself and the world. It's not looking outside for external salvation."

Sam West, the red-bearded Buddhist park ranger, was sharing his wisdom and experience. I had met Sam on the float trip down the Colorado River with Martin Litton, and felt a strong connection. He had followed a path that I was interested in pursuing. Thus, I went to spend Christmas of 1982 with Sam at the Grand Canyon. The weather was chilly and snow covered the ground, but the skies and air were clear. We passed our time on the rim of the canyon, hiking partway down, and in Sam's government quarters, a small old house clustered with those of other government employees.

Sam told me of how in high school and early in college he had found himself discontent with the values of life to which he had been exposed. He searched for alternatives and found the Tao, which uses nature as an expression of harmony; nature, rather than man, as teacher. He picked up the book of Tao from a shelf and read aloud these brief excerpts:

"'Stand before it, there is no beginning. Follow it, there is no end. Stay with the ancient Tao. Move with the present. . . .

"'The valley spirit never dies. It is the woman, primal mother. Her gateway is the route of heaven and earth, just like a veil barely seen. Use it, it will never fail. . . .

"'Heaven and earth last forever. Why do heaven and earth last forever? They are unborn, so ever living. . . .

"'The sage stays behind, thus he is ahead. He is detached, thus at one with all. Through selfless action he attains fulfillment. . . .

"'The highest good is like water. Water gives life to ten thousand things. It does not stride. It flows in places man rejects and so is like the Tao. . . .

"'In dwelling be close to the land, in meditation go deep in the heart, in dealing with others be gentle and kind, in speech be true, in ruling be just, in business be competent, in action watch the timing: no fight, no blame.'

"That gave me something I could relate to, a direct connection with something I somehow knew was inside of me. Then I came to the Colorado River. And this place, I think, has a power like no other place on earth. That awakened me further. I became more and more at home with wilderness, or nature, or whatever you want to call it.

"Once I was back in Seattle visiting my family. I went to have the shock absorbers changed on my car. The repair shop was in a busy mall. I didn't want to wait two and a half hours. I walked across the parking lot and found a clump of trees, like a little oasis. I just decided to lie down under the trees. It was one of the most peaceful times I ever had. I looked at the trees, fell asleep, woke up, got my car, and drove off.

"Those little places are reminders of the right way to live. Our western world has attained an intensity through technology that has stretched people, causing them all sorts of stress, perversions, and aberrations. Because society is caught in the spin of the technological world, people develop an alienation—they lose the connection with where we come from, which is wilderness, which is nature preserved. Once we lose that, all we have is what we've manufactured, where there are no true reference points. It's like when we lose the snow leopard, or the extinction of animals; then, we lose a part of ourselves.

"I've seen people who have spent a week or two on the river and changed their lives. They would go home and quit their jobs. That place has the power to do it. It has a precious kind of energy that can be tapped: just by knowing it's there and by going there in a respectful way and relating to it. The better the appreciation of harmony and interplay of life, the better chance we have of understanding our relation to each other as human beings and seeing the larger picture. Grass, birds, trees give subtle messages, but once you wipe them out, they're gone.

"My experience demonstrates over and over that there's a different flow of energy where people don't go. It doesn't have to be physically beat down; you can just tell when a lot of people have been to a place. Or when they haven't. In Alaska and Nepal, where you get into vast areas, mountain ranges, and whole river systems, then you can begin to sense and touch infinity."

Sam combined for me background in wilderness and spirituality. He was thirty-seven when I visited him at the Grand Canyon. Though medium in size, he appeared taller because of his wiry build and erect posture; he was modest, but self-assured and poised. Born in Seattle, he spent boyhood summers at a family place on one of the islands of Puget Sound, rowing, fishing, hiking in the woods. He continued rowing as a member of the crew at the University of Washington, from which he graduated in 1969. Though majoring in advertising and public relations, he preferred the outdoors and gravitated to the Colorado River, where he became a guide and subsequently field manager for OARS, one of the largest outfitting firms. The guides were quartered between trips in house trailers near Lee's Ferry, but after sleeping out for two or three weeks on the riverbank, Sam found trailer life claustrophobic and moved to a redwall canyon, Hislop's Cave, where he lived for the better part of two years. Winters he would spend in Mexico and Guatemala, often in native villages, fishing in the Pacific with a handline from a dugout. He worked for OARS on rivers in Alaska and California, living for a time with a lovely lady from whom he learned about healing, spirituality, and loving. Then he went to work in Nepal to establish a guide program employing Tibetans

and Nepalese. It was a powerful place spiritually, where he observed people caring about each other, and where he learned more
of Buddhism, Hinduism, and Eastern philosophy.

In the early 1970s at the Grand Canyon he had seen tourist use
of the Colorado River skyrocket in numbers. There were no sanitation regulations. Hundreds of people would wash their clothes in
the river without restraint—they knew no better, and no one told
them. There was no effort at scheduling rafts so that congestion
prevailed in the middle of wilderness. He and another concerned
guide petitioned the National Park Service to institute a system of
control and environmental protection. That didn't work, but when
he returned from Asia in the late seventies the National Park Service had finally established a river management unit and offered
him a job. The assignment required discipline, but no more so
than guiding. Half the time he would travel down the Colorado
River, often by kayak, checking sanitation, consulting groups on
regulations, answering questions and interpreting natural history,
working on trails, and cleaning littered beaches. The other half of
the time he worked in the office and on search-and-rescue missions. There was also a third half—when he took time off and time
out for Buddhism.

The Colorado River flowing between the walls of the Grand
Canyon was Sam's cathedral, a magic place in which to pursue his
religion. When we traveled the river together with Martin, Sam
didn't make any show of it, but I sensed that he had something
going, a process of self-realization in an environment of nature.
Then, at times, he would leave the Grand Canyon for Buddhist
retreats. This caused a problem: He was valued at the park, but
needed freedom from it to avoid stifling his individualism and integrity. Then he met Paul Winter, to complicate things further.
Winter, a well-known musician (an instrumentalist on the sax-
ophone and clarinet), had been the leader of a jazz group who
turned to joining music with the sounds of wild animals and wilderness. His album *Callings* was about a sea lion pup, utilizing recorded voices of sea lions, dolphins, and blue whales. He had come
to the Grand Canyon in 1980 to attend and perform at a conference
on clean air, which led to a fourteen-day trip down the river the
following year, complete with sound engineers, vocalist, and Sam

as trip leader. Sam also bonged on a huge, old Indian drum. Subsequently, Paul Winter's "Missa Gaia" (or Mass for Mother Earth) was performed and recorded at the Cathedral of St. John the Divine in New York, a moving composition, highly praised, combining pipe organ, vocals, wolf howls, whale songs, and the sounds of the Grand Canyon.

The drum sat in a corner of the living room of Sam's little house. He bought it for four hundred dollars at the Museum of Northern Arizona, which had gotten it at the Indian pueblo at Taos, New Mexico. It was larger than any drum I had ever seen and I venture that drum embodied a tale in itself: of who had made it, how it sounded when first performed in some traditional ceremony at old Taos, and its adventures in different hands from then till now. Sam's quarters consisted of kitchen, living room, and bedroom. I had the bed while he slept on the living room floor, probably in greater comfort. He had some unusual furnishings: paintings and photographs of the Grand Canyon, a beautiful Navajo rug, bronze Buddhist figures, a silver and gold tea stand from Tibet, a handwoven Tibetan carpet with an intricate design of the mythical *garuda*, the celestial hawk, and the snow lion. Sam, I thought, was in control of his life as much as anyone can be, living simply, without craving superfluities. From partway down the trail inside the Grand Canyon, Sam earlier in the day had pointed to the sacred mountains of the Navajo and Hopi peoples visible more than a hundred miles away. To one who releases the barriers of his mind and allows perceptions of spirit and sacredness to penetrate and register, life surely must take on broad dimensions.

"Once you're on the path," said Sam, "you see yourself with clarity; you become friends with yourself. You decide that material wealth isn't important. You become available to other people; you can cut them a little slack, understand why they're pissed off when they're pissed off. We all have the same essential form and nature, like water, ice, and vapor, all the same material, just manifest in different ways. Learning that changed my attitude a great deal.

"Buddhism is a way of life. It provides me with tools and insights that help me to live to what I think is my fullest potential. It relates to wilderness by getting in touch with yourself so you can see clearly, appreciate details, be awake in whatever situation you're in. Once you start tuning in to who you are, then it's much easier to relate to the elements, the powers that exist.

"Wilderness is a relative thing, relative to perception dependent upon experience. Personally, I like relating in wilderness with people. There need to be places in wilderness completely untrammeled, in their wild state—or they will be lost. But there need to be places, intermediate places, where people can come to experience their desires and learn about wilderness and its importance.

"To stand at the rim of the Grand Canyon, or at the edge of any wild sanctuary, is not the answer. It's so vast, like looking at a picture. You have to go to the inside of it, on a walk down the trail, or a float down the river. Those experiences touch people inside of themselves. The human relationship and interaction are vital.

"For people who come out from New York City and go down the river on a motorized boat—well, that's *absolute* wilderness to them, though it may not be to you. It's valid to have that spectrum: with trails for people; no trails with people; no trails without people. You can't go to the extreme of saying let's lock up everything that's left, but we should include places that are wild, the larger the better. The trouble is that it's a battle to maintain a park with any decent conditions!

"There has to be some kind of elevation of consciousness to reevaluate the path we're on, a recognition that we're exploiting the world at an incredible rate and we had better slow down. Where I used to go on summer vacation, where there were only five houses, now there are three houses deep for five miles: four hundred where there were five. It's all going away. No wonder wilderness becomes more evident, more valuable as it disappears.

"In Christianity there is too much separation between the spirit, or God, and human needs. 'Subdue and conquer the earth.' Well, you can interpret that from the Bible any way you want. If you take it literally, that gives you carte blanche to run over anything; whereas, if you look at a Native American religion, or an Eastern religion, it says the earth is my mother. It's a sacred place; all the animals are sacred, all the animals are my brothers and sisters. Maybe that's the difference in some sense. There are different ways of looking at the earth and wilderness. Technology is different in dimension than spirit recognition. There has to be a balance, based on that elevation of consciousness."

Yes, wilderness changes people. It humbles and uplifts. Conventions fade and cooperation replaces competition. I've seen that again and again. On the trip down the Colorado River, The Unit, our portable outhouse, at first seemed alien, almost hostile, but as we became drenched, worn, and weary, that unit became a symbol of life's simplicity and directness.

My friend Sam was popular at the Grand Canyon. The park superintendent wanted to promote him. Sam had security and a career future. But it didn't surprise me a few months following our visit to hear from him that he had gone back east to join Paul Winter in getting the message out through music. But then, security is neither his need nor goal.

To identify closely with natural features of the earth changes an individual, in attitude, direction, in body, mind, and spirit. "The earth is part of my body," said Too-Hool–Hool-Zute, a fiercely spiritual leader of the Nez Perce Indians, who dwelled in the Idaho wilderness. Alvin M. Josephy, Jr., in his classic book on these Native Americans, writes as follows:

"The Nez Perces, without the amenities of civilization but with respect for the earth, lived in a state of balance and harmony with their surroundings, almost a natural part of the country itself. They were brothers to the animals and trees, to the grasses seared by the sun, to the insects on the rocks, the brooks running through snowbanks in winter, and the rain dropping from the leaves of bushes. Everything about them, the inanimate objects as well as the creatures that lived, was bound like themselves to the earth and possessed a spiritual being that was joined through a great unseen world of powers to the spirit within an individual Indian."

That is an ancient and universal way. The pre-Confucian Chinese described a society wherein "not only a man's family is his family but all men are his family and all the earth's children his children." Reverence for life is implicit in the Buddhist doctrine of rebirth. "The forest," according to Gautama Buddha, "is a peculiar organism of unlimited kindness and benevolence that makes no demands for its sustenance and extends generously the products of its life activity. It affords protection to all beings, offering shade even to the axeman who destroys it."

In my visits to the Himalayan Institute in Pennsylvania I learned how Eastern practices apply this philosophy to individual well-being. The Oriental mind views all illness as "a loss of oneness inside oneself," a disharmony that weakens the body and opens it to disease. Deliberate activities such as Tai Chi and yoga are designed to achieve harmony and calm as the keystone of health. *Pranayama*, one of the key elements of yoga, is the process of isolating the inner self from influences of worldly thought, a means of understanding forces functioning within the body and gaining control over the *prana*, the vital energy. The process is best undertaken alone, in a quiet natural setting free of refinement, a lonely place to search one's soul and restore normal harmony to body and mind.

The idea is contemporary and demanding as well as ancient. On August 23, 1981, I was at the Grand Canyon attending a ceremony commemorating that marvel of creation as a World Heritage Site, a classification developed by the United Nations Educational, Scientific and Cultural Organization (UNESCO). Only the day before I had completed my eighteen days of travel on the Colorado River with Martin Litton. It was hardly enough, yet as I looked down at the river, I felt that I had touched something vital that others at the ceremony had not. A military band played patriotic music and government officials delivered packaged speeches that could have been given anywhere. But I was caught up short and brought to full attention when the principal speaker, an assistant director general of UNESCO named Abdul Razzak, quoted these lines of James Baldwin:

"For you must say Yes to Life wherever it is found, and it is found in some terrible places. But there it is, and if the father can say Yes Lord, then the child can say that most difficult of words, Amen. For the sea does not cease to grind down rock; generations do not cease to be born and we are responsible to them for we are the only witnesses they have."

Where are we, America? That this urgent message should be delivered by an Abdul, a citizen of a Middle Eastern nation, in behalf of a James, who felt constrained to leave his own homeland for Paris, struck me as incongruous, if not downright disheartening. How could I respond—except, of course, to say Yes to Life wherever it is found? In wilderness, and in contemplation of wilderness, the true utopia becomes myself. Which marks neither end nor beginning, but a step forward on the trail to the promised land, where spirit and substance meet.

Index

INDEX